RELIGIOUS
LITERACY

RELIGIOUS LITERACY

*What Every American
Needs to Know—and Doesn't*

Stephen Prothero

HarperSanFrancisco

A Division of HarperCollins*Publishers*

Unless otherwise noted, scripture citations are taken from the King James Version of the Bible.

HarperCollins Web site: http://www.harpercollins.com
HarperCollins®, ®, and HarperSanFrancisco™ are
trademarks of HarperCollins Publishers.

FIRST EDITION
Designed by Joseph Rutt

Library of Congress Cataloging-in-Publication Data
Prothero, Stephen R.
Religious literacy : what every American needs to know / Stephen Prothero. — 1st ed.
p. cm.
Includes bibliographical references and index.
ISBN: 978–0–06–084670–1
ISBN–10: 0–06–084670–4
1. Religious education—United States. 2. Religious—Dictionaries. I. Title.
BL42.5.U5P76   2007
200.71'073—dc22   2006041310

07 08 09 10 11 RRD(H) 10 9 8 7 6 5 4 3

To my daughters,
Molly and Lucy Prothero

Contents

Contents

Introduction

A few years ago I was standing around the photocopier in Boston University's Department of Religion when a visiting professor from Austria offered a passing observation about American undergraduates. They are very religious, he told me, but they know next to nothing about religion. Thanks to compulsory religious education (which in Austria begins in elementary schools), European students can name the twelve apostles and the Seven Deadly Sins, but they wouldn't be caught dead going to church or synagogue themselves. American students are just the opposite. Here faith without understanding is the standard; here religious ignorance is bliss.

The religious differences between Europe and the United States are typically described in terms of beliefs and practices: Europeans are far less likely than Americans to join and attend houses of worship or to believe in heaven and hell. This book, however, focuses on religious knowledge. It begins with a paradox I had been wrestling with for some time when my Austrian colleague helped to clarify it for me. That paradox is this: Americans are both deeply religious and profoundly ignorant about religion. They are Protestants who can't name the four Gospels, Catholics who can't name the seven sacraments, and Jews who can't name the five books of Moses. Atheists may be as rare in America as Jesus-loving politicians are in Europe, but here faith is almost entirely devoid of content. One of the most religious countries on earth is also a nation of religious illiterates.[1]

Bible Babble

The civic implications of this paradox began to dawn on me on February 25, 1993, the day the Bureau of Alcohol, Tobacco, and Firearms (BATF) raided the Waco, Texas, compound of an obscure religious sect called the Branch Davidians. I was at the time the proud owner of a freshly minted PhD trying to hold onto my first teaching job. My specialty was (and is) American religions, but I had no real expertise in new religious movements, and certainly no close encounters of the apocalyptic kind. Still, as I watched television coverage of the raid (which left six Branch Davidians and four BATF officials dead) and followed subsequent events in the media, I felt I knew how it was going to go down. The FBI, which took over the case from the BATF after the botched raid, thought it was calling the shots. But as I saw it, the Branch Davidians' leader, David Koresh, was luring FBI agents into playing roles he had assigned to them in an end game of his own imagining—an end game whose logic derived not so much from FBI profiles or SWAT team tactics as from Koresh's own idiosyncratic interpretation of the biblical book of Revelation.

"It's going to burn," I told myself, and I remember thinking that I should pick up the phone and call the FBI, tell them what Koresh must be thinking, tell them to give him the time he had requested to unlock the cryptic meanings of the book of Revelation's Seven Seals, show them how perfectly, how eerily, they were playing the parts he had assigned to them, let them know that, if they persisted, the whole thing would end in fire. But how do you call the FBI? (Do they have an 800 number?) And why would they listen to a thirty-something like me?

I did not call. I hoped instead. I hoped that the federal government knew what it was doing—that President Bill Clinton and Attorney General Janet Reno were getting good advice from people far more knowledgeable than I about end times theology. Unfortunately, no such counsel was forthcoming. And so the siege did end in fire. As the FBI attacked the compound with tear gas and combat vehicles on April 19, 1993, flames engulfed the buildings, and Koresh and about seventy-five followers (including twenty-one children) perished.

Waco was a case of death by religious ignorance. Perhaps the outcome was fated; perhaps the Branch Davidians were, as many believed, an incendiary cult and Koresh a megalomaniac hell-bent on death and destruction. Still, it might have ended differently if there had been someone, anyone, in the White House or the FBI who knew something, anything, about apocalyptic Christianity, if federal officials had not blithely dismissed Koresh's theology as "Bible babble" unworthy of engagement.[2]

Religious ignorance proved deadly again in the aftermath of September 11, 2001, when an Indian American man was shot and killed at an Arizona gas station by a vigilante who believed the man's turban marked him as a Muslim (and therefore for assassination). But what killed Balbir Singh Sodhi, who was actually a Sikh, was not simply bigotry. It was ignorance: the vigilante's inability to distinguish a Muslim from a Sikh. The moral of this story is not just that we need more tolerance. It is that we need better education—and not because it is nice to be multicultural but because the world's religions, no longer quarantined in the nations of their birth, now live and move among us: yoga in our church halls, *nirvana* in our dictionaries, and Sikhs at our gas stations.

Religious ignorance was also rife after 9/11 in Washington DC, where, I soon learned to my dismay, hardly anyone spoke Arabic or understood the basics of Islam. And so the nation was treated for months to theology by sound bite. "Islam is peace," President Bush stated repeatedly, as if that mantra were all Americans needed to know about the Islamic tradition. Meanwhile, the televangelist Jerry Falwell denounced Muhammad as "a terrorist," and Paul Weyrich and William Lind, prominent voices in American conservatism, called Islam "a religion of war."[3] Who was right? Unfortunately, Americans had no way to judge, because, when it comes to understanding the Islamic tradition, most Americans are kindergarteners at best.

Cultural Literacy

Cultural literacy has been hotly debated ever since E. D. Hirsch's best seller of that name injected the term into the culture wars in 1987. In *Cultural Literacy,* Hirsch, a University of Virginia English professor, argued that much of our common cultural coin had been drastically devalued. ("Remember the Alamo"? Um, not really.) Hirsch traced this problem to John Dewey and other Progressive-era education reformers, who gave up in the early twentieth century on content-based learning in favor of a skills-based strategy that scorned "the piling up of information." This new educational model produced, according to Hirsch, "a gradual disintegration of cultural memory," which caused in turn "a gradual decline in our ability to communicate." Hirsch rightly understood that there are civic implications of this descent into cultural ignorance, particularly in a democracy that assumes an informed citizenry. "Having the right to vote is meaningless," he observed, "if a citizen is disenfranchised by illiteracy or semiliteracy." So Hirsch called for a return in America's schools to "core knowledge," beginning with his book's appendix of five thousand or so names, dates, concepts, and phrases essential in his view to cultural literacy.[4]

When I first began teaching in the early 1990s I was a follower of Dewey and the Progressives. In high school I had come to see the subject of history as nothing more than the mindless accumulation of names and dates, and I vowed upon entering college in the late 1970s that I would study every subject I could manage *except* history. Happily, I came across a professor who taught me that the vocation of history is not about memorizing names and dates but about forming judgments and contributing to debates about what happened in the past. So when I finished graduate school and became a professor myself, I told students that I didn't care about facts. I cared about having challenging conversations, and I offered my quiz-free classrooms as places to do just that. I soon found, however, that the challenging conversations I coveted were not possible without some common knowledge—common knowledge my students plainly lacked. And so, quite against my prior inclinations, I began testing them on simple terms. In my world religions classes I told my students that before we could discuss in any detail the great religious traditions of the world, we would need to have some shared vocabulary in each, some basic religious literacy. In this way I became, like Hirsch, a traditionalist about content, not because I had come to see facts as the end of education but because I had come to see them as necessary means to understanding.

Today religious illiteracy is at least as pervasive as cultural illiteracy, and certainly more dangerous. Religious illiteracy is more dangerous because religion is the most volatile constituent of culture, because religion has been, in addition to one of the greatest forces for good in world history, one of the greatest forces for evil. Whereas ignorance of the term *Achilles' heel* may cause us to be confused about the outcome of a Super Bowl game or a statewide election, ignorance about Christian crusades and Muslim martyrdom can be literally lethal. When Madeleine Albright was secretary of state in the Clinton administration, she had an "entire bureau of economic experts" at her disposal but only one adviser with any expertise in religion. In *The Mighty and the Almighty* (2006) she notes that currently US ambassadors to Muslim-majority countries don't have to have any training in Islam. That is not only foolhardy, it is dangerous. The same goes for ambassadors to India who don't know anything about Hinduism or to China who don't know anything about Confucianism.[5]

Religion has always been a major factor in US politics and international affairs. Neither the American Revolution nor the Civil War is comprehensible in a religion vacuum. The same goes for social reform movements such as abolitionism, temperance, women's rights, civil rights, and environmentalism—and, of course, for contemporary debates about abortion, stem cell research, capital punishment, animal rights, global warming, intelligent design, state lotteries, birth control, euthanasia, gay marriage, welfare policy, military policy, and foreign policy.

To be sure, the political, cultural, social, and economic force of religious ideas and institutions has not always been recognized. For much of the twentieth century, most American intellectuals dreamed of a public square empty of religious actors and religious arguments, and many imagined that this not-so-noble dream had become a reality—that religion had been quarantined to its rightful realm of the purely private and politics had been inoculated against the dangers of faith. Advocating for a politics stripped entirely of religious reasons—what the Catholic critic Richard John Neuhaus decried in the mid-1980s as a "naked public square"[6]—made sense as long as intellectuals were convinced, as they had been for the prior two decades, that religion was fading away. According to the prevailing secularization thesis, modernity and faith were antagonists in a zero-sum game; as modernity advanced, faith would retreat. But then came the deluge: the election of Jimmy Carter, the Iranian Revolution, the rise of the Moral Majority, the Reagan Revolution, 9/11, and the faith-based presidential election of 2004.

Today far too many thinkers, on both the left and the right, cling to the illusion that we live in a "post-Christian" country and a secular world. But evidence of the public power of religion is overwhelming, particularly in the United States. As Boston University law professor Jay Wexler has observed, "A great many Americans rely on religious reasons when thinking and talking about public issues. Ninety percent of the members of Congress, by one report, consult their religious beliefs when voting on legislation. A majority of Americans believe that religious organizations should publicly express their views on political issues, and an even stronger majority believe it is important for a President to have strong religious beliefs." All this is to say that the "naked public square" has been, as Wexler puts it, "substantially clothed with religion." At least in the United States, religion matters. In fact, religion is now emerging alongside race, gender, and ethnicity as one of the key identity markers of the twenty-first century.[7]

"A Nation of Biblical Illiterates"

If religion is this important, we ought to know something about it, particularly in a democracy, in which political power is vested in voters. But the average voter knows embarrassingly little about Christianity and other religions.

Evangelical pollsters have lamented for some time the disparity between Americans' veneration of the Bible and their understanding of it, painting a picture of a nation that believes God has spoken in scripture but can't be bothered to listen to what God has to say. The Democratic presidential aspirant Howard Dean, when asked to name his favorite New Testament book, mistakenly cited an Old Testament text (Job) instead. But such confusion is not restricted to Dean's home state of Vermont. According to recent polls, most American adults cannot name one of the four Gospels, and many high school seniors think that Sodom and Gomorrah were husband and wife. A few years ago no one in Jay Leno's *Tonight Show* audience could name any of Jesus' twelve apostles, but everyone, it seemed, was able to list the four Beatles. No wonder pollster George Gallup has called the United States "a nation of biblical illiterates."[8]

One might imagine that ignorance of Christianity and the Bible is restricted to non-Christians or at least to non-evangelicals. But born-again Christians do only moderately better than other Americans on surveys of religious literacy. In a 2004 study of Bible literacy among high school students, most evangelical participants were not able to identify "Blessed are the poor in spirit" as a quote from the Sermon on the Mount.[9]

When it comes to religions other than Christianity, Americans fare far worse. One might hope that US citizens would know the most basic formulas of the world's religions: the Five Pillars of Islam, for example, or Buddhism's Four Noble Truths. But most Americans have difficulty even *naming* these religions. In a recent survey of American teenagers, barely half were able to come up with Buddhism and less than half with Judaism when asked to list the world's five "major religions." Far fewer could name Islam or Hinduism. According to Harvard religious studies professor Diana Eck, "Christians in the United States are pretty abysmally ignorant about the religious traditions of the rest of the world."[10]

Religion as a Chain of Memory

In *The Man Who Mistook His Wife for a Hat* (1987), neurologist Oliver Sacks wrote about patients with Korsakov's syndrome, a neurological illness characterized by profound amnesia. Not knowing in any given moment what they are doing or why, these patients wander around in a state of profound disorientation; in losing their memory, they have lost themselves. Societies suffer from similar syndromes. The French sociologist Danièle Hervieu-Léger has written eloquently about the loss of faith in Europe as a sort of amnesia. The rise of secularism in Europe, she contends, is rooted not so much in doubt as in forgetting. Religion is a "chain of memory," she argues, and Europeans have broken the chain.[11]

Faith is more robust in the United States, but Americans are forgetters too. Catholics have forgotten the words of the Baltimore Catechism their parents and grandparents once knew by heart. Protestants have forgotten the key plot points in the Exodus story, which beckoned New England's colonists to a New World Zion. Methodists have forgotten what distinguishes them from Baptists. And whatever Americans once knew about Islam and Asian religions, well, they have forgotten most of that too.

Many of the institutions that once forged the "chain of memory" that is religion are now some of its weakest links. Because of grave misunderstandings about the First Amendment and the separation of church and state, the subject of religion is taboo in many public schools. Moreover, churches, synagogues, and other religious congregations, which once inculcated "the Fourth R" effectively (though doubtless in their own manner) are now doing so ineffectively, or not at all.[12] Basic religious literacy is lacking even in seminaries, where many ministers-in-the-making are unable to describe the distinguishing marks of the denominations they are training to serve.

Half a century ago, in *Protestant-Catholic-Jew* (1955), sociologist Will Herberg wrote that "the religion which actually prevails among Americans today has lost much of its authentic Christian (or Jewish) content." The postwar religious revival, which saw church membership and attendance rates rocket to all-time highs, came according to Herberg at a cost. And the cost was religious content. In conforming themselves to American culture, Protestantism, Catholicism, and Judaism had become little more than parallel paths up the mountain of the American dream. Instead of quaking in the presence of the Almighty, Herberg observed, Americans blithely pledged their allegiance to "religion that makes religion its own object." In the process Protestantism, Catholicism, and Judaism became, at least in their American incarnations, "so empty and contentless, so conformist, so utilitarian, so sentimental, so individualistic, and so self-righteous."[13]

Today what Herberg decried as "the growing 'religious illiteracy' of the American people" remains a major challenge to believers hoping to keep their children in the faith or to bring up the next generation of ministers, priests, rabbis, and imams.[14] Catholic leaders lament how quickly and deeply their youth descended into Catholic illiteracy after the reforms of the Second Vatican Council (1962–65) did away with rote memorization of the Baltimore Catechism. Evangelicals mourn the passing of biblical literacy at the hands of television, video games, and the Internet. Jews worry about what Jewish illiteracy portends for their community's survival. Religious literacy also troubles educators, who know how much our appreciation of literature, music, and art depends on our knowledge of the Bible—how difficult it is to understand the musical compositions of J. S. Bach and the paintings of El Greco as long as we are deaf and blind to artists' spiritual impulses and religious idioms. In 2002 the official magazine of the National Association of Independent Schools decried "a high level of religious illiteracy" even in the nation's elite private schools.[15]

But broken links in the chain of memory that sustains faith through the generations should not be of interest solely to believers or educators. Americans' inability to think clearly and speak confidently about Christianity and other religions should concern anyone who cares about American public life.

A Civic Problem

I am by training a professor of religious studies. That means, among other things, that just about every time I step onto a plane or attend a party I have to explain to someone that, no, I am not a minister, no, I do not teach theology, and, no, I do not work in a divinity school. Theology and religious studies, I often say, are two very different things—as different as art and art history. While theologians *do* religion, religious studies scholars *study* religion. Rather than ruminating on God, practitioners of religious studies explore how other human beings (theologians included) ruminate on sacred things. Scholars of religion can be religious, of course, but being religious is not our job. Our job is to try to understand what religious people say, believe, know, feel, and experience. And we try to do this work as fairly and objectively as possible.

Working as a religious studies professor also means being committed to seeing the study of religion as an indispensable part of a liberal education—to viewing religious literacy as a key component, perhaps *the* key component, of what Hirsch called cultural literacy. So I share with philosopher Warren Nord the conviction that our current inattention to religion in secondary and higher education today is a failure of the highest order—that "current American education is profoundly illiberal in its refusal to take religion seriously."[16] In this book, however, I write more as a citizen than as an educator. I am convinced that one needs to know something about the world's religions in order to be truly educated. And I will admit to a sneaking suspicion, likely rooted in my Episcopal upbringing, that faith without knowledge is dead. However, the argument of this book is neither that liberal education needs religious studies nor that real faith requires religious knowledge. The argument is that you need religious literacy in order to be an effective citizen.

When antebellum Americans weighed the pros and cons of slavery—almost exclusively on the basis of the Bible—most citizens could make sense of that debate's references to the runaway slave in the New Testament book of Philemon and to the year of the Jubilee (when slaves could be freed) in the Old Testament book of Leviticus. When the Seneca Falls convention of 1848 put female suffrage on the national agenda, most citizens knew that suffragettes would have to contend with the injunctions in 1 Timothy and 1 Corinthians (two New Testament letters attributed to the apostle Paul) that women should keep silent in the churches and submit to male authority. Today it is a rare American who can follow with any degree of confidence biblically inflected debates about abortion or gay marriage. Or, for that matter, about the economy, since the most widely quoted Bible verse in the United States—"God helps those who help themselves"—is not actually in the Bible.[17]

Religious illiteracy makes it difficult for Americans to make sense of a world in which people kill and make peace in the name of Christ or Allah. How are we to understand protests against the Vietnam War, which compelled Catholic priests to burn draft records in Maryland and Buddhist monks to set fire to themselves in Vietnam, without knowing something about Catholic just war theory and the Buddhist principles of no-self and compassion? How are we to understand international conflicts in the Middle East and Sri Lanka without reckoning with the role of Jerusalem in the sacred geography of the Abrahamic faiths and with the differences between Hinduism and Buddhism in Southeast Asia? Closer to home, how are we to understand faith-based electioneering if the "reds" on the Religious Right and the "blues" on the Secular Left continue to stereotype one another as distinct species? Is it possible to weigh the merits of Supreme Court rulings on religious liberty if we are unaware of the legacies of anti-Catholicism, anti-Semitism, anti-Mormonism, and anti-fundamentalism in American life?[18]

From the time of the nation's founding, the success of the American experiment in republican government was rightly understood to rest on an educated citizenry. If suffrage was to be extended first to white males with property and eventually to men and women of all races, then it would be essential for all Americans to understand the issues on which they were voting. How could we act responsibly as citizens if we did not know how to read, if we did not know something about politics and history and science and economics?

Today, when religion is implicated in virtually every issue of national and international import (not least the nomination of Supreme Court justices), US citizens need to know something about religion too. In an era in which the public square is, rightly or wrongly, awash in religious reasons, can one really participate fully in public life without knowing something about Christianity and the world's religions? Without basic religious literacy? How to decide whether intelligent design is "religious" or "scientific" without some knowledge of both science and religion? How to determine whether the effort to yoke Christianity and "family values" makes sense without knowing what sort of "family man" Jesus was? How to adjudicate the debate between President Bush's description of Islam as a religion of peace and the conviction of many televangelists that Islam is a religion of war without some basic information about Muhammad and the Quran? How to determine whether the current Supreme Court's First Amendment jurisprudence discriminates against minority religions without knowing what Sikhs and Buddhists hold dear?

Unfortunately, US citizens today lack this religious literacy. As a result, they are too easily swayed by demagogues on the left or the right. Few Americans are able to challenge claims made by politicians or pundits about Islam's place in the war on terrorism or what the Bible says about homosexuality. This ignorance imperils our public life, putting citizens in the thrall of talking heads and effectively transferring power from the third estate (the people) to the fourth (the press).

The Roots of Religious Illiteracy

How did this happen? And what can we do about it?

In order to answer these questions, we need to understand how one of the most religious countries in the world slipped into religious amnesia. When did we forget what we once knew about the Bible, the Apostles' Creed, the Westminster Confession, the Ten Commandments, the Exodus story, and the crucifixion? How was the chain of memory that once transmitted religious knowledge from parents to children, priests to parishioners, and schoolteachers to students severed?

This book answers these questions by going back, first, to an Eden of sorts in which basic literacy and religious literacy (at least of the Protestant sort) went hand in hand—when young people learned to read by learning to read the Bible, and Christian doctrines and stories were part of the mental furniture of virtually all adults. It then locates a moment in US history—call it the Fall—when religious faith and religious knowledge went their separate ways. Observers of today's culture wars might imagine that my account of the decline of religious literacy will turn on the events of the 1960s, notably the 1962 and 1963 US Supreme Court rulings that banned school prayer and Bible reading in the public schools. After all, the justices behind *Engel v. Vitale* (1962) and *Abington v. Schempp* (1963) have long been the whipping boys of the Religious Right, which itself emerged out of the rancor these rulings unleashed.[19] But public schools are not the only places where religious literacy has been cultivated (or ignored), and religion ceased to be a topic of instruction in these schools generations before the hippies became hip.

The historical portion of this book focuses instead on two religious revivals: the Second Great Awakening of the first third of the nineteenth century and the postwar revival of the 1940s and 1950s. In each case the villains were not activist judges or ACLU-style secularists hell-bent on hounding religion out of the public square but well-meaning religious folks intent on doing just the opposite. In one of the great ironies of American religious history, it was the nation's most fervent people of faith who steered Americans down the road to religious illiteracy. Just how that happened is one of the stories this book has to tell.

Defining Religious Literacy

After making a historical diagnosis of religious illiteracy, this book goes on to prescribe a remedy. Given a problem like ignorance, the solution is obviously going to be knowledge. But what kind of knowledge do we need? And what sort of education will deliver it?

Before answering these questions, we must define more precisely what religious literacy is and what it is not. Like the term *cultural literacy,* religious literacy is obviously a metaphor of sorts. On its home ground in linguistics, literacy refers to the ability to use a language—to read and perhaps to write it, to manipulate its vocabulary, grammar, and syntax. In this sense religious literacy refers to the ability to understand and use in one's day-to-day life the basic building blocks of religious traditions—their key terms, symbols, doctrines, practices, sayings, characters, metaphors, and narratives.

Like languages, however, religions are particular creatures. Just as it is not possible to speak language in general (one must choose to speak one particular language), religious literacy in the abstract is an impossibility. (One cannot be literate in *every* religion; neither is there one generic religion to "speak.") It would probably be most precise, therefore, to refer to specific *religious literacies:* Protestant literacy, Buddhist literacy, Islamic literacy (or, even more accurately, Methodist literacy, Zen literacy, Sunni literacy, and so on). In this context Protestant literacy might refer to knowing the basic history of the Protestant Reformation, the core beliefs of the Christian creeds, and the basic symbols, heroes, and stories of the King James Bible, while Islamic literacy might refer to knowing basic Islamic history, the key practices of the Five Pillars of Islam, and the basic symbols, heroes, and stories of the Quran. Religious literacy might also be divided into a variety of functional capacities; for example, ritual literacy (knowing how to cross yourself during the Catholic Mass or how to perform ablutions before Muslim prayers); confessional literacy (knowing what Christians affirm in the Apostles' Creed or what Muslims affirm in the *Shahadah*); denominational literacy (knowing salient differences between Episcopalians and Catholics or between Reform and Conservative Jews); and narrative literacy (knowing what Adam and Eve are said to have done in the Garden of Eden or how the Buddha came to abandon his palace for the life of a wandering ascetic). It might even be useful to refer, as has Professor Francis Clooney of the Harvard Divinity School, to "interreligious literacy."[20] But all this specificity can get unwieldy at times, so this book will refer to religious literacy in general as a shorthand for one or more of these particular religious literacies.

In the United States today the most important of these particular literacies is Christian literacy. Inside the academic study of religion it is decidedly out of fashion to emphasize Christianity over other religions. In fact, many a college course in American religion devotes more time to Vodou than it does to Methodism. The point of this multicultural approach to American religion is to underscore the fact that the United States is one of the most religiously diverse nations on earth. But the United States is also the world's most Christian country. With a Christian population of about 250 million, there are more Christians in the United States today than there have been in any other country in the history of the world.

Christianity's dominance, moreover, swells as you enter the corridors of power. Of all the members of the 109th Congress, 92 percent were Christians, as were 100 percent of fifty state governors in 2000. Among this elite group of state and national politicians, there were zero Muslims, zero Buddhists, and zero Hindus.[21] So it should be obvious that Christian literacy is more important than other religious literacies when it comes to understanding US politics. A quick search of the *Congressional Record* (the official source for Senate and House debates) reveals in excess of a thousand usages of the Golden Rule and more than five hundred invocations of the Good Samaritan over the last two decades. This same search yields hundreds of references to the Promised Land, Armageddon, and the Apocalypse. In a nationally televised address on September 11, 2001, President George W. Bush quoted from the Twenty-third Psalm. One year later, on the first anniversary of the 9/11 attacks, he concluded with a reference to John 1:5 ("The light shines in the darkness, but the darkness has not understood it").[22] You may be a Hare Krishna, a Jain, or an atheist yourself, but to be religiously literate in contemporary America you need to be familiar with Bible characters such David and Goliath, Bible stories such as the trial and crucifixion of Jesus, and Bible phrases such as "an eye for an eye" and "the love of money is the root of all evil."

Christian literacy is not enough, however. To understand foreign policy on Tibet, for example, one needs to know something about Buddhist monasticism and the Dalai Lama. To follow the ramifications of the "under God" language in the Pledge of Allegiance, one needs to know something about the nuances of both atheism and polytheism. And to fully engage in debates about the war in Iraq, one needs to be informed about jihad and the Islamic tradition of martyrdom (a tradition, it might be noted, that Muslims adapted from Christians and Jews). The war on terrorism is to a great extent—a far greater extent than most American politicians recognize—a war of ideas. To wage that war, one needs to be equipped with ideas—to understand, among other things, the religious underpinnings of Osama bin Laden's strategy to engage "the crusader-Zionist alliance" in a clash of civilizations.[23]

Religious Literacy in Practice

In this book religious literacy refers to the ability to understand and use the religious terms, symbols, images, beliefs, practices, scriptures, heroes, themes, and stories that are employed in American public life. Some of this is factual information, which might be learned, as students often learn vocabulary words, by simple memorization. So this book's proposals are open to the criticisms of "rote learning" that descended upon Hirsch when he published his controversial list of "what every American needs to know." But religious literacy is not just the accumulation of facts. Tempting as it is to define this book's core concept entirely in terms of doctrine—as the ability to work with such Christian teachings as the atonement or such basic practices as baptism—religious literacy cannot and should not be reduced to memorizing and regurgitating dogma. To return again to the Christian example, surely religious literacy also includes knowing the key characters, images, and stories in the scriptures, rites, and history of the church. And so, in addition to doctrine, this book's definition of religious literacy includes narrative. To be religiously literate today is to be familiar with the creation story in Genesis and the apocalyptic horrors of Revelation. It is to know that David triumphed over Goliath, even though David was small and Goliath was big, perhaps to know as well that David felled the giant with a stone. Religious literacy, in short, is both doctrinal and narrative; it is conveyed through creeds and catechisms, yes, but also through creation accounts and stories of the last days.[24]

Like other forms of literacy, religious literacy is more a fluid practice than a fixed condition.[25] It is the ability to participate in our ongoing conversation about the private and public powers of religions. But that ability itself depends on knowing basic information about Christianity and other religions, and that basic information changes over time. Certain religious terms that were widely employed in American public life in 1776—Socianism, to take just one example—are no longer in circulation today. And terms, such as Wahhabism, that were not noteworthy as recently as the 1990s now circulate widely. Because of the rapid rise of religious diversity in the United States since Congress opened up immigration from Asia in 1965, understanding the basics of Islam, Buddhism, and Hinduism is far more important than it was a half century ago. Nonetheless, understanding Christianity and the Bible must remain the core task of religious literacy education, if only because Christian and biblical terms are most prevalent on our radios and televisions, and on the lips of our legislators, judges, and presidents.

There are many uses to which religious literacy can be put. Religious literacy can be used to firm up the faith of young people raised in the Lutheran Church–Missouri Synod or Reform Judaism. It might be seen, in other words, as a way to keep teenagers on the straight and narrow, to convince young adults to marry inside the faith, or to give adults the courage to share their deepest convictions with their friends. Some readers might assume that this is my agenda. After all, many who speak out on religion in public life have theological axes to grind; they are out to promote Roman Catholicism or to ridicule fundamentalism or to turn the United States into a theocracy of this or that sort. But my agenda is not religious. It is civic and secular. I was raised an Episcopalian and, if pressed, will fess up to being a Christian. I prefer, however, to describe myself as religiously confused. Like many Americans, I find far more questions than answers in the world's religious traditions, and my attitude toward people who possess firmer faith than my own is awe rather than fear. Regardless of the measure of my faith (and doubt), however, I write here not as a believer (or unbeliever) but as a citizen. My purpose is not to foster faith or to denigrate it. Neither is it to advance the liberal arts or to boost high school students' SAT scores (though these are both laudable educational ends to which religious literacy might be put). My goal is to help citizens participate fully in social, political, and economic life in a nation and a world in which religion counts.

To put this goal in more personal terms, my hope is that readers will come away from this book empowered to talk about religion in their homes, at work, in houses of worship, and in the rough-and-tumble of local and national politics. I hope that readers will be emboldened to ask questions about their own faiths and to learn about the religious traditions of others. A neighbor of mine—a conservative Catholic—told me recently that she and many of her Catholic friends go mum whenever the topic of religion comes up in everyday conversations out of a fear that, if they speak up, their ignorance will be quickly found out (presumably by biblically literate Protestants). At least one study supports this anecdotal evidence, reporting that many Catholics harbor "feelings of inadequacy" in the face of conservative Protestants "better versed in Bible knowledge." Catholics may find it reassuring to learn that the average American Protestant knows very little about the Bible. I find it troubling, however, that members of America's largest religious group (Roman Catholicism) feel that they cannot discuss religion even with their friends, not because of qualms about mixing religion and politics but because of fears about making fools of themselves. I doubt, moreover, that such anxieties are confined to Catholics. This book aims to allay these anxieties and quiet these fears by offering readers of all faiths (and none at all) the confidence they need to participate in religious discussions.[26]

What to Do?

So much for what religious literacy is and does. How might we cultivate it?

One way of course is for individuals to read the Bible or the Quran, or both. Individuals can also peruse the Dictionary of Religious Literacy in chapter 6 of this book. This dictionary defines key terms from Christianity and other religions, focusing on the religious symbols, beliefs, rituals, holidays, scriptures, people, places, and historical events employed in public life for political purposes. It also refers in many cases to specific instances in which these terms have been used—references to Adam and Eve and Sodom and Gomorrah in the gay marriage debate, for example, or President George W. Bush's description of the war on terrorism as a crusade, or Senator Hillary Clinton's characterization of restrictive immigration legislation as contrary to the spirit of the Good Samaritan. This dictionary delivers, in other words, the basic vocabulary one needs to become a religiously literate US citizen, and to allay anxieties about discussing religion over the water cooler or in the living room.

In addition to empowering individual readers with the basic building blocks of religious literacy, this book suggests how religious literacy might be cultivated in our collective lives. Churches, synagogues, mosques, and temples can do much to address our collective ignorance— to follow the commandment to "remember" made repeatedly in the Hebrew Bible. Religious leaders can preach from their scriptures more plainly and more regularly. Religious congregations can go "back to basics" in their Sunday schools and religious camps. But even if America's religious congregations were to step up and start teaching effectively the faiths of their fathers and mothers, that would affect only regular attenders. And even they would come to know only their own religious tradition (and from one particular perspective).

The media could help too. Since 9/11 mainstream print and broadcast media have gotten religion. Many major newspapers have religion beat writers, and it is no longer rare to see an intelligent program on religion broadcast on national television. But it no longer appears to be the media's vocation to educate the public—entertainment is the new god— and even if it were, the media's own plague of religious illiteracy would prevent them from doing much good.

The most effective way forward, therefore, is to focus on secondary schools and colleges. America's private and public educational institutions need to get religion, to start seeing teaching about religion not as a third rail but as the "Fourth R." Two barriers currently stand in the way: misinformation about the constitutionality of teaching about religion in schools, and a misguided approach to religious studies in colleges and universities. Each of these barriers can be overcome if American citizens come to understand what the US Supreme Court has actually said about religion in the public schools, and if religious studies experts stop preaching the gospel of religious relativism.

This book argues for both the constitutionality and the necessity of teaching about religion in public schools and higher education. In this respect its proposals might be understood as advocating "civic education," which one group defines as the inculcation of the knowledge, skills, dispositions, and virtues necessary for "self-government" in our "constitutional democracy."[27] And my proposals do engage the "civic education" debate. This book shares with the writings of Professors Eck and Wexler the conviction that teaching about religion is first and foremost a civic enterprise. However, unlike others who have advanced civic arguments for the study of religion in our schools, I focus on spreading knowledge rather than inculcating virtues. Today many are not so sure that morality needs religion as a prop or that religion's first order of business should be performing such a role. Scores of books have been written about America's moral decline. This book addresses a different problem: our descent into religious ignorance.

My argument concerning the academic study of religion in secondary and higher education is threefold: first, that teaching about religion is an essential task for our educational institutions; second, that the primary purpose of such teaching should be civic; and third, that this civic purpose should be to produce citizens who know enough about Christianity and the world's religions to participate meaningfully—on both the left and the right—in religiously inflected public debates. High school and college graduates who have not taken a single course about religion cannot be said to be truly educated.

Like the scene in *The Wizard of Oz* in which Dorothy opens the door to a Technicolor munchkin land, many key chapters in US and world history leap from black-and-white to color once you realize the role religion played in them—how the Inner Light of Quakers shaped the abolitionist movement, how biblical criticism lent the women's rights movement much of its early brio, and how the theological mouthful of "dispensational premillennialism" fed the bottom line of software firms during the months before Y2K. The same is true of the stories that appear in the morning paper and on the nightly news. Suicide bombings in the Middle

East, the enduring popularity of *The Da Vinci Code,* the latest diet fad, the Yankees–Red Sox morality play, and the ritual cycles of presidential elections all make far more sense (and are far more intriguing) if these tales are not stripped of the coat of many colors that is religion.

But more intriguing is not the whole story here, since in addition to making the world more interesting, religious literacy also makes it less dangerous. Of course, getting past religious ignorance is not the panacea some advocates of interreligious dialogue imagine it to be. (People sometimes kill their enemies not because they do not understand them but precisely because they do.) Still, it is hard to avoid the conclusion that some of the bloodletting in such places as Waco and Afghanistan and Iraq might have been avoided if we had understood a bit better our own religions traditions, and those of others.

Part 1

The Problem

One

A Nation of Religious Illiterates

B oth the Religious Right and the Secular Left feel besieged. In the *Left Behind* novels popular in conservative Christian circles, true believers are "raptured" into heaven at the end of times; everyone else is "left behind." Today secularists are attesting to a Last Days scenario of another sort, in which the old order of reason, rights, and the separation of church and state is being replaced by a new medievalism in which the president and his acolytes answer to God rather than to the American people. This disquiet can be heard in port cities across the country, but it is particularly palpable in Manhattan, the mecca of the Secular Left, where many report that their island is starting to feel, well, like an island again, cut off from the heartland by (among other things) its cosmopolitanism. At least for New Yorkers, it is as if the iconic Saul Steinberg cartoon of the United States according to Manhattan—an image that looks west across Ninth Avenue and the Hudson River and New Jersey to a Kansas City the size of a yellow cab and a Los Angeles no bigger than a courier's bicycle—is eerily mutating into a Grant Wood landscape, its bucolic foreground anchored not by yellow cabs but by the corn rows and church spires of Kansas, with nary a skyscraper on the horizon. "I feel assaulted," one New Yorker told me. "I feel like these Christians are hiding a crucifix in their shoe. Any minute they'll pull it out and gut you."[28]

Bill O'Reilly of *The O'Reilly Factor* on Fox News feels assaulted too. Whereas secularists are sure that the Religious Right has taken over US politics, he is morally certain that "secular progressives" are winning the culture wars. Christmas is "under siege," O'Reilly says. An "anti-Christian jihad" is banishing Christmas trees from holiday parades, Christmas carols from public school pageants, and Christmas greetings from department stores. In the world according to O'Reilly, the ultimate aim of these criminalizers of Christmas is nothing less than banishing religion from the public square and thereby clearing the way for "secular progressive programs like legalization of narcotics, euthanasia, abortion at will, gay marriage." Televangelist Jerry Falwell also believes that "radical secularists" are "aggressively attempting to redefine America in their own Godless image," and religious broadcaster Pat Buchanan complains about "hate crimes against Christianity." The mission of the Secular Left, concludes Buchanan, is "to expunge from the public life of the West all reminders that ours was once a Christian civilization and America once a Christian country."[29]

The emotions on both sides of this question are understandable, though the irony of the situation—in which each camp sees itself as a victim and believes that the other is seizing control of the country—seems lost on everyone concerned. The fact of the matter is that, in the American marketplace of ideas, neither faith nor faithlessness is close to either bankruptcy or monopoly. Though O'Reilly may rage, Christmas (which remains a national holiday) is not fading into that good night. And theocracy—in the true sense of church-run government—is not even a twinkle in the Bush administration's eye. Much ink has been spilled, and many megabytes expended, trying to pigeonhole the nation into either "secular America" or "Christian America." It has always been both.

The United States is by law a secular country. God is not mentioned in the Constitution, and the First Amendment's establishment clause forbids the state from getting into the church business. However, that same amendment also includes a free exercise clause safeguarding religious liberty, and Americans have long exercised this liberty by praying to God, donating to religious congregations, and hoping for heaven. So there is logic not only to President John Adams's affirmation in the Treaty of Tripoli in 1796 that "the government of the United States of America is not in any sense founded on the Christian religion" but also to the Supreme Court's 1892 observation that "this is a Christian nation." In short, the long-standing debate about whether the United States is secular or religious is fundamentally confused. Thanks to the establishment clause, the US government is secular by law; thanks to the free exercise clause, American society is religious by choice.[30]

Ever since George Washington put his hand on a Bible and swore to uphold a godless Constitution, the United States has been both staunchly secular and resolutely religious. Church and state have never been completely separated in the United States; religion and politics were bedfellows from the start. Traditional liberals such as the political philosopher John Rawls insist that religion restrict itself to the individual heart, the pious home, and the religious congregation; religion is a private matter that will contaminate civil society if not quarantined from public life. Because religion is a "conversation stopper," political discourse must be conducted entirely in terms of "public reason," which by definition excludes religious reasons. According to this strict separationist perspective, the wall between church and state is supposed to form, as one nineteenth-century activist once put it, "a barrier high and eternal as the Andes." The only alternative is "politics as holy war."[31]

George W. Bush caught a lot of flak for disrespecting this church-state divide at his 2001 inauguration, which included one prayer offered by the Reverend Franklin Graham (Billy's son) in the name of "the Father, the Son, and the Holy Spirit" and another offered by the United Methodist minister Kirbyjon Caldwell "in the name that's above all other names, Jesus, the Christ." But Bush's sin was also committed, in *flagrante delicto,* by Bill Clinton, whose inaugurations were unabashedly Christian affairs. Clinton's 1997 fete included a trinitarian prayer by Billy Graham, a benediction by a black Baptist preacher, and songs by no fewer than three gospel groups (one called the Resurrection Choir). Plainly, the celebrated wall of separation between church and state has never been particularly wide or sturdy. Breached nearly as often as it has been respected, this wall resembles a rickety picket fence far more than the eternal Andes. Washington and Madison, Reagan and Clinton all declared national days of prayer or thanksgiving, and the Supreme Court still opens its sessions with "God save the United States and this Honorable Court." As G. K. Chesterton once put it, the United States has long been "a nation with the soul of a church."[32]

Churched and Unchurched Believers

The contrast with Europe could not be sharper. Many theological doctrines that Europeans now dismiss as fables—heaven and hell, angels and the devil—are enthusiastically affirmed by the vast majority of Americans. Out of every ten adults in the United States, more than nine believe in God, more than eight say that religion is important to them personally, and more than seven report praying daily. Believers here also put their money where their faith is; annual giving to houses of worship—about $88 billion—is larger than the gross domestic product of many nations. What the apostle Paul once said to the Athenians—"I see that in every way you are very religious" (Acts 17:22, NIV)—applies to Americans too.[33]

Conservatives often claim that "secular humanism" is running amok in America—that the United States has become "post-Christian." But that is simply not the case. The kind of hard-nosed secularism that is common in Europe—"Eurosecularity," in the neologism of sociologist Peter Berger—is hard to find even in the bluest boroughs of America's bluest states. Some surveys show that the portion of "Nones" (those who claim no religious preference) is rising in the United States—doubling by one account over the course of the 1990s from 7 percent to 14 percent. But those who have distanced themselves from organized religion have done nothing of the sort when it comes to God or spirituality. In a recent survey of US adolescents, sociologist Christian Smith found that, of the teenagers who claimed "no religion," fewer than one out of five rejected the possibility of life after death. In a recent study of American adults, nine out of ten of the "no religion" respondents told researchers that they pray. These "Nones," in short, are about as irreligious as your average nun. Few are Euro-style atheists or agnostics; the vast majority are "unchurched believers"—spiritual people who for one reason or another avoid religious congregations.[34]

Of America's religions, the most popular of course is Christianity. Half of Americans describe themselves as Protestants, one-quarter as Catholics, and 10 percent as Christians of some other stripe. This makes the US population more Christian than Israel is Jewish or Utah is Mormon. Moreover, members of this Christian majority are extraordinarily observant. About two-thirds of Americans are church members, and two-fifths report attending a religious congregation either weekly or almost every week.[35]

Inside American Christianity, evangelical or "born-again" Protestantism is particularly robust. Forty percent of Americans call themselves born-again Christians, and nearly half report a born-again experience. When it comes to biblical literalists—those who say they believe that the Bible is the literal word of God—only the Philippines (54 percent) and Poland (37 percent) rank higher than the United States (34 percent).[36]

America's buoyant religiosity repeatedly flows beyond the rivers of our private domains onto the banks of our public life. The land of Thomas Jefferson and church-state separation is now the land of *The Passion of the Christ* and the passions of born-again politicians. Candidates for elected office call Jesus not only their Savior but also their favorite political philosopher. National news magazines repeatedly put Jesus and Mary on their covers, not least because such magazines race off the shelves. In the world of entertainment, Christian music sales exceed $1 billion annually, and songs such as "Jesus Take the Wheel" by *American Idol* winner Carrie Underwood top the charts. Although conservative radio and television commentators rail against the exile of Christianity from American public life, their own ratings belie the huffing and puffing. Even heated debates about the proper role of religion in the public square—court cases about posting the Ten Commandments on public property or about accommodating God in the Pledge of Allegiance—attest to the power of the Christian majority to put such matters on the national agenda.[37]

A Nation of Religions

If the United States is both secular and religious, it is also both Christian and pluralistic. Christianity dominates, but this nation of immigrants is also "a nation of religions."[38] Los Angeles, the most religiously heterogeneous city in the country, boasts more than three hundred Buddhist temples and is likely home to more Buddhist schools than Tokyo. According to a recent study, one in every eight Americans, including many Christians and Jews, say that Buddhism has influenced their religious lives. There are only about a million Hindus in the United States, but many of the largest companies in the Silicon Valley are run by them. And yoga, which began in ancient India as a technique for spiritual liberation from the cycle of life, death, and rebirth, is now a Main Street phenomenon, practiced in community centers and churches alike. Taoism is present too—in thousands of martial arts academies scattered in cities and small towns across the United States. Islam is even more visible. Now represented in over 1,200 mosques nationwide, it will soon outrun Judaism as America's second largest religion (that is, if it hasn't already).

Harvard's Diana Eck exaggerates when she calls the United States "the most religiously diverse nation on earth." With a Christian majority of roughly 85 percent, the United States is far more homogeneous than dozens of countries with no religious majority. (For every hundred people in Singapore, for example, there are forty-two Buddhists, fifteen Muslims, fifteen Christians, eight Taoists, and four Hindus.) Still, Eck is right that the United States offers its citizens one of the world's largest menus of spiritual options. The fare is mind-boggling in Flushing, New York, which religious studies scholar R. Scott Hanson has described as "perhaps the most extreme case of religious pluralism in the world." Over two hundred houses of worship, including six different Hindu temples and one hundred Korean churches, are crammed into this small community of a few square miles. There are buildings for Buddhists, Sikhs, Muslims, Taoists, Mormons, and Protestants. Jews can choose among Reform, Conservative, and Orthodox synagogues.[39]

Given America's religious diversity, it should not be surprising that Jesus and Mary have company in the public square. Kanye West may not be rapping about the Dalai Lama, but the spiritual and political leader of the Tibetan people has become an American icon, celebrated on billboards for Apple computers as someone who "thinks different." A gaggle of celebrities, not least the actor Richard Gere, has championed the cause for Tibetan independence. Perfumes have been named after such Hindu concepts as om (a sacred sound), samsara (the cycle of life, death, and rebirth), and karma (the law of actions and their consequences). American Hindus Against Defamation, a pressure group modeled after the Anti-Defamation League, is working hard to combat negative stereotypes of Hindus. More than any of these religious newcomers to American society, however, Islam has pushed powerfully into politics. Thanks to groups such as the Council on American-Islamic Relations and the Muslim Public Affairs Council, Muslims were quite active in both the 2000 and 2004 presidential elections. (They voted overwhelmingly for Bush in the former and for Kerry in the latter.) In Dearborn, Michigan, Muslims constitute a potent political force.

All this is to say that both the private and the public lives of Americans are "awash in a sea of faith." Unfortunately, however, Americans' knowledge of religion runs as shallow as Americans' commitment to religion runs deep. Many cannot recognize the phrase "Hail, Mary" except as the name of a football play; many are unaware that the pop singer Madonna was actually named after someone. In fact, most Americans lack the most basic understanding of their own religious traditions. Americans, writes historian R. Laurence Moore, "are stupefyingly dumb about what they are supposed to believe."[40]

Religious Literacy Quiz

Over a century and a half ago Henry David Thoreau complained in *Walden* (1854) about the religious ignorance of his neighbors in Concord, Massachusetts. "As for the sacred Scriptures, or Bibles of mankind, who in this town can tell me even their titles?" he asked. "Most men do not know that any nation but the Hebrews have had a scripture." Things are a bit better today. Most major bookstores carry translations of such scriptures as the Bhagavad Gita and the Quran. After the Bible itself, Lao Tzu's Taoist classic, the Tao Te Ching, is likely the most widely translated book in the United States. Still, one wonders who is actually reading these sacred texts, and with what sort of care. In Thoreau's time the Unitarian minister turned Transcendentalist sage, Ralph Waldo Emerson, mistook the Bhagavad Gita to be "the much renowned book of Buddhism." Closer to our time justices for the United States Court of Appeals for the Fifth Circuit made a similar mistake. While considering in 1982 whether the International Society for Krishna Consciousness (the Hare Krishnas) is a religion, they said that the Bhagavad Gita (which is a Hindu scripture) is "as important in the Buddhist religions [sic] as the Bible is to Christians and Jews." Today most Americans are no better prepared to distinguish between Hinduism and Buddhism. Only a tiny minority can name a single scripture from any Asian religion. In a recent book on religious diversity in the United States, sociologist Robert Wuthnow discovered that American Hindus, Buddhists, and Muslims don't just want to be tolerated, they "wish to be understood." If so, that wish is going unfulfilled.[41]

In an effort to determine just how far we are from this goal of inter-religious understanding, I gave a religious literacy quiz to my Boston University students at the start of an introductory course I was teaching in the spring of 2006 called "Death and Immortality." Before I parse the results, readers might like to take the test for themselves. (The answers appear in the appendix.)

Religious Literacy Quiz

1. Name the four Gospels. List as many as you can.

2. Name a sacred text of Hinduism.

3. What is the name of the holy book of Islam?

4. Where according to the Bible was Jesus born?

5. President George W. Bush spoke in his first inaugural address of the Jericho road. What Bible story was he invoking?

6. What are the first five books of the Hebrew Bible or the Christian Old Testament?

7. What is the Golden Rule?

8. "God helps those who help themselves": Is this in the Bible? If so, where?

9. "Blessed are the poor in spirit, for theirs is the kingdom of God": Does this appear in the Bible? If so, where?

10. Name the Ten Commandments. List as many as you can.

11. Name the Four Noble Truths of Buddhism.

12. What are the seven sacraments of Catholicism? List as many as you can.

13. The First Amendment says two things about religion, each in its own "clause." What are the two religion clauses of the First Amendment?

14. What is Ramadan? In what religion is it celebrated?

15. Match the Bible characters with the stories in which they appear. Draw a line from one to the other. Hint: Some characters may be matched with more than one story or vice versa.

Adam and Eve	Exodus
Paul	Binding of Isaac
Moses	Olive Branch
Noah	Garden of Eden
Jesus	Parting of the Red Sea
Abraham	Road to Damascus
Serpent	Garden of Gethsemane

Most of my students flunked this exam. The results, however, were not entirely discouraging. Almost everyone was able to associate "Adam and Eve" with the "Garden of Eden," and nearly nine out of ten knew that the holy book of Islam was the Quran. But most students could not list the four Gospels, only one out of eight could name the first five books of the Hebrew Bible or Old Testament, and only one in four could name a single Hindu scripture. National surveys have shown that most Americans cannot name five of the Ten Commandments; my students averaged four. They were equally unfamiliar with what may be the most important piece of oratory in Western civilization; only one in six knew that "Blessed are the poor in spirit" is a quote from the Sermon on the Mount.[42]

My class also fared poorly on the exercise that required them to match Bible heroes with Bible stories. In their creative retellings, the most basic elements of the most influential Bible narratives were shuffled and reshuffled like so many cards at a poker table. In their imaginations Paul bound Isaac, Noah led the Exodus of the Israelites out of Babylon, Moses was the recipient of the dove's olive branch, Abraham was blinded on the road to Damascus, and Jesus was nearly as likely to be born in Jerusalem or Nazareth as in Bethlehem. Ben Franklin once proposed that the United States adopt as its national seal a depiction of Moses leading the Israelites across the Red Sea. Some of my students thought that this was Jesus' job. On these quizzes Gospels were credited to such scriveners as Isaac, James, Michael, Simon, Peter, and Paul. In fact, 10 percent of my class thought that Paul was one of the four Gospels. Perhaps most disturbingly, the vast majority of my students did not know that the First Amendment both guarantees religious freedom (the free exercise clause) and prohibits the government from endorsing religion (the establishment clause). In fact, only one in six of my students knew both of the First Amendment's religion clauses.

Joan of Arc

If things are this bad at Boston University—and in fairness to my students I should note that professors at the University of North Carolina at Chapel Hill and Wheaton College (Illinois) have reported equally dispiriting results on similar quizzes—how is it elsewhere in the country? Unfortunately, there is not much data on Americans' religious knowledge. Experts can tell you how many American Baptists there are in the United States and what portion of the population in Maine's Aroostook County belongs to that denomination's churches. We know that Catholicism is the largest religious group in thirty-six states, that Southern Baptists dominate in ten, and Mormons in two (Utah and Idaho). We know that women are more likely than men to believe in angels and witches, that liberals are more likely than conservatives to believe in haunted houses, that 20 percent of evangelicals believe in reincarnation, that the vast majority of Americans support the rights of women to act as clergy, and that only a small minority concur with the apostle Paul's view that wives should submit to their husbands. Unfortunately, researchers have devoted far less attention to what Americans know about their own religions or the religions of their neighbors. Some polling data is instructive, however. And both the current situation and the trends are alarming.[43]

Biblical illiteracy has been fairly well documented. In fact, according to the Gallup Organization, which has tracked trends in US religion for over fifty years, Bible reading has declined since the 1980s and "basic Bible knowledge is at a record low." Virtually every American home has at least one Bible, publishers sell about twenty million Bibles annually, and Gideons International gives away a new Bible every second of every day. Moreover, nearly two-thirds of Americans believe that the Bible holds the answers to all or most of life's basic questions, and a majority claims that it reads that book at least twice a month. If so, Americans are not reading particularly carefully.[44]

The Gospel of John instructs Christians to "search the scriptures" (John 5:39), but little searching, and even less finding, is being done. In 1997 *Tonight Show* host Jay Leno took to the streets of New York to find out how much average Americans know about the Bible. Interviewees told him that God created Eve from an apple, that Jacob gave his son Joseph a new car, and that Matthew was swallowed by a whale.[45] But biblical illiteracy is not limited to Manhattan. Consider these sobering facts gleaned from more scientific surveys:

- Only half of American adults can name even one of the four Gospels.[46]

- Most Americans cannot name the first book of the Bible.[47]

- Only one-third know that Jesus (no, not Billy Graham) delivered the Sermon on the Mount.[48]

- A majority of Americans wrongly believe that the Bible says that Jesus was born in Jerusalem.[49]

- When asked whether the New Testament book of Acts is in the Old Testament, one quarter of Americans say yes. More than a third say that they don't know.[50]

- Most Americans don't know that Jonah is a book in the Bible.[51]

- Ten percent of Americans believed that Joan of Arc was Noah's wife.[52]

In 2005 an enterprising journalist called up the ten cosponsors of an Alabama bill that sought to protect public displays of the Ten Commandments. Just one of those cosponsors could name all ten. But journalists are just as religiously ignorant as politicians. After President George W. Bush referred to the Good Samaritan story in his first inaugural address in 2001, Dick Meyer of CBS News confessed that that portion of the speech left him stumped. "There were a few phrases in the speech I just didn't get," he said. "One was, 'When we see that wounded traveler on the road to Jericho, we will not pass to the other side.'" Meyer later added, "I hope there's not a quiz."[53]

Mount Cyanide

One might hope that we are at a nadir here—that the only way out is up. But as pollster George Barna has observed, "The younger a person is, the less they understand about the Christian faith." A recent Gallup poll found that "Bible illiteracy is common" among US high school students. (Fully 8 percent of the teen respondents thought that Moses was one of the twelve apostles.) And teachers are five times more likely to say that Bible knowledge is decreasing than to say that it is increasing.[54]

One of this Gallup poll's most intriguing findings is that born-again Christians are only marginally better informed about the Bible than other students. Only 44 percent of born-again respondents correctly identified "Blessed are the poor in spirit, for theirs is the kingdom of heaven" as a quote from the Sermon on the Mount, versus 37 percent of the broader group. And while born-again students did better than the general population in identifying Cain as the person who said, "Am I my brother's keeper?" and in knowing that the apostle Paul was blinded by a vision on the road to Damascus, private school students did better than evangelicals on both questions.[55]

In an early study of Americans' biblical knowledge, dating to 1968, conservative Protestants did better than liberal Protestants and far better than Catholics. For example, when asked whether "Blessed are the strong: for they shall be the sword of God" appears in the Bible (it does not), only 20 percent of the Southern Baptists (a theologically conservative group) were fooled compared with 28 percent of the Congregationalists (a liberal Protestant group) and 41 percent of the Catholics. On some recent surveys, however, evangelicals actually display *less* biblical knowledge than other religious adherents. For example, when asked whether the Bible locates Jesus' birth in Jerusalem (it does not), only 51 percent of the Jews surveyed were fooled, while 60 percent of evangelical Protestants got the answer wrong.[56]

America's youth—evangelical or otherwise—are not learning the Bible at home or in religious congregations. But they are not learning about it in school either. In a 1997 study on "The Place of Bible Literature in Public High School English Classes," only 9 percent of the high school English teachers surveyed said that they taught either a course or a unit on the Bible. And in 2005 only 8 percent of public school teens reported that their school offered an elective Bible course.[57]

Perhaps the most damning data to come out of studies on teenagers and the Bible is that there is hardly any difference in Bible knowledge between younger teens (seventh to ninth graders) and older teens (tenth to twelfth graders). This means that students are learning almost nothing about the Bible during high school—that schools (at least public schools) are failing to function as "chains of memory."

There is a humorous list of biblical bloopers, supposedly drawn from actual student papers and exams, that used to circulate fairly widely among teachers. For example (from the Hebrew Bible or Old Testament):

- "Moses led the Jews to the Red Sea where they made unleavened bread which is bread without any ingredients."

- "The Egyptians were all drowned in the dessert. Afterwards, Moses went up to Mount Cyanide to get the Ten Commandments."

- "Moses died before he ever reached Canada. Then Joshua led the Hebrews in the Battle of Geritol."

And, from the New Testament:

- "Jesus enunciated the Golden Rule, which says to do one to others before they do one to you. He also explained, 'A man doth not live by sweat alone.'"

- "The epistles were the wives of the apostles."

- "St. Paul cavorted to Christianity. He preached holy acrimony, which is another name for marriage."

These bloopers don't pop up as often as they used to. That may be because to get the humor you have to know something about Judaism, Christianity, and the Bible—that God gave Moses the Ten Commandments on Mount Sinai, that Joshua led the Battle of Jericho, and that Jesus said, "Man shall not live by bread alone" (Matthew 4:4; Luke 4:4).

Religiously Befuddled

Broader Christian literacy is also hard to find. Many a proponent of inter-religious dialogue assumes that Christians know their own religious tradi-tions. In fact, interreligious dialogue assumes basic knowledge on both sides of the religious divide that the discussion is designed to bridge. But this assumption is hollow, at least in the United States. Many American Christians here do not know that Easter commemorates the resurrection of Jesus or that the Trinity comprises the Father, Son, and Holy Spirit. Many Baptists cannot tell you how their denomination understands its signature rite of adult baptism. Many Methodists will simply shrug if you ask them about their denomination's distinctive doctrine of sanctification. And many Lutherans have no idea who Martin Luther is. A professor at a prestigious seminary in the South reports that she spends considerable time in her church history courses on what might be called "Denomina-tions for Dummies," basic information that in the past would have been covered in the elementary grades of Sunday schools (or public schools) but is lost on her ministers-in-training today.

Over the last few presidential election cycles, evangelicals have emerged as key players in American politics. In 2005 "The 25 Most Influential Evangelicals in America" merited the cover of *Time*. Still, many Americans confuse evangelicals with fundamentalists, and two-thirds of Americans report that they have no clue what evangelicalism means. Church members routinely report that they are happy with the religious education their congregations offer, but there is little evidence that offerings such as the Catholics' ubiquitous CCD (Confraternity of Christian Doctrine) courses or Lutheran and Episcopalian confirmation classes are accomplishing much, except perhaps as social events.[58]

Broader religious literacy—understanding of non-Christian religions—is far more difficult to gauge, largely because polling organizations rarely ask about it. In one of the earliest efforts to quantify this sort of religious knowledge, a 1954 Gallup poll asked Americans to name the founder of any religion other than Christianity. Only about a third were able to do so. In a more recent study the overwhelming majority of Americans freely admit that they are not at all familiar with the basic teachings of Islam, Buddhism, or Hinduism. One reason for this may be that most Americans do not know a Muslim, Buddhist, or Hindu. A surprisingly high portion of the Boston University students who took my religious literacy quiz (nearly nine out of ten) knew that the Quran was the Muslims' holy book, but fewer than a quarter were able to name a single Hindu scripture, and only one student was able to list Buddhism's Four Noble Truths. No wonder sociologist Christian Smith has concluded that young Americans are "remarkably inarticulate and befuddled about religion."[59]

Is the Pope Catholic?

Religious groups in the United States have long lamented declines of religious knowledge in their ranks. The US Catholic hierarchy has fretted for decades about a yawning knowledge gap between Catholics who came of age before the Second Vatican Council of the early 1960s and those who did so after its reforms rocked the church. In the Golden Age of Catholic education, students in CCD classes memorized the Baltimore Catechism by heart; virtually all Catholic school students were Catholics, and nearly all the teachers were priests and nuns. Today Catholic school courses are taught almost exclusively by laity, and non-Catholic students are a surging presence. Moreover, efforts to update catechetical training have replaced time-honored instruction about church traditions with touchy-feely conversations about one's personal values. "The problem is that somehow the doctrines got lost and we were left with only our desires, hopes, fears, and dreams, together with broad-stroke connections to a few marquee items like Jesus, God (the relation between them left fuzzy), the Spirit," writes John C. Cavadini of Notre Dame's Department of Theology. "Most other items were left behind in a penumbra of distinguished but cozy irrelevance." As a result, nearly half of American Catholics say that they "often feel that [they] cannot explain [their] faith to others."[60]

A 2001 book called *Young Adult Catholics* found among US Catholic youth "a low level of knowledge of the Catholic tradition and a limited command of Catholic cultural symbols," which the authors attributed to (among other things) a shift in emphasis from participating in the sacraments to loving Jesus and a growing tendency to reduce the sum of religion to moral behavior. What others have called cafeteria Catholicism these researchers refer to as "selective Catholicism," and what these "selective Catholics" are choosing to discard are the narratives, doctrines, and symbols of the church. The most striking finding in *Young Adult Catholics,* however, is that CCD attendance does not correlate in any way with knowledge about Catholicism. Nearly two-thirds of American Catholic youth attend after-school CCD classes, but they aren't learning much there. "We got God loves you but not much else," one interviewee told the authors of *Young Adult Catholics.* Other participants were equally critical:

"Nothing in depth, just Jesus is love."

"No content; touchy-feely."

"I was confirmed and had no idea of what was going on."[61]

A Catholic friend of mine told me that CCD is "lame and useless." When I asked Catholic students in my 2006 "Death and Immortality" course what they did in CCD, the first answer I got was: "Color!" A less flip response was that these classes focus almost exclusively on social service projects. Either way, Catholic youth are not being taught much about their tradition.

One Catholic theologian, noting that "the religious illiteracy of so many otherwise well-educated young Catholics" may be "too familiar to bear mentioning again," refers to Catholic ignorance of Catholicism as akin to a "retinal detachment" in which "a whole field of vision" is "pulling inexorably away toward blindness." The fear is that, as American Catholics are losing sight of what is distinctive about being Catholic, they are becoming indistinguishable from Americans in general. Responding to this troubling situation, Catholic leaders have called for stern measures to address the "crisis in religious literacy" among young Catholics, including attempts to effect the "conversion of Catholics to Catholicism." Meanwhile, theologians in Notre Dame's Department of Theology have called for "a renewed pedagogy of the basics," bishops have made fostering Catholic literacy a high priority, and a Web site called *Catholics Read* is trying "to encourage Catholics to read the Bible and related books." Not to be outdone, entrepreneurs have come up with innovative ways to catechize wayward Catholics, such as Trivial Pursuit–style board games called Catechic and Is the Pope Catholic?[62]

The Greatest Story Never Read

Evangelicals also lament a "tragedy of religious illiteracy" in their ranks. Mark Noll, a Notre Dame history professor and an evangelical himself, opened his book *The Scandal of the Evangelical Mind* (1994) by arguing that "the scandal of the evangelical mind is that there is not much of an evangelical mind." Os Guinness, an evangelical writer, put it equally starkly: "Most evangelicals simply don't think." While evangelicals once followed Jonathan Edwards, John Wesley, and others in affirming both heartfelt experience and hard-won education, evangelicalism today has become, as another born-again Christian wrote, "less a matter of learning than it is a matter of experiencing." Pop psychology has elbowed biblical exegesis out of many born-again pulpits (including some of the most successful megachurches), self-help books outsell theological works in most Christian bookstores, and loving Jesus has replaced affirming the Westminster Confession as the soul of evangelical piety. Despite their conviction that the Bible is the Word of God, evangelicals show scant interest in learning what scripture has to say or wrestling with what it might mean. "I have watched with growing disbelief as the evangelical church has cheerfully plunged into astounding theological illiteracy," writes evangelical theologian David E. Wells. Even in the Bible Belt, the Good Book is fast becoming, as another evangelical puts it, "The Greatest Story Never Read."[63]

In an effort to get evangelical youth to read that unread story, Christian publisher Thomas Nelson initiated in 2003 a series of "Biblezines," which reprint the entire New Testament in a format guaranteed to attract American teens. The glossy magazine *Revolve* (for teen girls) looks like a Christian *Seventeen,* complete with beauty secrets, a feature called "Are You Dating a Godly Guy?" and fashion tips ("Just make sure you look like a child of God"). *Refuel* (for guys) has the frenetic feel of *ESPN: The Magazine* and offers tips on such "practical" matters as wrestling an alligator and handling a jalapeño. ("Man, it's like dealing with the burning problem of sin. You need to grab the right solution. Get Jesus.") *Real*— for hip-hoppers—offers "Dope Christian Rhymes" and a series of articles by ex-cons called "Jail Ain't No Joke." The concept here is simple: young people don't read the Bible because it's too imposing, too hard to understand, too square; but if you put it in a friendly format they'll eat it up. This concept has been a huge commercial success. Thomas Nelson claims that *Revolve* "became America's #1 selling Bible in less than 3 months after it was originally released" in July 2003. It is doubtful, however, that these godly glossies are doing much to wipe out biblical ignorance among American youth. When I assigned *Refuel* one week to students in a seminar on the Bible in American culture, many admitted that they skipped entirely over the New Testament text, reading instead the "extreme" sidebars, which gyrated around the edges of each page, demanding attention like a hyperactive child. One student was convinced that *Refuel* was an *Onion*-style parody. In either case the biblical message was literally lost in translation.[64]

Jews also fret about a lack of basic understanding of Judaism among Jewish youth. "At a time when Jewish life in the United States is flourishing, Jewish ignorance is too," writes one rabbi. "Tens, if not hundreds of thousands of teenage and adult Jews are seeking Jewish involvements— even Jewish leadership positions—all the while hoping no one will find out their unhappy little secret: *They are Jewishly illiterate.*" Convinced that ignorance of Judaism and the problem of out-marriage are inextricably intertwined, groups such as the Jewish Literacy Foundation have dedicated themselves to addressing the problem of "uneducated" and "unaffiliated" Jews.[65]

Even atheists and agnostics have a religious illiteracy rant. The Weststar Institute, the think tank behind the notorious Jesus Seminar (which took it upon itself in the 1980s and 1990s to decide what Jesus *really* said and did), describes itself as "an educational institute dedicated to the advancement of religious literacy." Its Web site contends that "religious literacy is essential" to (among other things) "liberation from religious bullies" and "inoculation against fanaticism." Other freethinkers promote teaching about religion on the theory that the more you know about religion, the less likely you are to be suckered by one of its elaborate cons.[66]

An Eye for an Eye

What these diverse constituencies share is a rhetoric of lament, and tucked inside that rhetoric is a certainty that not so long ago in a place not so far away things used to be much, much better. In the 1790s, or the 1890s for that matter, how might eleven average Americans have responded to a fellow juror who cited the Old Testament book of Leviticus in a 1995 murder trial in Colorado? During jury deliberations a juror pulled out a Bible and referred to the "eye for an eye, a tooth for tooth" passage in Leviticus 24:20–21, which concludes: "He that killeth a man, he shall be put to death." The juror in question then reportedly urged his colleagues to go home to their own Bibles and prayerfully ponder this passage for themselves. The next day the jury returned a unanimous decision for the death penalty. In 2005, after a long appeals process, the Colorado Supreme Court, in a 3–2 decision, ruled that the jurors were not permitted to consult the Bible (which it referred to as "extraneous prejudicial material") and ordered a new trial. In the ensuing hue and cry, conservative Christians, drawing on time-honored culture wars rhetoric, denounced the decision. "Today's ruling further confirms that the judicial branch of our government is nearly bereft of any moral foundation," said a spokesperson for Focus on the Family, a Colorado-based evangelical group. "It is a sad day when the Bible is banned from a jury room." Colorado Governor Bill Owens also decried the decision as "demeaning to people of faith." Few noticed, however, just how impoverished were the exegetical skills of the jury.[67]

There are very few passages from the Hebrew Bible that are explicitly rejected in the New Testament, but Leviticus 24:20–21 (which is echoed in Exodus 21:23–25 and Deuteronomy 19:21) is one of them, since in Matthew 5:38–39 Jesus says, "Ye have heard that it hath been said, An eye for an eye, and a tooth for a tooth: But I say unto you, That ye resist not evil: but whosoever shall smite thee on thy right cheek, turn to him the other also." The purpose of citing this passage is neither to provide divine sanction for nonviolence nor to forestall a reading of the Bible in favor of capital punishment, but simply to offer yet another case study in the dangers of religious illiteracy. Were any jurors aware of Jesus' refutation of "an eye for an eye"—his invocation of a new morality of "turn the other cheek"? Might this defendant have been spared a decade on death row if they had been? At least for me, the moral of this story is neither (as the Colorado Supreme Court ruled) that Americans should not bring Bibles into the jury box nor (as Focus on the Family argued) that they should. The moral is rather that if jurors are going to consult scripture— and, court rulings aside, they doubtless are—then those jurors should at least have the decency (and the piety) to try to get the Bible right.

Two

Religion Matters

In 1966 *Time* magazine asked, on a stark, black cover reminiscent of a Victorian funeral card, "Is God Dead?" Today, when books on spirituality crowd the best-seller lists, God is a recurring character on television, and Jesus is big at the box office, this question seems, well, a little European. "Is Secularism Dead?" seems the pertinent question. Whereas red-state believers once felt marooned in a sea of secularists, now unbelievers in the blue states feel adrift in a sea of patriotic piety. The challenge is not to decide whether it is time to pay our last respects to the Almighty but to figure out how anyone ever could have imagined that God was anything other than alive and well and living in America. Was there really a time when people actually believed that the world was outgrowing religion?

As the 1966 *Time* cover indicates, the answer to that question is yes. Social theorists of such stature as Auguste Comte in the nineteenth century and Max Weber in the twentieth were convinced that wherever modernity advanced, religion would fade. Their acolytes multiplied in the early 1960s, as the religious revival that followed the Second World War was fading into the countercultural camp meeting of the late 1960s and early 1970s. At the height of this flirtation with secularity, theologians weren't just predicting the eclipse of God, they were bragging about doing God in. To be clear, these "Death of God" theologians were not saying that God was literally deceased; many of them didn't believe that God had ever been literally alive in the first place. What they were saying was that God was as good as dead—that divinity had ceased to matter in the modern world.

The academic culture that produced "secularization theory," as the social-scientific species of this prognosticating is called, is a curiously parochial enclave, by no sights as cosmopolitan as its natives imagine, and by no means representative of modern societies. Among academia's curiosities is the persistent skepticism of its inhabitants, their tendency to dismiss faith as fanaticism. Theorists who postulated the death of religion under modernity's crush (or, at a minimum, its retreat into the closet of the private) often based their predictions on nothing more substantial than the vague air of skepticism they detected at the dean's sherry hour; if academia was marching away from God—or so the logic went—the rest of the modern world would surely follow. So it seemed safe for social scientists to ignore religion as a force in the modern world. Religion, after all, had no force over them. When it came to truly important matters such as politics, economy, and society, religion must be as vestigial as the appendix; whether you had one or not didn't matter a whit (though having one might make you deathly ill). Or so went the conventional wisdom.

Pop Goes Jesus

That such wisdom now begs for an adjective as dismissive as *conventional* owes much to the vitality of religion in American popular culture, which is indebted in turn to the collective decision of evangelicals—made around the time the novel was still a scandal and no self-respecting church would cotton to an organ—to join modernity rather than fight it. Since that time religion and modernity have become fast friends, with evangelicals borrowing (and sanctifying) virtually every accoutrement of modern life: theater, radio, rock music, marketing, advertising, television, and the Internet, to say nothing of individualism and consumer capitalism.

We now know that prophecies of God's death, however passionately or poetically argued, were but fingers in the wind, measuring little more than the climate of faith in, say, Sigmund Freud's Vienna, Jean-Paul Sartre's Paris, or the environs of Harvard Square. Secularization theory has run aground, as grand theories often do, on the shoals of historical facts. Today the hard-core atheist, once a stock figure in American life, has gone the way of the freak show. The best-seller lists, long obsessed with sex, lies, and other virtues, are now salted with titles ripped from the hymnals. Sales of *The Purpose-Driven Life* (2002) by the megachurch pastor Rick Warren and Tim LaHaye's and Jerry B. Jenkins's apocalyptic *Left Behind* novels are sufficient (20 and 60 million, respectively) to turn even John Grisham green. On the other side of the spirituality spectrum Dan Brown's *The Da Vinci Code* (2003) and Ron Howard's 2006 movie of the same name combine a caustic critique of Catholicism with a provocative retelling of the life of Jesus. Spirituality and religion, angels and vampires, the Son of God and the supernatural suffuse all sorts of television shows. And on the radio, supposedly secular artists now invoke the J-word with impunity—all the way to the bank. "If I talk about God my record won't get played, Huh?" Kanye West raps in "Jesus Walks." Not exactly. The song won a Grammy.

It was politics rather than pop culture, however, that drove a stake into the heart of the assumption that modernity was sucking the vitality out of religion. The story of the recent rediscovery of the force of faith—that is to say, the story of the shipwreck of secularization theory—begins with the US Supreme Court, which outlawed prayer and devotional Bible reading in the public schools in 1962 and 1963 and upheld abortion in 1973 in *Roe v. Wade*. Democrats defended these rulings (and the freedoms of the counterculture) in the name of Thomas Jefferson, individual rights, public reason, and the First Amendment. Republicans decried the same rulings (and the licentiousness of the counterculture) in the name of God, family values, revelation, and the Judeo-Christian tradition. In this way religion became a player once again in American political life.

The first beneficiary of this rechristening of US politics was of course the peanut farmer and Sunday school teacher from Plains, Georgia, Jimmy Carter. Before Carter it was possible to see the United States as a secular nation with a citizenry that, while individually religious, had nevertheless agreed to quarantine religion from the public square. The White House had been dominated until Carter's 1977 inauguration by a New England ethos that viewed public professions of religion as bad manners or bad faith (or both). Senator John Kennedy, while campaigning for the presidency in 1960, felt obliged to pledge to make policy on subjects such as birth control, gambling, and education without any regard to his Catholicism. Carter, however, in keeping with the emergent southern style in US politics, spoke repeatedly and unabashedly about his piety (not least in *Playboy*, where he famously confessed to lusting in his heart). Governor Ronald Reagan was swept to victory on the wings of the Moral Majority, which from its founding in 1979 had urged the nation to repent of its godlessness and amorality and return to its ostensibly Judeo-Christian roots. President Reagan's speeches repeatedly invoked themes from the biblical commonwealth of New England's Puritans, notably Governor John Winthrop's metaphor of the Massachusetts Bay Colony as a "city upon a hill" (an image that Winthrop himself borrowed from Matthew 5:14: "Ye are the light of the world. A city that is set on a hill cannot be hid").

By the mid-1980s the line between religion and politics had become exceedingly fuzzy, and the Supreme Court was flummoxed about where to draw it. As the ranks of born-again Christians swelled to over one-third of the population and preachers strutted their stuff (and their favorite political candidates) on Christian radio and television stations, religion became more conservative, more public, and more political. (It was during this decade that George W. Bush repented of his alcohol use—and his father's liberal Episcopalianism—and accepted Jesus as his Savior and Lord.)

In the early 1990s a double-digit "God gap" opened up among frequent worshippers between the Democrats (now understood as the secular party) and the Republicans (the "faith-based" alternative). During the 1960s and 1970s there had been no discernible party preference among religious practitioners; religious affiliation was politically irrelevant. In 1992, however, frequent worshippers (those who attend religious congregations at least once a week) preferred Bush the Elder over Bill Clinton by 14 percentage points. That gap widened to 20 percent in the 2000 Bush-Gore and the 2004 Bush-Kerry elections, dwarfing the proverbial gender gap. Gore and Kerry, of course, did better among those who never darken the door of a religious congregation, but such voters constitute a much smaller portion of the electorate than frequent attendees do. After the Republicans triumphed in the 2004 election, there was considerable debate about whether "values voters" really turned the election. That remains questionable. Not in doubt is the fact that regular attendance at religious services is now one of the best predictors of political affiliation and voting behavior.[68]

Jesus-Loving Politicians

The sociologist Peter Berger once remarked that, if India is the world's most religious country and Sweden the least, then the United States is a nation of Indians ruled by Swedes. Not exactly. Like citizens of India, US citizens are extraordinarily religious. But so are their leaders. Since Jimmy Carter, born-again bona fides seems to have become a requirement for the Oval Office, and Jesus-loving politicians are as thick on the ground in Washington DC as Bush haters in Paris. Berger's observation, in short, is now as wet as it once was dry: the United States is plainly a nation of believers ruled by the same.

All this is to say that the old wishful thinking about religion's death at the hands of modernity is starting to look delusional, at least in the

American instance. Some still label the United States "post-Christian," but smart sociologists and historians have admitted the errors of their ways. Berger, one of the star secularization theorists of the 1960s, confessed in a book called *The Desecularization of the World* (1999) that secularization theory is bunk, at least as a general proposition. "The world today, with some exceptions ... is as furiously religious as it ever was, and in some places more so than ever," Berger wrote. "This means that a whole body of literature by historians and social scientists loosely labeled 'secularization theory' is essentially mistaken."[69]

International events also had a hand in overturning the secularization myth. The Iranian Revolution of 1979, which saw Mohammad Reza Shah Pahlavi and his US-backed secularists displaced by Muslim clerics, demonstrated that the old "realist" strategy of conducting foreign policy as if religion didn't matter was not so realistic after all. The rise to power of the Bharatiya Janata Party (BJP) in India in the late 1990s showed that right-wing political activism was not unknown even to the Hindu faith. And 9/11 brought home as never before the public power of religious ideologies. After the horrors of that day we knew not only that piety could elect presidents and overturn governments but also that it could hijack jets, attack the Pentagon, and take down two of the world's largest buildings. Since 9/11 events in Afghanistan, Iraq, and Iran have brought home to Americans, perhaps as never before, the relevance of religion to world affairs. Observers disagree about whether we have entered into a "clash of civilizations" pitting the Judeo-Christian West against the Muslim world. But there is little doubt that groups such as the Wahhabis—virtually unknown to the average American politician just a decade ago—will play a role in shaping the next world order.[70]

One response to these events might be to imagine that religion emerged as a historical force with the rise to power of the Iranian cleric Ayatollah Khomeini in the late 1970s or of the televangelist turned politician Pat Robertson in the early 1980s. That response would be misguided since religion has always mattered, not least in American public life. Today what needs explaining is not the persistence of religion in modern societies but the emergence of unbelief in Europe and among American leaders in media, law, and higher education. If there is any general rule to follow regarding the place of religion in modern life, that rule is that God is alive and well and shaking things up in places as distinct as California and Utah, Zimbabwe and Brazil, India and Pakistan, Israel and Tibet.

Textbook Ignorance (American Style)

High school textbooks blatantly disregard this rule, following instead Emily Post's dictum not to discuss religion in polite company. So US high school students learn virtually nothing about the powerful historical and contemporary effects of religious beliefs, religious practices, religious people, and religious institutions.

When religion is mentioned in US history schoolbooks, it is all too often an afterthought or an embarrassment (or both) and clearly a diversion from what is presumed throughout to be a secular story. Historian Jon Butler has called this the jack-in-the-box approach: Religious characters pop up here and there, typically with all of the color and substance of a circus clown, but their appearances—prosecuting witches in Salem in the 1690s or making monkeys of themselves at the Scopes Trial in Dayton, Tennessee, in the 1920s—are always a surprise (or a scare), and, happily, they go back into hiding as quickly as they emerge. Readers of American history textbooks might learn something about the religious bigotry of the Puritans and the quaint customs of Native Americans of bygone days. And when the Civil War rolls around there may be a brief discussion of the Quakers' abolitionist sentiments. But after President Abraham Lincoln is buried, religion typically goes underground too, leaving students with the distinct impression that, insofar as religion has had any historical effects, those effects are now safely behind us. In fact, according to one study of US history textbooks, there is typically more discussion of railroads than of religion in the postbellum period.[71]

Secularists love to chuckle at evangelicals for their quaint take on American history—for forcibly converting the Founding Fathers to Christianity and for reading the godless Constitution as part of God's divine plan for "Christian America." But secularists have their foibles too, including their own odd take on American history—an interpretation enshrined, unfortunately, in all too many history textbooks. According to this view—call it the secular myth of America—American civilization is on the march from religion to reason, superstition to science. True, religion intrudes occasionally to retard this advance, but zealots always retreat dutifully into the backwaters from whence they came. A thirst for freedom sends the Pilgrims to the New World, but when they get here all they want to do is catch cod, and when Thanksgiving rolls around they give thanks not to God but to the Indians, or to the land itself. The revivals of the early nineteenth century send Americans scurrying to the pews (and away from bars and brothels), but their real purpose is to dupe factory workers into thinking that "God" loves a happy laborer. According to one major study of thirty-one history textbooks up for adoption in Texas, "The treatment of religion as a force in US history continues to receive short shrift."[72]

A Very Short History of Religion in US History

The tendency of textbook authors and publishers to reduce religion, as one critic has put it, to "either a quaint relic or a chronic source of strife" cannot erase the fact that what sociologist Gerhard Lenski called "the religious factor" has been a major factor in US history—and not always on the Dark Side.[73] In fact, none of the classic events in American history—the Revolution, the Civil War, the New Deal, the Reagan Revolution—can be understood without some knowledge of the religious motivations of the generals, soldiers, thinkers, politicians, and voters who made them happen. As the following very short history indicates, religion has always mattered in American society.

Religion mattered in North America's English colonies. As Alexis de Tocqueville observed in *Democracy in America* (1835), "It must never be forgotten that religion gave birth to Anglo-American society."[74] The Puritans came here at least in part to worship God as they saw fit. In virtually everything they thought and did (fishing and farming included), they understood themselves to be in a covenantal relationship with God. According to the terms of this conditional covenant, God would bless them if they acted well and curse them if they did otherwise. In this way every aspect of life among the Puritans, including their economics and their politics, was brought under the sacred canopy of their faith.

In *The Protestant Ethic and the Rise of Capitalism* (1904–1905), Max Weber argued that religious ideas give rise to economic realities (not, as Karl Marx had argued, the other way around). More specifically, Weber contended that the "Protestant ethic" of the Puritans birthed capitalism—by providing a divine mandate for hard work, savings, and other essentials of a capitalist economy. That may or may not be the case. It is indisputable, however, that Puritanism in colonial New England profoundly influenced the course of American literature, art, economics, society, and politics.[75]

Puritanism also affected the founding of Rhode Island, which Roger Williams established as a haven for Baptists and other religious dissenters from Puritan orthodoxy. Anglicanism mattered in the founding of Virginia, and Roman Catholicism in the founding of Maryland. And Quaker

William Penn established Pennsylvania as a "holy experiment" in religious liberty.

Religion mattered in the encounters of British, French, and Spanish colonists with the Indians, and of these colonists with one another. These encounters have often been understood chiefly in military, economic, technological, and even biological terms (since so many Indians died of European diseases), but they were also religious exchanges. Colonists converted Indians to Protestantism and Catholicism, and some colonists taken captive by Indians took up Indian religious practices. Spanish missions included both forts and churches. The French traded furs with the Mohawks, but they also preached to them the Catholic Christ. Later in US history, Native Americans responded to efforts to "civilize" and "Christianize" them with new religious movements such as the Ghost Dance, which played a major role in the Wounded Knee Massacre of 1890.

Religion mattered in the American Revolution too, which proceeded very differently from France's more secular revolt. The Great Awakening of the 1730s and 1740s, a grand revival that stretched up and down the eastern seaboard, helped to knit the colonists into one people and in so doing paved the way for a rebellion against the British Crown that many understood theologically—as a quest to make good in the political realm on the liberty they had already found in the spiritual. The revolution may not have been, as historian J. C. D. Clark has argued, "the last great war of religion in the western world," but it was motivated in part by religious dissenters who saw Anglicanism and monarchy as parts of a single tyrannical force and termed their rebellion "the cause of heaven against hell." As this rhetoric intimates, Americans in the making were careful to direct their revolt against the British monarchy rather than Christianity. Those who drafted the Constitution and the Bill of Rights were influenced far more by Deism than by anticlericalism. The early republic experienced, as historian Henry May has observed, a moderate, pro-Christian Enlightenment as opposed to the more radical, anti-Christian Enlightenment of the French.[76]

This moderate Enlightenment transformed American religion, chiefly by making Protestantism more egalitarian. Having cast off George III, Americans became chary of the tyranny of Calvin's capricious God. In the spiritual marketplace brought on by the First Amendment, "populist preachers" and the "sovereign audience" reigned. Ordinary people took control of their churches just as they had taken control of their government. In the process the God-fearing faith of Calvinism yielded to the Jesus-loving faith of evangelicalism, and American religion became less intellectual and more enthusiastic. Americans, the Baptist firebrand Elias Smith proclaimed in 1809, must be "wholly free to examine for ourselves what is truth, without being bound to a catechism, creed, confession of faith, discipline or any rule excepting the scriptures."[77]

Religion mattered as well during the early nineteenth century, when a series of social reforms swept the country. The movements to abolish slavery, reform the prison system, prohibit alcohol consumption, care for the insane, bring education to the masses, and win for women the right to vote· were all led by evangelical Protestants and justified on biblical grounds. (Abolitionist William Lloyd Garrison put Jesus on the masthead of his newspaper, *The Liberator.*) Moreover, these social reformers drew the resources required to fight these fights from a deeply theological well of postmillennial optimism. They pushed to free slaves and to shut down saloons because they believed that such reforms would usher in the kingdom of God, which in turn would bring on Christ's Second Coming. And if these efforts also preserved the Protestant character of the nation in the face of the Catholic hordes washing ashore from Europe, well, so much the better.

Religion mattered in the Civil War also. This defining moment in American history was of course a battle over slavery and state's rights. But it was also a holy war in which, as President Abraham Lincoln famously observed, both sides "read the same Bible and pray to the same God." The Presbyterian Church of the Confederate States of America argued that slavery was "a gracious Providence" sanctioned in the Bible, while Frederick Douglass, disgusted over Christendom's complicity in the sin of slavery, divided Christianity into two irreconcilable factions: "the corrupt, slaveholding, woman-whipping, cradle-plundering, partial and hypocritical Christianity of this land" and "the pure, peaceable, and impartial Christianity of Christ." When the war ended, both sides saw it as an Armageddon of sorts. Southerners fastened onto the Myth of the Lost Cause, which embraced Confederate soldiers as martyrs and the South as something of a resurrected Christ, while Northerners anointed Lincoln, who was assassinated on Good Friday, as a Christ of their own who shed his blood to atone for the sins of the nation.[78]

After the Civil War Americans debated the pros and cons of capitalism with much of the theological passion they had devoted to the slavery question. Steel magnate and philanthropist Andrew Carnegie promulgated a "gospel of wealth," which understood getting rich as a religious obligation. This theology was later popularized by the Baptist minister and Temple University president Russell Conwell, who contended in

"Acres of Diamonds," a sermon he reportedly preached six thousand times to 13 million people, that "to make money honestly is to preach the gospel." Progressive proponents of the Social Gospel, by contrast, saw capitalism as a sin. The novel *In His Steps* (1897) by the Congregationalist minister Charles M. Sheldon is remembered today for bequeathing to us the query "What would Jesus do?" but its original purpose was to drive home the point that if Jesus were out and about in Victorian America he would be caring for slum dwellers, not selling steel.[79]

Religion mattered as the United States expanded its empire overseas in the late nineteenth century. Earlier, the doctrine of Manifest Destiny had propelled Americans west into the frontier on the theory that it was God's will for them to civilize and Protestantize the continent. After bumping up against the Pacific, Americans looked farther afield, forcibly opening Japan to trade in 1853, and annexing Hawaii and waging war in Cuba and the Philippines in 1898. This expansion, which would soon extend to Haiti, Nicaragua, and many other Latin American countries, was motivated and justified by commercial and military interests, to be sure, but also by a desire to missionize the "heathen."

Religion mattered during World War II, when the federal government packed virtually every Japanese American Buddhist in the country off to an internment camp, in part because government officials confused Buddhism with Shinto (in which the Japanese emperor was worshipped as a god). As in the Civil War, Americans again gave theological reasons both for supporting and opposing this war. Partisans of "muscular Christianity," recalling that Jesus "came not to send peace, but a sword" (Matthew 10:34), contended that their "manly Redeemer" would want them to fight for what is right. Christian pacifists, who worshipped a "sweet Savior," countered with the story of Jesus rebuking followers after they drew blood from his captors in the Garden of Gethsemane (Matthew 26:51–52).[80]

During the Cold War, of course, religious considerations were paramount. In this era "reds" were atheists, Americans were monotheists, and the Cold War was spiritual warfare that, in an era of nuclear weapons, carried portents of the Apocalypse. Religion mattered too in the civil rights movement, which as one historian has written was "led by ministers, fortified by Scripture, exhorted in massive church meetings, and buoyed by gospel music."[81] And it mattered as a thousand freedoms bloomed during the Beat movement of the 1950s and the counterculture of the 1960s and 1970s, which were fueled not only by jazz, rock 'n' roll, and marijuana but also by Zen, Transcendental Meditation, and Jesus piety.

Religion mattered as well in each of America's great waves of immigration since, in addition to hopes and dreams, pilgrims from Ireland and Germany, Japan and India brought to America their religious traditions. Catholicism arrived in force with the Irish in the 1830s and Judaism with Eastern Europeans in the 1880s. After the passage of new immigration legislation in 1965 Buddhists, Hindus, Sikhs, and Muslims came in numbers too. Each of these immigration waves set off nativist opposition, on the one hand, and renewed calls for tolerance and pluralism, on the other. It was largely through the force of immigration that Americans came to debate whether the United States is a secular or a Christian country and (more recently) whether it is Judeo-Christian, Judeo-Christian-Islamic, or multireligious.

Finally, religion mattered in the culture wars of the 1980s and beyond, which were set off by Supreme Court decisions banning school prayer and upholding abortion, and by a little-known 1978 IRS ruling that eliminated the tax-exempt status of segregated Christian schools. These events in turn catapulted evangelicals back into US politics, something they had remained aloof from since their embarrassment at the Scopes "Monkey Trial" in 1925.

Presidential Piety

President George W. Bush has been criticized for seeking to transform the United States into a theocracy. But the public display of religion is nothing new in the White House. In fact, it is older than the White House building itself. When George Washington became the country's first president in 1789, he placed his hand upon a Bible and punctuated his official oath of office with "So help me God." In his inaugural address, he asked "the benign Parent of the Human Race" for "His divine blessing." Since that time, no president has failed to invoke "the Infinite Power," as Jefferson once called God. In fact, presidents have long used their bully pulpit to hold forth on such matters as military chaplains, school prayer, state aid to religious schools, faith-based social services, and creationism. James Garfield, "the Preacher President," was a Disciples of Christ revivalist who occasionally mounted a real pulpit during his years as commander-in-chief. James Polk forbade liquor and dancing in the White House and refused to conduct official business on the Sabbath. Benjamin Harrison, who like John Adams considered going into the ministry, may have been the most active churchman, serving as a deacon and an elder in his Presbyterian church, teaching Sunday school, organizing Bible studies, and participating actively in the YMCA.[82]

When it comes to American history, religion is, as historian Edwin Gaustad once argued, "a datum and point of reference as omnipresent and inescapable as the rivers and the mountains, the laws and the courts, the trade routes and the labor unions, the political parties and the national presidents." That datum is inescapable today in the Supreme Court, which every year or so must decide how to define religion, if only to keep the government out of its hair (and vice versa). Religion is omnipresent in congressional elections, where some Democrats are making an effort to learn the vocabulary of faith and speak it with a native twang. It matters in public debates over environmentalism (which most evangelicals wholeheartedly support) and stem-cell research (which they generally oppose), and whenever and wherever born-again Christians try to apply the "What would Jesus do?" test to public policy—to tax rates in Alabama, the ethics of gas-guzzling SUVs, and the war in Iraq. It matters too in presidential elections since, like it or not, there is a religion test for the presidency. When New York governor Al Smith ran on the Democratic ticket in 1928 he lost in part because he was Catholic. Today you might not have to be a Protestant or even a Christian to earn the Oval Office—92 percent of Americans say they would vote for a Jew—but you do have to be a person of faith. Only 49 percent of Americans say they would even consider making an atheist commander-in-chief.[83]

Textbook Ignorance (Global Style)

The influence of religion is by no means confined to American history. World events have been shaped by Confucian ritual, Jewish law, Christian love, and Buddhist compassion. Chinese history was influenced by Confucian conceptions of family and society, which influenced in turn both Japanese and Korean life. Jain concepts of nonviolence inspired Gandhi's campaign for Indian independence and the US civil rights movement. The Bible inspired (and the Roman Catholic Church funded) Michelangelo's work on the Sistine Chapel. Slogans such as *sola scriptura* ("Bible alone") and "the priesthood of all believers" led Protestant reformers to redraw the map of Europe. Jerusalem has long been a flash point because Jews, Christians, and Muslims alike see it as holy ground. Catholic condemnations of scientists, most famously in the case of Galileo's heliocentric theory of the solar system, retarded the scientific revolution, yet virtually every early scientific pioneer was a believer who was convinced that he was uncovering the secrets of the Creator's Book of Nature. Most of the great conflicts in world history—between Protestants and Catholics in early modern Europe, between Communists and Buddhists in contemporary Tibet, and among Christians, Jews, and Muslims in fifteenth-century Spain—have been largely or partly religious. And some contemporary nation-states, including Israel and Pakistan, emerged out of such conflicts.

Atheists and agnostics, pointing to such horrors as the Holocaust, routinely claim that religion has been the most powerful force for evil in world history. That is probably true. But religion has likely been the world's most powerful force for good too. While it is plausible to claim that religion no longer counts for much in Sweden, Holland, and France, religious beliefs and practices continue to have undeniable impacts on social, economic, and political life in virtually every other country in the world. Religion matters today in hot spots such as the Balkans, northern Ireland, Kashmir, Sri Lanka, and the Middle East. But it also affects Indian tourism (since some high-caste Hindus consider traveling outside of India polluting), AIDS in Africa (where the Roman Catholic Church forbids artificial birth control), and banking throughout the Muslim world (since Islamic law prohibits the giving and receiving of interest).

You wouldn't know any of this by reading high school world history textbooks, however. Hinduism, Buddhism, Judaism, Christianity, and Islam all fare a bit better in these sources than they do in US history schoolbooks. Most world history textbooks offer quick-and-easy accounts of the origins of these religions and, in some cases, of the key beliefs and practices of contemporary adherents. But despite strongly worded calls for teaching about religion in state and national standards for world history, these accounts rarely extend beyond a few pages, and here too religion disappears with the rush of modernity—in this case around 1750. Once again students are led to believe that religion somehow belongs to the past; the present (and, presumably, the future) belongs to secularity. As philosopher Warren Nord has observed, in the case of Islam, the typical textbook teaches students a bit about Islam's origins in the seventh century only to see the tradition disappear for more than a millennium before popping up, quite unexpectedly, in the form of the Iranian hostage crisis of the 1970s. "Religion remains," Gaustad writes, "a classroom pariah."[84]

While one US history text describes Christmas as nothing more than "a warm time for special foods," these world history texts may actually skip altogether the life of Jesus, the Protestant Reformation, and even the Holocaust—all on the theory that religion is too hot to handle in the public schools. The result, according to a report released by the Association for

Supervision and Curriculum Development, is "massive ignorance of any faith beside one's own (and sometimes even of one's own)."[85]

Textbook authors are probably not actively trying to disrespect religion. They are likely just attempting to avoid controversy. Textbook publishers are notoriously allergic to controversy, and religion has a way of stirring up controversy in a country where so many people have invested so much in so many different faiths. Simple prudence might suggest it is best to steer clear of this minefield of potential parental protests.

But ignoring religion can be explosive too. During the 1980s textbook controversies broke out in Tennessee and Alabama when parents charged that schoolbooks that ignored religion were violating the Constitution by preaching the religions of "secular humanism" and the "New Age." These cases brought to light a history textbook that identified the Pilgrims as "people who make long trips" and a home economics text whose teacher's guide listed Jesus and Martin Luther as examples of a hyperreligious "irrational-conscientious" personality type whose "repressed hostility makes them far too literal-minded and rigid in their righteousness."[86]

The current booms in homeschooling and evangelical private schooling can be credited in part to a widespread perception among conservative Christian parents that public schools have gone over to the secular side. Recently some conservative Christians have called for what might be termed a "second disestablishment" of the public schools. Whereas the first disestablishment, effected over the course of the nineteenth century, got rid of a sectarian bias toward Protestantism in public schools, this second disestablishment takes aim at sectarian bias toward "secular humanism." Turning the tables on liberal critics of fundamentalists' efforts to censor such books as *Catch-22* and *Heather Has Two Mommies,* conservative Christian critics contend that secular humanists are now effectively censoring schoolbooks and, through them, the public schools themselves. In this way complaints about the exclusion of religion from schoolbooks have become part of a broader protest against the erasure of religion from American public life—yet another case of antireligious bias.[87]

In 1985, while the cultural conservative William Bennett was overseeing the Department of Education, the DOE's National Institute of Education commissioned a study on the role of religion in some sixty grade school and high school textbooks. In *Censorship: Evidence of Bias in our Children's Textbooks* (1986), the study's principal investigator, Paul Vitz, called attention to the scandal of the excision of religion from elementary and high school textbooks and, by extension, elementary and secondary schools: "Are public school textbooks biased? Are they censored? The answer to both is yes. And the nature of the bias is clear: Religion, traditional family values, and conservative political and economic positions have been reliably excluded from children's textbooks." A few years later historian Timothy Smith accused the authors and publishers of the thirteen high school US history textbooks he reviewed of "ignoring or distorting the place of religion in American history."[88]

Many of these textbook watchers are evangelicals, and as Vitz's comments about "traditional family values" and "conservative political and economic positions" suggest, some are concerned about more than just religion. But conservative Republicans are not the only constituency scandalized by the trivialization of religion in the public schools. Liberals and libertarians are angry too, though their focus is typically on the religion clauses of the First Amendment and America's heritage of religious diversity. While Vitz and those on the right are more likely to be worried about a lack of attention to Puritan New England, critics on the left want to give Roger Williams, William Penn, and other scions of religious liberty their due. A textbook review published by People for the American Way said, "While history textbooks talk about the existence of religious diversity in America, they do not show it: Jews exist only as the objects of discrimination; Catholics exist to be discriminated against and to ask for government money for their own schools; there is no reflection of the diversity within American Protestantism.... The Quakers are shown giving us religious freedom and abolition, and then apparently disappear off the face of the earth."[89]

This muzzling of religion is not only unfair, it is likely unconstitutional. As a series of recent Supreme Court rulings has made plain, the First Amendment requires that the public schools be neutral with respect to religion. That means not taking sides among the religions, not favoring Christianity over Buddhism, for example, or the Baptists over the Lutherans. But it also means not taking sides between religion and irreligion. As Justice Tom Clark wrote in *Abington v. Schempp* (1963), public schools may not preach the "religion of secularism." But pretending that you can understand the world without reckoning with one of the most influential forces in world history comes perilously close to doing just that. One elementary school teacher told researchers that she had celebrated Christmas with her students for twenty-three years and had never mentioned Jesus even once. Is that fair to Christianity? Is it neutral? Does it make educational sense to study American poetry without attending to the Psalms? Or world literature without reading the words of Confucius and Jesus? As Nord noted, "For some time now, people have rightly argued that ignoring black history and women's literature (as texts and curricula have traditionally done) has been anything but neutral. Rather, it betrays a prejudice; it is discriminatory. And so it is with religion."[90]

Reasons for Neglect

Many reasons have been offered for this not-so-benign neglect of religion in US and world history textbooks, which appears to have begun in the 1960s and 1970s. A desire to steer clear of controversy has already been mentioned. Another reason is confusion about Supreme Court decisions on religion and public education. Many teachers, parents, principals, superintendents, curriculum committees, textbook authors, textbook publishers, and members of textbook selection boards are simply unaware that the Court has repeatedly and explicitly given a constitutional seal of approval to teaching about religion "when presented objectively as part of a secular program of education."[91] In fact, many teachers wrongly believe that any mention of religion is unconstitutional. A related reason for the silence on religion in public schools is confusion about the crucial distinction between theology and religious studies—between what the Supreme Court Justice Arthur Goldberg called "the teaching of religion" (which is unconstitutional) and "the teaching about religion" (which is not).[92] Religion has been neglected because of demands for coverage of other "new" subjects—from women and blacks to Native Americans and Latinos. Religion has also been squeezed out by the "back to basics" movement, by the mania for testing (such as Massachusetts's high-stakes MCAS examinations), and by President Bush's "No Child Left Behind" initiative. In each of these cases an emphasis on so-called essentials has pushed to the sidelines supposed inessentials, such as the study of religion.

Schoolbooks also tend to trivialize religion because of the secular biases of those who write and publish them. Eurosecularity is rampant in both higher education and the media, textbook publishing's two homes. The former answers to the Enlightenment and the latter to Romanticism, but neither takes religion as seriously as the American public does. Many authors and publishers are as a result convinced that religion just doesn't matter, except perhaps to the ancient past. In other words, while historians and sociologists are finally coming around to repudiating secularization theory, that theory continues to animate, consciously or unconsciously, the writing and editing of high school textbooks.

So perhaps Peter Berger is not all wrong; perhaps those who lord over this country still have a bit of Sweden's secularity in them. The United

States is ruled, to be sure, from the White House, the Capitol, and the Supreme Court, and none of these institutions is in danger of going over to the secular side any time soon. But knowledge is power too, and textbooks have long functioned in the United States as the scriptures of our schools, which are themselves, as Frances Fitzgerald once put it, "Ministries of Truth for children."[93] Schoolbooks tell us what we need to know and what we ought to value. They tell us what matters and what can be ignored, what is worth dying for and what (or who) is to be shunned. They tell us what America is, both as an ideal and as a reality, and they interpret the wider world—the beaker in which the American experiment is forever bubbling up. This is no small power: telling children what to think about themselves, their country, and the world—telling them as well what to think of Islam and Christianity and Judaism or whether to think of religion at all. At least for the time being the gospel that these ministries are peddling is that religion is moribund—that God is dead.

Things were not always so. Not long ago high school textbooks were filled with references to the living God and the resurrected Christ. They quoted freely from the Gospel of Matthew and the five books of Moses. The truths these schoolbooks told were religious to the core: that the United States was a chosen nation, that good boys and girls would go to heaven, and that cleanliness was next to godliness. You may not agree with these messages, but there is no gainsaying the fact that this sort of education cultivated religious literacy, at least of the Protestant sort. In fact, in the colonies and the early republic, basic literacy and religious literacy were intimately intertwined. It was impossible to learn how to read without learning basic facts about the Christian tradition. To understand how we fell into the predicament we find ourselves in today, we need to go back to this educational Eden and see how teachers and students in that time heeded the biblical commandment to "remember."

Part 2

The Past

Three

Eden (What We Once Knew)

Once upon a time, Americans were a people of the book. Colonists did not just believe in the Bible, they knew what it said. They carried with them on their New World pilgrimages not only a thirst for adventure but also Psalters, New Testaments, and Bibles, which they read and memorized, cited and recited, searched for meaning and quoted for authority. They named their children after Bible heroes: Sarah, Hannah, and Mary; Joseph, Samuel, and David. And when these colonists' descendants became patriots and then citizens, they found themselves in a world animated not only by Adams and Washington and Jefferson but also by Adam and Moses and Jeremiah. They called their towns Eden and Bethlehem, Mount Ararat and Canaan, Shiloh and Jericho, and they knew the Bible stories these place names evoked. Sayings from the Gospels salted their everyday speech, as surely as knowing references to the exploits of the Israelites flavored their presidents' speeches. Among those presidents, Thomas Jefferson likely had the least conventional theology, but when prompted to propose a seal for the new nation, he suggested a biblical image: the people of Israel being led through the wilderness by a pillar of cloud and fire. In the colonies and the early republic, biblical wisdom was literally in the air.[94]

That wisdom had taken flight in sixteenth-century Europe, where Martin Luther, John Calvin, and other renegades had gotten up a religious revolution on the theory that ordinary folks should be able to read the Bible in their own languages and interpret it for themselves. During the Protestant Reformation, as that revolution came to be called, the focus of Christianity shifted—at least for the Reformers—from sacraments to scripture, from the idolatry of images to the veracity of words. *Sola scriptura* ("Bible alone") was the new rallying cry; God's grace now flowed not just through baptism and the Lord's Supper but also, and more importantly, through God's Word. And so clergy became first and foremost interpreters and teachers of that Word, the printing press became a gift from God, the translator became a new saint, and reading became a means of grace. To receive this grace, however, to free oneself from the tyranny of priestly mediation and papal bulls, one had to be able to read. So teaching reading became an act of nearly unparalleled piety, and acquiring basic literacy a religious duty.

The Protestants who peopled the North American colonies in the seventeenth century were heirs of this religious revolution, so among them too the fates of reading and religion were closely tied. But more than salvation hung on the colonists' ability to read; the success of the New World experiment itself depended on the profusion of basic literacy. In both Europe and North America it had long been understood that social order depended on morality, and morality on religion. As early as 1516 the Spanish crown had instructed its explorers that every New World village "was to have its own school and church, and it was the duty of missionaries to see that each individual was taught and instructed ... in the Catholic faith." Among New World Protestants, it was an article of faith that church and state alike depended on a populace able to read and understand the Word of God. Bible reading would foster faith, which would foster ethical behavior, which would sustain social order, even (God willing) in the wilds of this new wilderness. Or so the theory went. The point is that the effort to teach colonial children to read was a high-stakes project. On its success hung not merely the job prospects and spiritual destinies of individual children but the fate of the New World experiment itself. No wonder the colonists passed a series of laws in the seventeenth century requiring apprentices and children to "attain at least so much, as to be able duly to read the Scriptures, and other good and profitable printed Books in the English tongue."[95]

"The Most Literate Place on Earth"

With the American Revolution came a new rationale for basic literacy, and a new aim. Whereas the revolution of Luther and Calvin had provided a theological justification for reading, the revolution of Washington and Adams provided a civic one. Now children needed to read not only to be good Protestants but also to be good citizens—to free themselves from the tyranny of popes as well as kings. The theory here was simple, and it was rooted in a shared sense of the fragility of democratic government. Unlike European monarchies, which saw educated citizens as a bother at best, the American experiment in republican government, which vested sovereignty in the people and, by the 1820s, extended suffrage without regard to economic means (though, it must be noted, still in regard to race and sex), depended for its survival on an informed citizenry. Or, as James Madison put it, "A people who mean to be their own Governors, must arm themselves with the power which knowledge gives."[96] And so two potent justifications for literacy developed side by side. Children would learn to read both to free themselves from sin and to liberate themselves from monarchs—both to save their souls and to save the republic.

These two impulses—one religious and one secular—would eventually conspire to produce the public school system we have today. In the shorter term they produced literacy rates unparalleled in Europe, leading John Adams to write (in 1765) that "a Native of America, especially of New England, who cannot read and wright is as rare a Phenomenon as a Comet." That was hyperbole. Nonetheless, historian David Paul Nord's characterization of seventeenth- and eighteenth-century New England as "perhaps the most literate place on earth" seems warranted. "There is scarcely an adult individual in all New England," Philadelphia's *Analectic Magazine* reported in 1817, "who cannot read, and write, and keep accounts."[97]

Literacy came more slowly to African Americans and Indians. For African Americans the main barrier was a concern among slaveholders that, if slaves learned to read the Bible (including Galatians 3:28, ASV: "there is neither slave nor free ... in Christ Jesus") they would demand freedom in this world as well as the next. According to W. E. B. DuBois, only 5 percent of African Americans could read on the eve of the Civil War. Of course, many did learn to read, through the instruction of ministers or privately funded schools for black children. Some Massachusett Indians acquired literacy through the efforts of Congregationalist missionary John Eliot, who wrote both an *Indian Grammar* (1666) and an *Indian Primer* (1669), the latter promising to train its users "in the good Knowledge of God, in the Knowledge of the Scriptures, and in an ability to Reade." An Indian school in the "Praying Town" of Natick (one of fourteen such settlements) taught Massachusett-speaking Indians to read; the Reverend Cotton Mather of Boston's North Church oversaw an evening school for both Indians and blacks; and Harvard College enrolled Native Americans in its Indian College. Still, literacy was hard to find among these groups.[98]

Among whites, reading literacy was not as common in the southern and middle colonies, where scattered settlements made schools less feasible than they were in New England's towns and where Puritanism's power was muted by a preponderance of Anglicans, Quakers, and Lutherans. Still overall literacy rates for whites were higher—for both men and women—in the colonies than on the Continent.[99]

"Scripture Learnt"

Colonists and early Americans used this literacy first and foremost to read the Bible, which throughout American history has been both the best-selling book and the most influential cultural artifact. There may have been Bibles in as many as nine out of ten homes in the early republic, and the Bible was *the* book for reading in households and schools well into the nineteenth century. Many children read the Bible cover to cover multiple times before adulthood, and families gathered regularly in the morning or evening (or both) to pray, sing hymns, and read the scriptures, which they received as "a manual of law, literature, history, and warfare, as well as a primer for reading and, of course, religion." In fact, the controversial traditions of prayer, hymn singing, and Bible reading in public schools likely developed out of these domestic rituals.[100]

Early Americans' knowledge of religious matters was by no means confined to scripture, however. A few renegades understood the Reformation's *sola scriptura* imperative to mean that they should interpret the Bible solely by the light of individual conscience, without regard to creed, clergy, or catechism. But most Protestants understood that ordinary folk would need some assistance if their society was to avoid lapsing into a Babel of competing Bible interpretations. So Americans imported, published, purchased, read, and memorized countless catechisms—"no less than five hundred" by 1679, according to Puritan divine Increase Mather. The Westminster's Assembly's Shorter Catechism (1647) was the most popular in New England, and the Anglican catechism predominated in New York and such southern colonies as Maryland, Virginia, and the Carolinas. In 1717 a teacher in Rye, New York, reported that his school, sponsored by the Anglican Society for the Propagation of the Gospel, boasted twenty-one boys and fifteen girls who had memorized the entire Anglican catechism.[101]

Seventeenth- and eighteenth-century Americans (undistracted by such technological graces as radio, television, and the Internet) also heeded lengthy sermons on the Incarnation, the crucifixion, and the Trinity. According to church historian Harry Stout, "The average weekly churchgoer in New England ... listened to something like seven thousand sermons in a lifetime, totaling somewhere around fifteen thousand hours of concentrated listening"—roughly ten times the listening load of a four-year college student today. Many of these churchgoers, moreover, returned in print to sermons they had heard in church, making the sermon "the central ritual" in colonial New England and its dominant mode of "public communication." New England laypeople, moreover, were expected to offer their own sermon of sorts as a condition of admission to full membership in their Congregational churches. These "relations," which were delivered in public before the entire congregation, typically included a narrative about the candidates' conversion and a "heavily doctrinal" synopsis of Calvinist theology.[102]

While novels were the most popular books in some European countries in the late eighteenth century, religious books predominated in the colonies and the early republic. In fact, books on religion were far better sellers than books on politics, science, medicine, or law. Full Bibles and New Testaments were the most popular works retained in family libraries, and ministers were the most popular authors—the J. K. Rowlings of their time. Roughly half of the books printed in the British colonies between 1639 and 1689 were religious tomes. During and after the Revolution, political works increased in popularity, as did books that aimed simply to amuse, but religious works predominated; as late as the early nineteenth century roughly two-fifths of the books in family libraries in rural New England were devoted to sacred subjects. Among early America's "steady sellers" (a term coined by historian David D. Hall to denote popular volumes that stayed in print for decades, even centuries) were Philip Doddridge's *The Rise and Progress of Religion in the Soul,* Richard Baxter's *The Saints Everlasting Rest,* and John Bunyan's *Pilgrim's Progress.*[103]

Religion mattered more in New England than in other areas, but religious knowledge was widespread in Virginia too. Like colonial New Englanders, colonial Virginians were a people of the book, convinced that God had "Caused all holy Scriptures to be written for our learning." They supplemented the Bible, however, with the Anglican Book of Common Prayer. As a result, their literacy was liturgical as much as scriptural. "The entire drama of the faith, an explanation of the meaning of existence, a rule of conduct, and an apprehension of the spiritual," writes historian John Nelson, "were laid out for worshippers in the weekly recitation of confession, creed, collects, responses, Psalms, canticles, Old Testament, Gospel, and Epistle lessons." Priests and parents alike catechized youth, and courts instructed parents to teach their children to read the Bible. African American slaves did not convert in Virginia in large numbers, but those who did were catechized on Sundays and generally attended church services with whites.[104]

In the wider Chesapeake region in the seventeenth century, the Bible was far and away the most popular book, followed by Lewis Bayly's Protestant steady seller, *The Practice of Piety,* making Protestantism "something of a common denominator" even in Jefferson's Virginia and once-Catholic Maryland. Like the Bible itself, devotional books such as Bayly's were typically read intensively rather than casually—for knowledge more than entertainment—at least through the early nineteenth century. In other words, they were read and reread, studied and pondered, memorized and recited. In the process, the wisdom shared in these texts became part of the common culture on which colonists and early Americans of all social classes and regions drew. This common culture was not lost on visitors. After a brief sojourn in Connecticut, an Englishwoman wrote in 1775, "They are all politicians, and all Scripture learnt."[105]

All this is to say that, in colonial and early national America, basic literacy and religious literacy were one. Americans acquired, as they learned to read, at least the rudiments of a Protestant worldview, which (because of widespread literacy) was by no means confined to elites or, for that matter, to Protestants. To put it another way, it was not possible to learn how to read without learning biblical idioms; with basic literacy came religious literacy of the Protestant sort. If the early nineteenth century was, as orator and statesman Daniel Webster noted, an "age of knowledge," and the early republic was, as historian William Gilmore argued, a "republic of knowledge," then religious knowledge was one of the grand achievements of that age, and of that republic.[106]

This religious literacy, it should be emphasized, was limited to Christianity. More specifically, it was limited to Protestantism, since anti-Catholicism was one of its key components. Neither the colonists nor early Americans knew much about Judaism or Mohammedanism (as Islam was then called). And only the most sophisticated scholar or well-traveled sea captain knew anything at all about such Asian religions as Buddhism, Hinduism, or Sikhism. When Benjamin Franklin observed in his *Autobiography* that his father's library "consisted chiefly of books in polemic divinity," he was not talking about Islamic divinity.[107] The religious literacy that early Americans possessed was Protestant literacy of a sectarian sort. What they knew were the basic teachings, core practices, key values, and Bible stories of Protestant Christianity as their particular denominations understood it.

Household

Historians once imagined that education was confined to the formal instruction offered in schools. We now know that education occurs whenever human beings teach and learn—that the province of education extends to homes and religious congregations, newspapers and almanacs, publishers and booksellers, libraries and museums, theological tracts and political pamphlets, camp meetings and revivals, social reform organizations and religious denominations, Sunday schools and workplaces.[108] In the colonies and the early republic, all these sites functioned as links in the chain of memory passing religious knowledge down from generation to generation. Newspapers printed not only news stories but also sermons, while almanacs included the positions of the planets alongside quotations from the Psalms. Six venues, however, were particularly important in delivering to early Americans the religious information so many of us have now forgotten. These six venues were: homes, churches, schools, Sunday schools, Bible and tract societies, and colleges, which together warded off, at least through the early nineteenth century, the sort of religious amnesia now rampant among America's faithful.

In the colonies and the early republic, instruction in both reading and religion took place first and foremost in the home, which served as the primary institution of social organization and cultural transmission. Today homeschooling is a countercultural activity, but in seventeenth- and eighteenth-century America it was the norm. In 1642 the Massachusetts Bay Colony passed legislation requiring families to teach their children "to read and understand the principles of religion." Connecticut followed suit in 1650 with a law mandating that children and servants be taught to read and catechized weekly. New Haven, New York, Plymouth, Pennsylvania, and Virginia later passed similar laws.[109]

In early American households children learned to read and write on the laps of their parents. Writing, which was understood as a skill for the counting house, the government office, and the pulpit, was typically restricted to boys. But reading, understood as a religious skill (preparation for God's grace), was taught to girls as well, particularly after the onset of "republican motherhood," which charged eighteenth-century mothers with the task of turning their sons into patriotic citizens.[110]

This was an era of oral reading, which means not only that people read aloud in groups but also that children learned to read via the ears and the mouth as much as the eyes—through both recitation and memorization. In this era the Bible was the core text, and many children imbibed Bible stories by listening to parents and siblings long before they themselves learned to read. In many homes religious instruction was a daily task, and children as young as four or five were drilled repeatedly in the 107 questions and answers of the Westminster Assembly's Shorter Catechism (or in some suitable substitute, such as the 64 questions and answers of *Spiritual Milk for Babes: Drawn out of the Breasts of Both Testaments* by Puritan divine John Cotton). As Cotton's title implies, religious education was to the Puritans as essential as mother's milk, and it too was delivered by mothers to children, who memorized the Ten Commandments and learned of sin, salvation, and sanctification long before they could read. Cotton Mather, another Puritan divine, admonished mothers to drill their children in the catechism "continually," adding that nothing less than the eternal state of their souls hung in the balance:

> The Souls of your Children made a Cry in your Ears, O parents; ... They are Born Children of Wrath; and when they grow up, you have no way to Save them from the dreadful Wrath of God, if you do not Catechise them in the Way of Salvation. They cry to you; O our dear Parents; Acquaint us with the Great God, and His Glorious Christ, that so Good may come unto us! Let us not go from your Tender Knees, down to the Place of Dragons.... What, but more cruel than the Sea-Monsters are the Parents, who will not be moved by such Thoughts as these, to Draw out the Breasts of the Catechism, unto their Young Ones![111]

Household religious instruction did not end with British rule. According to his 1852 memoir, newspaper editor Joseph Buckingham (who was born in 1779) read at least one Bible chapter daily for years, completing the entire work ("with no other omissions than the jaw-breaking chapters of the Chronicles") at least a dozen times before the age of sixteen. In the process, "the incidents and the language became almost as familiar as the grace ... said before and after meals." But Buckingham was nearly as intimate with popular devotional works. "In her devotional exercises," Buckingham remembered, "my mother often introduced passages from Watts and Doddridge." Eventually Buckingham "could recite Watts's version of the Psalms from beginning to end, together with many of his Hymns and Lyric Poems."[112]

Church

Early Americans also learned about religion in the church, which since the time of Jesus' Great Commission has been mandated to go forth not only to baptize but also to "teach all nations" (Matthew 28:19). Meeting-house attendance was required by law as early as 1635 in Massachusetts, and on the eve of the Revolution there were religious establishments in nine of the thirteen colonies. Puritans, in keeping with their emphasis on religious knowledge, recognized not one clerical office but two. Each congregation was to have, in addition to a pastor, a teacher, whose job was to deliver sermons and catechize and tutor youth.

Puritanism was the reigning theology in the colonies, and Puritan sermons were arranged in a four-part scheme of text, doctrine, reasons, and uses. The niceties of this method, which goes back to *The Arte of Prophecying* (1592) by the English Puritan William Perkins, can be left to experts. The important point here is that sermons emphasized scripture—reading it, understanding it, and applying it. Particularly in New England, preachers rarely colored their sermons with tales from their own lives or the lives of their parishioners. They did biblical exegesis in the plain style, often for as long as two hours at a stretch, typically from notes or a complete manuscript. Anglican preaching, popular in Virginia, South Carolina, Georgia, and Maryland, where the Church of England was established, was more essay than exegesis, but Anglican clergy too steered clear of commonplace tales to focus on the Bible. If, as Augustine wrote, preaching is about teaching, delighting, and persuading, early American preachers focused on the first and third desiderata.

The Great Awakening of the mideighteenth century injected into the popular sermon a wider emotional range, including overt appeals to the horrors of hell, chiefly because such appeals induced conversions. Some Great Awakening preachers spoke extemporaneously, and a few waited on the Holy Spirit to inspire whatever they might say that day. But for the most part colonial and early American sermons remained rigorously theological. Most ministers were educated, and biblical preaching was the rule.

Lessons learned from the pulpit were supplemented with individual and group instruction. In Virginia a 1631 law required each minister to "examine, catechize, and instruct the youth and ignorant persons of his parish in the Ten Commandments, the Articles of the Belief and the Lord's Prayer." New England ministers took the duty to transmit basic religious literacy to the next generation at least as seriously. According to

Cotton Mather, "Few pastors of mankind ever took such pains at *catechis-ing,* as have been taken by our New-English divines." Even the traveling evangelist George Whitefield was committed to catechesis. Though he spent most of his seven sojourns to America in the 1730s and 1740s preaching and otherwise stirring up the Great Awakening, he also cate-chized youth and established a school in Savannah, Georgia.[113]

To be sure, not every colonist attended church or submitted to cate-chesis. Even in New England eighteenth-century ministers "complained of ignorant children who knew nothing of their catechisms, parents who failed to present infants for baptism, and brash Sabbath profaners who mocked their sermons, took the Lord's name in vain, or spoke lightly of the Devil."[114] But when it came to religion, a mixture of piety and knowl-edge was the rule.

Both of these ingredients were enhanced by the ratification in 1791 of the First Amendment, which outlawed any federal religious establish-ment. Though state establishments lingered until the demise of the Con-gregational standing order in Massachusetts in 1833, the American preference for persuasion over coercion in all things religious was firmly in place before the end of the eighteenth century. Many feared that reli-gious freedom would weaken the churches, but instead Christianity sprang to life, thanks largely to the Baptists and the Methodists, the two great revivalist denominations that by the midnineteenth century had trounced such old colonial standbys as the Congregationalists and the Episcopalians (as the Anglicans were renamed after the Revolution). In time, the vast spiritual marketplace brought on by the First Amendment would provide virtually all Americans with a religious option they could call their own. So church attendance boomed, and religious congregations became even more effective transmitters of religious knowledge.

Ministers also labored to convert and catechize Indians and African Americans. John Eliot, who has been called "perhaps the quintessential minister-educator of the seventeenth-century colonies," worked with the Indian Job Nesutan to translate the Bible into Massachusett (an Algon-quian language) in 1663. The first book Eliot produced for Indians, howev-er, was a catechism, and he drilled his native students in it relentlessly, teaching them the Ten Commandments and the basic outlines of the Chris-tian story: God's creation, humanity's fall, Christ's redemption. The family of Thomas Mayhew did similar work among Wampanoags on the islands of Martha's Vineyard and Nantucket, though unlike Eliot the Mayhews did not insist that the Indians cut their hair, wear English clothing, and congregate in "Praying Towns." Outside Puritan New England, Anglicans, Lutherans, Roman Catholics, and the Dutch Reformed conducted Native American missions too. One of the most successful, perhaps because it followed the example of the Mayhews in confining its work to Christianizing (as opposed to "civilizing"), was conducted among Mohawks in what is now upstate New York by Anglicans in the Society for the Propagation of the Gospel. Some Indian converts demonstrated exceptional religious literacy. Elisha Paaonut, a Wampanoag preacher from Martha's Vineyard, was said to know the Bible nearly by heart, and the Iroquoian leader T'hayendanegea (Joseph Brant), perhaps the best-known Indian of the Revolutionary period, translated the Gospel of Mark into Mohawk.[115]

African Americans converted to Christianity in far greater numbers, first in the Great Awakening of the early eighteenth century and especially in the revivals of the early nineteenth century. Some slaves acquired basic literacy, but most got their Protestantism orally: through master-approved white preachers, who often confined their sermons to such fare as Ephesians 6:5 and Colossians 3:22: "Slaves, obey your masters"; through black preachers partial to biblical narratives such as the Exodus story (in which God delivers his chosen people from slavery to freedom); and, perhaps most important, through spirituals that celebrated Jesus as a Moses figure who promises both salvation from sins and liberation from slavery. The Reverend William Sturgeon, an Anglican minister who taught African Americans at the Negro Charity School in Philadelphia, reported in the 1750s that many of his students could recite the Lord's Prayer, a creed, and some of the catechism.[116]

School

The United States was the first country to take universal free education as an ideal and the first to transform that ideal into a reality. This transformation began as early as 1647, when Massachusetts Bay Colony legislators passed a law intended to ward off the efforts of "that old deluder, Satan, to keep men from the knowledge of the Scriptures."[117] This law instructed towns of fifty households to appoint teachers of reading and writing, and towns of one hundred households to establish grammar schools. Virginia passed similar legislation during the same decade, and by the 1670s every New England colony except Rhode Island had such a law.

Over the course of the seventeenth century much of the burden of education passed from homes to schools. This happened quickest in New

England, where a population gathered in towns made schooling efficient. But even a settlement as scattered as Virginia had eleven schools by 1689 (to New England's twenty-three). Schools were as multiform as local conditions, ranging from "dame schools" run out of housewives' kitchens to "grammar schools," which taught Hebrew and Greek grammar to aid in the reading of the Bible, to private academies, "petty schools," and evening schools. These were variously funded: by parents, communities, employers, patrons, or churches.

Education was catch-as-catch-can in most southern colonies, which did not mandate education the way New Englanders did. In New York, New Jersey, and Pennsylvania, denominational schools—for Quakers, Mennonites, Lutherans, and so on—were the standard. In them children learned denominational doctrines alongside Bible stories. But across the colonies and then the early United States, teachers relied on similar textbooks. As historian Lawrence Cremin argued, "There is every reason to believe that the curriculum was fairly standard." And from the start this curriculum emphasized religion in a manner that doubtless would be ruled unconstitutional today. Children learned their ABC's from scripture-saturated schoolbooks or from the Good Book itself. And they aimed to read not so much to get rich as to get right with God. According to historian Jennifer Monaghan, early literacy education amounted in essence to "a course in Christianity." "If there was an overriding purpose to American colonial education," adds philosopher Warren Nord, "it was to nurture and sustain a Christian civilization."[118]

This notion of the pious schoolhouse endured well into the nineteenth century, notably in common schools (as public schools were then called). The publicly funded common school emerged in the 1820s in response to such developments as the rise of the "common man," aborning nationalism, the end of property requirements for voting, and, above all, fears about Roman Catholic immigration—the "great danger," as one nativist put it, posed by "the dark and stolid infidelity and vicious radicalism of a large portion of the foreign immigrating population." The goal of these schools, which by 1850 were instructing over 90 percent of the nation's white students, was to Americanize the school population—to make "of many, one." Beginning shortly after the Revolution, that population included girls, who were finally incorporated into the ideal of "universal education" between the 1780s and the 1830s. It embraced Southerners during the Reconstruction era of the late 1860s and 1870s, which finally saw public education take root south of the Mason-Dixon line.[119]

One of the myths of American education is that once upon a time (that is, before the Religious Right started to muck around in the public schools) public education was secular. This is simply not so. From their early-nineteenth-century beginnings, common schools were very much a part of an unofficial yet powerful Protestant establishment, which included the leading Protestant denominations and a "Benevolent Empire" of nondenominational voluntary associations dedicated to improving the world through peace, temperance, abolitionism, and other social reforms. These "little nurseries of piety and religion" preached this informal establishment's gospel of Protestant republicanism, teaching students to revere George Washington as a saint and Jesus as the Christ. They were religious in their leadership, faculty, curricula, and aims. Their textbooks called the Bible the Word of God, and their teachers endeavored to turn out not just good citizens but good Protestants.[120]

The New England Primer

Good Protestants were made during the colonial period through a process that English John Locke once referred to as the "ordinary Road" from illiteracy to learning. The first stop on this "ordinary Road" was the hornbook, a one-page lesson pasted onto a paddle-shaped board and laminated by transparent animal horn. This primitive primer, European in origin, was used in schools, homes, and churches—wherever colonists were taught to read. It came in a variety of forms, though it typically included the alphabet (in upper and lower case), followed by lists of vowels and a syllabary of common two-letter combinations. But the bulk of its limited space was given to religious matters: a cross in the upper left-hand corner, the Lord's Prayer, and a short invocation of the Trinity—"In the Name of the Father, & of the Son, & of the Holy Ghost. Amen."—sometimes called "The Exorcism" because of its alleged capacity to ward off evil.[121]

As printed books came to the colonies, publishers and booksellers became key links in the chain of memory that transmitted religious knowledge to early Americans, and the hornbook yielded to a series of best-selling schoolbooks, each of which combined lessons on spelling and syllabification with scripture readings and catechisms. The first great example was the *New England Primer.*

It is tempting to describe the *New England Primer* as the Bible of early American education. That is not quite right, since the Bible itself was the Bible of early American education. Many young colonists took the Bible as their first reader, laboring to decode in the letters, syllables, and words of the Gospel of Matthew the sounds of the Sermon on the Mount they had memorized as children. But after the Bible the *New England Primer* was the best-selling book in colonial and early America, and far and away the most important American schoolbook for over a century. Probably first published around 1690 (though the earliest extant edition dates to 1727), the *New England Primer* was printed, and plagiarized, by many publishers in hundreds of varying editions under a variety of different names—these were precopyright days—and was ubiquitous in both New England and the middle colonies. Print run estimates vary from two to eight million, but because schoolbooks were so highly prized, these copies were handed around to millions more. According to one historian, the *New England Primer* "influenced, probably more than any other elementary book for children, the character and creed of many leading actors in our country's history," including many of the nation's founders. It was, another historian wrote, "for a hundred years, beyond any other, the principal text of American schools."[122]

The purpose of any primer would seem to be to teach children to read. But like the hornbook, the *New England Primer* was first and foremost a primer on religion. Its 1777 edition, published in the midst of the American Revolution, championed not Enlightenment virtues so much as Calvinist truths. It began with "A Divine Song of Praise to God, for a Child," followed by a child's morning prayer and a child's evening prayer. Only then did it move on to letters, syllables, and words. Its word lists were shot through with religious terminology: one-syllable words such as *saint* and *vice,* two-syllable words such as *Ba-bel* and *Ja-cob.* Then, for more advanced readers (and theologians), *dam-ni-fy, ho-li-ness, be-a-ti-tude, be-ne-dic-ti-on, for-ni-ca-ti-on,* and *a-bo-mi-na-ti-on.*[123]

The heart of the *New England Primer,* however, was its series of rhyming couplets and accompanying woodcuts, which offered children a simple way to memorize the alphabet. In almost every case these couplets drew on a Bible story (more often the Old Testament than the New). The lesson began (again in 1777):

A *In Adam's Fall*
   We sinned all.
B *Heaven to find;*
   The Bible Mind.
C *Christ crucify'd*
   For sinners dy'd.

By the time students got to *Z* and Zacchaeus, they had been introduced to the Flood, Judgment Day, the Exodus, Peter's denial of Christ, Elijah, Job, Esther, Ruth, Samuel, Obadias, David, and many more Bible stories and heroes.

It has been widely remarked that the *New England Primer* taught the Calvinist theology of New England's Puritans, including its fear of God, its morbid preoccupation with sin and death, and its dread in the face of everlasting judgment. In addition to preaching Reformed truths, however, the book offered a wealth of basic information about the Christian tradition. Following immediately on its doggerel of the ABC's was a one-page catechism of the Old and New Testaments, which began:

Who was the first man?	*Adam*
Who was the first woman?	*Eve*
Who was the first Murderer?	*Cain*
Who was the first Martyr?	*Abel*

This catechism went on to teach schoolchildren about the oldest man (Methuselah), the strongest man (Sampson), and the wisest man (Solomon). It told readers who built the Ark (Noah), who led Israel into Canaan (Joshua), who saves lost souls (Jesus Christ), who betrayed his Master (Judas), and who was the first Christian martyr (Stephen). Later versions Americanized this list, asking: "Who saved America?": "George Washington"; and "Who betrayed America?": "Benedict Arnold."[124]

The *New England Primer* also included the Lord's Prayer and the Apostles' Creed, Bible quotations, lists of biblical names, "A Dialogue Between Christ, Youth, and the Devil," an account (accompanied by a gruesome woodcut) of the martyrdom of the Protestant minister Mr. John Rogers at the hands of Queen Mary, and a shorter version of the Westminster Confession, which educated its readers about such matters as monotheism, original sin, and the virgin birth. Finally, the *New England Primer* contained this famous prayer (which seems to have first appeared in this formulation in the 1737 edition):

Now I lay me down to sleep
I pray the Lord my soul to keep
If I should die before I wake
I pray the Lord my soul to take.

Today we often think of public schools as religion-free zones, as if the First Amendment guarantees not freedom of religion but freedom from it. In early America, however, religion permeated the classroom. Children learned both to conduct business and to get right with God. The primers they consulted were, as other historians have noted, "denominational texts," which focused as much on the Fourth R as the first. Or, to put it more precisely, religion was their first R, since in their hierarchy of knowledge theology towered above reading, writing, and arithmetic. Children who learned from the *New England Primer* would have acquired not only basic literacy in English but also basic literacy in Calvinism. From an early age they would have been conversant with the foundational beliefs, practices, stories, and heroes of their parents' faith.[125]

Noah Webster's Speller

The *New England Primer* dominated eighteenth-century education and was used sporadically into the early twentieth century, but its sales were minuscule when compared with the first great best seller in American history, Noah Webster's speller. Webster is best known for his efforts to standardize the writing and speaking of American English—by taking the *u* out of *honour* and the *k* out of *musick*—notably in his *American Dictionary of the English Language* of 1828 and his "American" translation of the Bible of 1833. But Webster's most popular creation was *The American Spelling Book,* which first appeared in 1783 (under the infelicitous title of *Grammatical Institute of the English Language, Part I*) and later came to be known, because of its vivid blue covers, as the "blue-back speller."

At a time when sales of a few thousand units qualified a book as an unqualified success, Webster's speller was shipped to dry-goods stores in crates of seventy-two dozen. The editions came fast and furious; publishers in Vermont alone produced some twenty-seven editions between 1787 and 1820. Webster estimated that ten million copies had come off printing presses by 1829, and by midcentury Americans were reportedly buying copies at a rate of a million per year (though sales spiked to over a million and a half copies in 1866, when newly freed slaves turned to Webster to grab the brass ring of literacy). Aggregate sales estimates converge in the range of seventy million, making Webster's speller one of the best-selling books of all time, behind only the Bible and perhaps *Quotations from Chairman Mao Tse-tung.*[126]

Given these figures, it is difficult to overestimate the influence of Webster's speller. Historian Henry Steele Commager, however, came close. "It established its sovereignty in the East; it went west with the Conestoga wagon, and in the knapsacks of countless itinerant pedagogues; it leaped the mountains and established its empire on the Pacific coast; it even invaded the South," Commager wrote. "No other secular book had ever spread so wide, penetrated so deep, lasted so long.... Under its benign guidance generations of young Americans learned the same words, the same spelling, the same pronunciations; read the same stories; absorbed the same moral lessons."[127]

But young Americans absorbed far more than morality from Webster, as this was no secular book. In fact, Webster's speller was chock-full of Bible quotations and other religious fare. Webster once criticized his most eminent predecessor, Thomas Dilworth, for never missing an opportunity to insert God into his popular speller, *A New Guide to the English Tongue* (1740). "Nothing has a greater tendency to lessen the reverence which mankind ought to have for the Supreme Being," Webster remarked acidly, "than a careless repetition of his name upon every trifling occasion." But Webster's speller, while doubtless more circumspect when it came to naming Names, hallowed God too. Its first reading lesson—the very words on which millions of American children began to read—begins with these pious lines:

> *No man may put off the law of God.*
> *My joy is in his law all the day.*
> *O may I not go in the way of sin!*
> *Let me not go in the way of ill men.*

This lesson goes on to discuss—in simple vocabulary that somehow manages to respect Webster's self-imposed limit of three letters (and one syllable) per word—such matters as repentance, the Golden Rule, loving one's enemies, salvation, the atonement, churchgoing, everlasting life, cursing, swearing, stealing, lying, and hell.[128]

Subsequent lessons, also intended (in keeping with pedagogical customs of the day) to be committed to memory and spoken aloud, quote from the Bible repeatedly, but Webster's speller emphasizes morality as much as theology. Webster called his narratives "Lessons of easy Words, to teach children to read, and to know their duty," and they echo the virtue and vice catalogs in Paul's Epistles. Repeatedly the man whom conservative Christians now laud as the "Father of American Christian Education" reminded his readers that both their fates and the fate of the nation hung on their moral scruples. His "Moral Catechism," printed near the back of the book, commends to readers lives of humility, mercy, peacemaking, purity of heart, justice, generosity, gratitude, charity, frugality, industry, and cheerfulness while steering them away from pride, cruelty, anger, revenge, deceit, laziness, drunkenness, wastefulness, and avarice. "God's word, contained in the Bible," this catechism proclaims, "has furnished all necessary rules to direct our conduct."[129]

Webster then tells his readers the words they need to read the Bible. He prints lists of hundreds of names of biblical characters, each parsed into syllables and with detailed notations on pronunciation. He includes a narrative of the creation of the world, which begins, "In six days God made the world, and all things that are in it." He prints various sayings of Jesus. His list of homophones—*pray* and *prey, rite* and *right, prophet* and *profit*—includes many words important to church history, and his lists of abbreviations cover more than a dozen biblical books.[130]

Webster's speller is a bit more secular and much less sectarian than the unapologetically Calvinist *New England Primer*. The *New England Primer* reads like a sacred text with some reading lessons thrown in, whereas Webster's speller is plainly a reading book with religious lessons interspersed. Nonetheless, by one account, one-third to one-half of the content of Webster's early spellers was religious fare.[131]

McGuffey's Readers

Both the *New England Primer* and Webster's *American Spelling Book* had lives of Old Testament proportions. In fact, each enjoyed a revival among evangelical homeschoolers in the 1980s and 1990s and remained in print in the early twenty-first century. In the 1830s, however, these two classics gave way to the hugely popular McGuffey readers, which like their predecessors conveyed to American youth considerable religious knowledge.

The McGuffey readers, which debuted in 1836, have been called "the most influential volumes ever published in America." Although more popular in the Midwest and the South than in New England, and in rural than urban America, they became by 1890 the standard school readers in some thirty-seven states. Over their long life they sold roughly 120 million copies, making them, along with the Bible, Webster's spellers, and the Harry Potter series, the most popular books in American history. Individual copies of these readers were almost certainly read by more people than the average Bible, however, since these volumes (which often remained in a schoolhouse for a dozen years) were, like the *New England Primer* and Webster's speller, read to rags. Their influence, moreover, extended well beyond schoolhouse walls since ministers, writers, and other culture brokers who memorized their contents as children went on to quote liberally from them as adults.[132]

The McGuffey readers were the brainchild of William Holmes McGuffey, a Scotch-Irish Presbyterian preacher and professor of ancient languages at Miami University in Oxford, Ohio, who became upon their publication the "Schoolmaster of the Nation." (His brother, Alexander Hamilton McGuffey, later assisted with the franchise.) These readers succeeded commercially because they told gripping stories about children to children, and in that sense anticipated and contributed to the midcentury mania for child-centered education. Today we owe to these volumes our collective memory of such ditties as "Twinkle, Twinkle, Little Star" and such sayings as "Where there's a will, there's a way."

Scholars have criticized the McGuffey readers for presenting a romantic image of rural and small-town life—a happy heartland free of racial, ethnic, religious, and class conflict. They have lamented the absence of blacks, Native Americans, Catholics, and Jews in these texts. And they have noted the readers' social conservativism—their middle-class morality of frugality, hard work, and self-control. At least as noteworthy, however, is the theology of these volumes. One biographer wrote that "two passions consumed McGuffey—educating the young mind and preaching the gospel." His popular readers did both. Many of the entries were written by notable American ministers; others came from the Bible itself. Early readers were saturated with the sort of Calvinist content that McGuffey would have gotten from the Westminster Confession during his Presbyterian childhood. God was these books' leading character, piety their cardinal virtue, and the Bible their ultimate source of wisdom. According to church historian George Marsden, the earliest editions of these readers taught "God's creation and Providence, the insignificance of the world, the sinfulness of humans, the primacy of salvation through Christ for the next life, and the necessity of righteousness and piety in this life."[133]

One of the problems faced by compilers of any nineteenth-century reader was which Bible translations to use. If you used the Protestants' beloved King James, Catholics would cry foul. But if you went with the Catholics' authoritative Douay-Rheims translation, Protestants would protest. McGuffey solved this problem ingeniously—by offering folksy translations of key passages. His readers rendered the Ten Commandments in rhyme:

Thou no gods shall have but me.
Before no idol bend the knee.

Take not the name of God in vain.
Dare not the sabbath day profane.
Give to thy parents honor due.
Take heed that thou no murder do.
Abstain from words and deeds unclean.
Steal not, for thou by God art seen.
Tell not a willful lie, nor love it.
What is thy neighbor's do not covet.[134]

And they delivered the Lord's Prayer too in an accessible (though cloying) rhyming format:

Our Father in heaven,
We hallow thy name;
May thy kingdom holy
On earth be the same;
Oh, give to us daily
Our portion of bread;
It is from thy bounty,
That all must be fed.
Forgive our transgressions,
And teach us to know
The humble compassion
That pardons each foe;
Keep us from temptation,
From weakness and sin,
And thine be the glory
Forever! Amen![135]

As popular schoolbooks evolved from the *New England Primer* through Webster's spellers and McGuffey's readers, things changed but much remained the same. These classic schoolbooks equipped generations of American schoolchildren not only with basic literacy but also with cultural literacy—what historian Elliot Gorn has called "a lingua franca . . . that went beyond common readings to a shared set of morals, aesthetics, and beliefs." More important for present purposes, these textbooks provided a shared set of religious information. Though the moralism characteristic of Victorian America undeniably accreted in the McGuffey readers over time—"Pure and undefiled religion is," one later reader said, "to do good"—key Protestant doctrines and stories were nonetheless plainly conveyed. Students reared on these schoolbooks typically learned the Ten Commandments and the Lord's Prayer by heart. They were familiar with the Sermon on the Mount and the Exodus story. They understood the rudiments of church history and the creeds. To put the matter more in civic terms, they were capable of understanding biblically inflected debates on such matters as slavery, temperance, women's rights, war, and poverty. They knew the religious heritage out of which these debates grew and without which they would have sounded bewildering.[136]

Other Pious Schoolbooks

Neither the *New England Primer* nor Webster's speller nor the McGuffey readers enjoyed a monopoly over the minds of American schoolchildren. According to one historian, the quantity of schoolbooks circulating in the early republic was so large as to be "almost beyond belief." But competing books also stressed the Fourth R alongside reading, writing, and arithmetic. There were spellers for Quakers and Lutherans, and primers and catechisms for Anglicans. Dilworth's hugely popular *New Guide* was even more theological than Webster's speller, and as a rule textbooks published in New England accented divinity more than the Cincinnati-based McGuffey franchise. Readers by Charles Sanders, which in some years outsold the McGuffey readers, included, in addition to lessons on "The Bears and the Bees" and "The Cat and the Lobster," such fare as "God Made All Things" and "The Child's Prayer." "The Bible" was the first lesson in Samuel Goodrich's popular reader. The *Franklin Family Primer* (1807) included numerous illustrations of Bible scenes, including "Noah's Ark," "Moses in the Bullrushes," and "Moses Smiting the Rock." And *The First Dixie Reader* (1868) somehow squeezed into a lesson called "The Frog" not only the fact that it is bad for boys to kill frogs but also this tidbit: that "God made [the frog's] tongue with glue on it, so he could thus get his food."[137]

Among these alternatives to Webster and McGuffey, Richard Gilmour's Catholic readers are particularly important. Widely used in parochial schools, these readers contained, in addition to such McGuffey staples as "Rip Van Winkle," such articles as "The Power of the Blessed Sacrament." Alongside requisite moral lessons on industry, honesty, and prudence, they included more specifically Catholic fare, including teachings on the evils of avarice and the importance of charity to the poor. Popes and saints—Mary the first among them—figured prominently, as did monks, missionaries, and martyrs.[138]

These examples, which could be multiplied a hundredfold, lend force to historian Ruth Miller Elson's claim that "a religious tone is evidence throughout the century" in American primers, spellers, and readers. Even arithmetic texts, she observes in her history of nineteenth-century schoolbooks, taught religious facts—for example, by asking students to calculate how many days had passed "since the birth of Our Savior." From these schoolbooks children learned that there is one God who created, ruled, and judged the world, and that Americans are God's chosen people. They also learned that Protestantism was the one true religion and that Roman Catholicism was an antidemocratic invitation to ignorance, immorality, and tyranny. (Catholic schoolbooks had their own prejudices, such as the claim in *Sadler's Excelsior Geography* (1878) that Catholicism is the "one true religion.")[139]

Sunday School

These pious schoolbooks were used in schools, households, and churches. They were also employed in another link in the chain of memory that helped to ward off religious amnesia, namely, the Sunday school, which according to one historian served as "the primary tool of Protestant religious education in the nineteenth century."[140]

Today Christian Sunday schools and Jewish Sabbath schools are places where children of congregation members are raised in a given faith. When the Sunday school movement migrated from England to the United States in the 1790s, however, Sunday schools had a very different purpose: teaching working-class children (including many African Americans) how to read. In the 1820s this British model gave way to the modern Sunday school under the auspices of the American Sunday School Union (ASSU), which was founded in Philadelphia in 1824. Now the children of church members made up the student body, and cultivating religious literacy was the mission.

This new model, which focused on learning "the leading doctrines of the Bible" through rote memorization and recitation, was an immediate success. By 1832, 8 percent of the nation's Sunday school age children were enrolled in ASSU-affiliated schools, with much higher numbers in some urban centers (28 percent in Philadelphia), and by 1837 there were roughly one million students in sixteen thousand Sunday schools across the country. One reason for these impressive numbers was the willingness of Sunday schools to enroll female students. Whereas common schools were initially largely for boys, girls constituted the majority of students in early Sunday schools. Sunday schools were less pluralistic when it came to region, however. Although today's Bible Belt is in the South, Sunday schools were initially concentrated in the North.[141]

Sunday schools fostered religious literacy by publishing and distributing religious tracts and by constructing a vast network of libraries, which just before the Civil War accounted for most of the nation's total libraries and nearly half its total library volumes. The ASSU's main emphasis, however, was Sunday school instruction. Initially, Sunday school teachers tried to spark a sudden conversion in each student. By midcentury, however, the emphasis shifted to a more gradual process that liberal Protestant theologian Horace Bushnell called "Christian nurture." Around this same time teachers started downplaying rote memorization of Bible sayings, focusing instead on grasping the meanings of Bible stories. *Lessons for Every Sunday in the Year* (1864), a popular Sunday school text published by the Methodist Episcopal Sunday School Union (but by no means confined to that denomination) guided students through fifty-two lessons on the Old and New Testaments. This book and its imitators prompted Sunday school book publishers to agree on a uniform lesson plan, which cycled through the same Bible passages each week for seven years, ensuring that Baptists in Texas and Methodists in Iowa were reading the same texts each weekend (though not through the same interpretive lenses). In this way Sunday schools became "a primary avenue for socializing the rising generations into evangelical culture."[142]

The growth of common schools in the 1820s and 1830s gave a huge boost to the Sunday school movement. In fact, these two types of schools settled almost immediately into a symbiotic relationship of separate spheres. As common schools and Sunday schools spread, the former focused on basic literacy while the latter emphasized religious literacy. This partnership would eventually have a double effect: divesting Sunday schools of their original mission of teaching literacy to the poor and underprivileged, and divesting common schools of their charge to make good Protestants. In the process, parents and ministers concerned about the religious education of their youth came to see the value added of the Sunday school.

Some restorationists (Protestants who wanted the modern church to mimic the New Testament church in all particulars) rejected Sunday schools as, to quote Disciples of Christ founder Alexander Campbell, "hobbies of modern times" and "inventions of men." But the Disciples of Christ eventually got on the Sunday school bandwagon, and denominations with proud histories of catechesis—notably, Episcopalians and

Methodists—were big Sunday school supporters from the start. In time, virtually every church in the country would offer Sunday classes to members' children, and Sunday schools would come to rival common schools as vehicles for cultural transmission.[143]

Like common schools, Sunday schools taught middle-class morality. They also delivered basic knowledge of evangelical Protestant theology (human depravity, Christ's atonement, and so on) as well as the distinctive beliefs, practices, and histories of their own Protestant denominations. (Though nonsectarian itself, the ASSU allowed individual Sunday schools to affiliate with particular denominational groups.) In this way Sunday schools became, in the judgment of Anne Boylan, the ASSU's foremost historian, "the primary locale—outside of the family—for religious indoctrination of Protestant youth." "A child who had spent any appreciable time in a Sunday school," Boylan concludes, "would be well equipped to participate in American public life, where references to Bible characters and events were commonplace."[144]

Bible and Tract Societies

The literacy fostered by Sunday schools and common schools was by no means evenly distributed across the United States. On the western frontier a scattered population made churches and schools scarce and libraries almost nonexistent. Missionaries to the frontier met illiterate pioneers whose encounters with Christianity were rare and fleeting, prompting one missionary to lament in 1815 "the dreadful famine of the *written,* as well as the *preached* word of God." Other evangelists were appalled to find families in Kentucky who "seem as stupid on the subject of religion as the stones of the street," a Virginia woman who mistook a biography of Washington for a Bible, and a group of young toughs who threw stones at the scriptures for target practice. This famine was particularly worrying in light of the feast of secular novels and other "vicious literature" available on the frontier. Pioneers seemed to expend the limited reading skills they possessed on literature that amused rather than edified. As a result, the masses on the frontier were left "in the grossest darkness and spiritual ignorance," "destitute" of both learning and religious books.[145]

Or so went the missionaries' literature of lament. Some suspicion is warranted here, however, since these lamentations were used to win support for a vast enterprise of evangelical organizations dedicated to bringing true religion to all Americans—to imploring readers on the frontier to "put down that novel!" and study the Bible.[146]

Beginning in the nation's first generation, hundreds of nonprofit Bible, tract, and missionary societies sprang up at the local, state, and national levels, each intent on imprinting the stamp of evangelicalism on American civilization. The earliest were local, starting with the Boston-based Society for Propagating the Gospel among the Indians and Others in North-America (SPGNA), which became in 1787 the first missionary society established in the United States. Many were denominational efforts, such as the General Baptist Tract Society. The most enduring and successful, however, were interdenominational associations with national reach—groups such as the American Bible Society (established 1816), the American Tract Society (established 1825), and, as already noted, the American Sunday School Union. As their names imply, these voluntary organizations had different missions. Each was founded, however, on the proposition that faith without knowledge is dead, and all grew into ambitious publishers with vast distribution networks. Together these organizations produced Bibles of all shapes and sizes, tracts that aped the salacious styles of the popular literature of the day, and spiritual literature for children. They collected these volumes in free libraries devoted to stamping out religious ignorance. And they cast them across the continent through a vast distribution network of preachers doubling as itinerant book distributors.

In the first decade after its founding the SPGNA distributed an impressive inventory of books: 1566 primers, 969 spellers, 768 New Testaments, 634 Psalters, and 310 Bibles. The Massachusetts Society for Promoting Christian Knowledge, which upon its founding in 1803 became the first US voluntary association devoted to religious publishing, had by 1815 distributed 30,350 tracts and 8,224 books. By the 1830s, however, such societies were counting their output in the millions. The American Tract Society, for example, was pumping out five million tracts annually, leading some enthusiasts to dream of placing a tract in the hands of each and every American. This would prove to be an impossible dream, but America's Bible and tract societies did create, as historian David Paul Nord argued, "the first genuine mass media in America."[147]

College

The last of the six links in the chain of memory that fostered religious literacy in the colonial and early national eras was the college. Among the generation of immigrants that arrived in New England before 1646 were one hundred men with Cambridge degrees and thirty-two with degrees from Oxford. Of these men, ninety-eight served as ministers. So it should not be surprising either that New Englanders valued higher education or that they understood the college to be, in the words of Jonathan Edwards (who would later serve as Princeton's president), "nurseries of piety."[148]

America's first three colleges—Harvard (established 1636), William and Mary (1693), and Yale (1701)—were all founded primarily to educate clergy, and each emphasized the Fourth R. Yale was dedicated to the "upholding and propagating of the Christian Protestant religion," and William and Mary was at its founding "a seminary of ministers of the gospel." At Harvard, where the vast majority of the library's titles were works in divinity, faculty taught students not only "to know God and Jesus Christ" but also to understand Jesus as "the only foundation of all sound knowledge and learning." Recipients of Harvard's AB degree had to be "able to read extempore the Pentateuch, and the New Testament in Latin out of the Original Tongues"—a good thing since most Harvard graduates through the late seventeenth century went on to become Protestant ministers.[149]

By the Revolution, there were nine degree-granting colleges (not counting various academies offering similar instruction), and none of them even contemplated education as a secular endeavor. Instruction in these colleges stressed, according to historian Lawrence Veysey, "discipline and piety," and religious concerns remained paramount in American higher education well into the nineteenth century.[150] Most colleges had denominational ties, and their courses inculcated without apology the specific theological and liturgical commitments of their particular denominations. Students were required to attend chapel services, and campus revivals were often stirred up by college presidents, who were typically Protestant ministers themselves.

Faculty (also top-heavy with Protestant clergy) offered a fixed curriculum focused on what we now call Classics. Following Noah Webster, who understood the goal of education to be "the preservation and transmission of the wisdom of the ages," faculty at these denominational colleges sought less to create new knowledge than to pass down the sacred truths bequeathed to them from antiquity.[151] In addition to Latin, professors taught Hebrew and Greek, with an eye to equipping students to read the Old and New Testaments in their original languages. The standard curriculum culminated in a yearlong course in moral philosophy typically taught by the college president. This course, which often included "evidences of Christianity," aimed to gather the disparate knowledge accumulated in prior college courses into a coherent theological vision. Its ultimate goal—and that of higher education generally—was to make learned Protestants.

Education reformers challenged this denominational college model throughout the 1820s, arguing (among other things) that some theological and philological instruction needed to give way to new subjects and that a preoccupation with something akin to theological correctness was impeding advances in science. But Protestant theology remained a staple of higher education long after it was run out of public schools. The old college paradigm, which favored teaching over research and Greek and Latin over geology and geography, triumphed in the influential Yale Report of 1828, which argued for the retention of classical language training on the basis of "an imperative obligation to read and know the Scriptures in their original simplicity and purity." The ministry remained the most popular career choice for college graduates into the late 1830s, and well beyond the Civil War private colleges continued to exude a Protestant ethos. Public colleges and universities did too. In fact, as historians Jon Roberts and James Turner have observed, state institutions were if anything more explicitly theological than their private counterparts "since they answered to electorates deeply suspicious even of Catholics, much more of outright unbelievers." As late as 1905 a study of religion at state universities would conclude that these institutions were "more intensely and genuinely Christian than the average community."[152]

Toward a New Religion

In this brief history of how households and churches, schools and Sunday schools, spellers and primers, voluntary associations and colleges conspired to plant religious knowledge in Americans, we see both the flowering of religious literacy and the seeds of its demise. Children who read, memorized, and recited passages in the *New England Primer*, Webster's spellers, and the McGuffey readers learned much about the basic beliefs and practices, stories and heroes of Protestant Christianity. But by the early nineteenth century the acids of nondenominationalism were starting to erode religious content. Sectarian Protestantism (most conspicuously of the Calvinist variety) was starting to give way to nonsectarian Protestantism. With this shift came a tendency to emphasize morality since it was in the domain of ethics that Protestants of different denominations could agree. As it became imperative to get along (at least with other Protestants), theology started giving ground to morality. If the point of the *New England Primer* was to teach children that they were sinners and that Jesus died to save them from their sins, the point of the later McGuffey readers was to teach children that God wanted them to work hard, save their money, tell the truth, and avoid alcohol. Their core text was not Paul's "for by grace are ye saved through faith" (Ephesians 2:8) but the Ten Commandments. Already Americans were inaugurating a new form of religion—less sectarian, less doctrinal, more emotional, and more moralistic. "Little children, you must seek," one reader put it, "rather to be good than wise."[153]

In other words, we had already taken one giant step toward the contemporary era in which morality is the essence of religion and the term *Christian* connotes opposition to abortion and gay marriage rather than faith in the incarnation and the redemption—an era in which having a relationship with Jesus is more important than knowing what he actually did, in which believing in the Bible matters more than knowing what the Bible has to say. More than the forces of secularism, it was this sort of religion that would do religious literacy in.

Four

The Fall (How We Forgot)

Historian Martin Marty tells a story about a heated debate at an early Methodist convention concerning whether Methodists should build seminaries to educate clergy. Rising to oppose the idea, one bishop said that faith was strongest in a soul unfettered by book learning. If pressed, the bishop added, he would opt any day for a preacher without education over a preacher without passion. A critic then asked the bishop whether he was thankful for his own ignorance, to which the bishop unabashedly answered yes. "Whereupon," Marty writes, "the critic moved that the convention sing a *Te Deum,* since the good bishop had so much for which to be thankful."[154]

This story encapsulates the nineteenth-century battle inside American Christianity between piety and learning—a battle that learning lost. In Marty's telling the bishop plays the fool. But for many American Christians, then and today, willingness to be a fool for Christ is a mark of true faith. Christianity is about loving Jesus; it does not require knowing much of anything at all. How did this happen? How did religious ignorance become a sign—perhaps *the* sign—of genuine piety? And what lessons might this story of our fall into religious illiteracy hold for Americans today?

Answers to these questions must begin with the fact that the divorce of piety and learning is nothing new. In the early 1950s Dean O. R. Sellers of Chicago's McCormick Theological Seminary was lamenting that demand for such practical subjects as home economics, shorthand, and shop had edged Bible courses out of high schools. College professors used to be able to presume the average incoming student would possess "an elementary acquaintance with the Book of Books," Sellers complained. "He would have learned the books of the Bible in order, the Lord's Prayer, the Twenty-Third Psalm, and the Ten Commandments.... He would have heard about Adam and Eve, Cain and Abel, David and Goliath, Joseph and Mary, Peter and Paul. At Christmas and Easter he would have learned about the birth, crucifixion, and resurrection of Jesus.... he would know that Moses led the children of Israel from Egypt, that Daniel was put into the den of lions, and that there were twelve apostles." But then a "great wave of secularism" washed away our collective memories of these Bible heroes and their exploits.[155]

When did that wave wash over America? And what seismic shocks caused it to crest and to crash? The conventional wisdom is that the Supreme Court broke the chain of memory that is religion when it banned prayer and devotional Bible reading in the public schools in the early 1960s. This has long been the complaint of leaders of the Moral Majority and the Christian Coalition, pressure groups that owe their genesis in large measure to the one-two punch of *Engel v. Vitale* (1962) and *Abington v. Schempp* (1963). But Sellers wrote his lamentations in 1951, and at least as early as the turn of the century a push by progressive reformers for greater attention to vocational education, athletics, and "life adjustment" skills had edged religion and many other traditional academic subjects out of public school curricula.

As has been noted, religious faith and religious knowledge were inseparable in the colonies and the early republic. America was, as the Great Awakening's grand itinerant George Whitefield once put it, "an excellent school to learn Christ in." But early Americans didn't just know Jesus; they knew the Sermon on the Mount (often by heart). They believed, as the Reverend John Lathrop of Boston's Second Church wrote, that "the connexion between knowledge and faith, is such, that the latter cannot exist without the former." And they were convinced, as historian David Paul Nord put it, that "genuine religion was not about miracles, enthusiasm, direct revelation, human will, or even uninformed faith; it was about knowledge, learning, and reading the word." All that changed, however, with the rise to public power in the early nineteenth century of a new form of Protestantism called evangelicalism. By the end of that century a lack of elementary knowledge of Christianity would constitute evidence of authentic faith. What for generations had been shameful—religious illiteracy—would become a badge of honor in a nation besotted with the self-made man and the spirit-filled preacher.[156]

Long-term trends are always the products of multiple causes, so it is often difficult to track their genesis with any precision. The story of the decline of religious literacy is particularly difficult to reconstruct. Even today we do not routinely survey Americans on their religious IQs. And we certainly did not do so in the colonial, antebellum, or Progressive eras. Historians of American religion know much about the rise and fall of particular denominations, theological debates, and practices such as preaching and hymn singing, but we know very little about the rise and fall of religious knowledge—what Americans knew and when they knew it.

Still, many of the causes of our collective Fall into religious illiteracy are plain, as are some of the villains. And here the evildoers were not, as one might expect, diabolical secularists conspiring to banish religion from the public square. Rather, they were well-meaning Protestants, Catholics, and Jews intent on rescuing religion from the acids of modernity. This story—a tale of the demise of religious knowledge at the hands of people of faith—begins with a catalytic event in American religious, cultural, and social history called the Second Great Awakening.

The Second Great Awakening

Like the Great Awakening of the 1730s and 1740s, the Second Great Awakening was a widespread religious renewal that produced powerful individual conversions, explosive church growth, and epochal cultural changes. It began at the turn of the nineteenth century with a series of revivals that burned hottest on the southern and western frontiers, most notably at a camp meeting held in 1801 in Cane Ridge, Kentucky—an event that Methodist evangelist Peter Cartwright later termed the greatest outpouring of the Holy Spirit since the biblical day of Pentecost. In these revivals the Puritans' harsh insistence that God had predestined each of us before birth to either heaven or hell gave way to the gentler Arminian conviction (named after John Calvin's Dutch critic Jacobus Arminius) that all are free to accept or reject the saving grace of Jesus and so to play a part in determining their eternal destinies. Equally important, the genteel revival style of colonial New Englanders (heartfelt but orderly) capitulated in these revivals to orgies of sobbing, shrieking, shouting, and other spiritual ecstasies. ("When I see a man preach," Abraham Lincoln once said, "I like to see him act as if he were fighting bees.") Out of the egalitarian impulses of Jacksonian America—an America in which someone as woodsy as Andrew Jackson could grow up to be president—the irreverent reverend was born, and he quickly learned to offer his audiences (and audiences they were) the potent mix of religion and entertainment we would later come to associate with American revivalism. Thanks to the efforts of Charles Grandison Finney, the lawyer turned evangelist who argued the case for Christ (and lent to US revivalism a variety of potent "new measures"), America's Pentecost spread like wild-fire in urban areas of upper New York State beginning in the 1820s, prompting observers to refer to these areas as the "Burned-Over District." Not until the great revival in Rochester, New York, in the winter of 1830–31 did this spiritual fire consume its fuel.[157]

By the end of the 1830s America's religious landscape had assumed its current shape. The population had been rapidly Christianized, but Christianity itself had become extraordinarily diverse. Evangelicalism had supplanted Puritanism as the dominant religious impulse, thanks in no small measure to the willingness of evangelicals to mix the ways and means of revivalism with those of republicanism. Methodists and Baptists—both prorevival groups—had displaced such eighteenth-century stalwarts as Congregationalists and Anglicans atop the denominational pecking order. With the disestablishment in Connecticut and Massachusetts of Congregationalism—"protestant popedom," Thomas Jefferson called it—in 1817 and 1833, respectively, the free-exercise promise of the First Amendment had been extended to citizens within their respective states. And as Roman Catholic immigration rose and a dizzying array of new religious options (including spiritualism, Adventism, Mormonism) fueled the "antebellum spiritual hothouse," religious competition became fierce, not just among the Protestant denominations but between Protestants and Catholics too.[158]

As the nation became both Christian and religiously plural, the links in the chain of memory that once bound the minds of Americans to the truths of the Christian tradition began to fracture. Ironically, the United States became a nation of forgetters at the same time it became a nation of evangelicals. And more than any other single event, the Second Great Awakening aided and abetted our national amnesia. True, revivalism made Christians. In fact, it made converts by the millions. Church membership rates more than doubled from roughly 17 percent of Americans at the start of the Revolution to 34 percent in 1850. And for the first time the Christian story traveled deep into the heart of the African American population. Earlier efforts, chiefly by Anglicans, to convert slaves through "a lengthy process of learning, memorization, and moral testing" had largely failed, probably because the religion slaves were being asked to adopt bore almost no resemblance to West African religious traditions. Now, however, God could be known in spirit as well as in truth—in sudden conversions, in ecstatic worship, in call-and-response preaching, and in shouting and song.[159]

Many of those who came to Jesus during the Second Great Awakening went on to learn the basics of the Christian faith. Religious literacy expanded among African Americans, who came to see the story of Israel's exodus from bondage to freedom as their own story and to praise Jesus for taking onto the cross both the world's sins and their own suffering. Presbyterians and Congregationalists remained faithful not only to Jesus but also to their traditions of learning. But for the most part the Christians made during and after in the Second Great Awakening were Christians of a very different sort from those who populated colonial and early America, since during the early nineteenth century religious faith and religious knowledge began for the first time to march to different drummers.

A revolution in print technology spurred explosive growth in sectarian religious periodicals such as *Calvinist Magazine* and *Arminian Magazine,* which fomented bitter religious controversies—between Calvinists and Arminians over salvation, between Unitarians and Trinitarians over Jesus, and between Mormons and their angry opponents over ongoing revelation—which in turn kept Christian teachings on the minds of ordinary Americans. These new technologies also put inexpensive denominational tracts, not least a massive *Baptist Library,* into the hands of the masses. As they read and debated these magazines and tracts, Americans learned much about the beliefs and practices of their denominations and of Christianity itself. But gradually nondenominational uniformity eroded the particularities of denominational life. What church historian Nathan Hatch described as the "the most centrifugal epoch in American church history" succumbed to centripetal pressures.[160]

Among these pressures was the vast network of nondenominational voluntary associations constituting the Benevolent Empire. One of the key features of American denominations had long been their neighborliness: their willingness to see other denominations less as rivalrous sects (the European model) than as friendly competitors. In the wake of the Second Great Awakening, this denominational ideal gave birth to the allied notion of nondenominationalism, which accented not so much competition as cooperation. Now Presbyterians and Methodists, Baptists and Congregationalists joined hands to form a united evangelical front dedicated to transforming the United States into a Christian civilization and to stamping the imprint of that civilization on the wider world. Most of these organizations—the American Anti-Slavery Society, the American Temperance Society, the American Bible Society, the American Tract Society, the American Sunday School Union, the American Home Missionary Society, and so on—foreswore any denominational affiliation. In order to accomplish their goals, the Protestants who staffed and led these groups agreed to disagree when it came to doctrine. Why argue about infant baptism when there were drunks to sober up and "heathens" to save? So the American Bible Society published scripture "without note or comment," and the literature distributed by the American Tract Society and the American Sunday School Union steered around such contentious matters as the Trinity, Holy Communion, and Judgment Day. Hymns also reinforced a nondenominational Protestant identity by stressing the shared experience of Jesus, a common morality, and what church historian Stephen Marini termed a "core of consensus beliefs"—a core, it might be noted, that seemed to be shrinking by the day.[161]

For the first half of the nineteenth century, the pendulum of American Christianity swung back and forth between denominational specificity and nondenominational vagueness—between the thirty-three-volume *Baptist Library* and the more irenic forty-five-volume *Evangelical Family Library*. After the Civil War, however, many Americans grew tired of theological controversies. Desperate for union in church as well as state, they gravitated—in churches, schools, and colleges—toward a lowest-common-denominator faith. If the measure of such developments is growth, then this one is to be applauded, since over the course of the century American Protestantism boomed and missionaries expanded its footprint worldwide. But this growth came at a cost, and once again the cost was religious literacy.

Dimensions of the Sacred

Philosopher Ninian Smart argued that the world's great religions exhibit at least six important family resemblances, which he terms "dimensions of the sacred." These dimensions are: the doctrinal/philosophical, the narrative/mythic, the ritual/practical, the experiential/emotional, the ethical/legal, and the social/institutional. Different religions exhibit these dimensions in varying degrees. In fact, the inclination of believers to emphasize some dimensions while downplaying others—Confucianism's focus on ritual, for example, or Orthodox Judaism's on law—is one way to tell religions apart. As we have seen, Puritanism celebrated the doctrinal and experiential dimensions of religion. Puritans emphasized both experiencing the "new birth" and learning true doctrine. Jonathan Edwards, the grand synthesizer of Puritan thought, saw the Christian life as a dance of the head and the heart, the intellect and the emotions.[162]

Historians disagree about the nature of the relationship between Puritanism, which dominated the American religious landscape in the seventeenth and eighteenth centuries, and evangelicalism, which dominated from the early nineteenth century forward. These two religious impulses certainly share much, not least a reverence for the Bible and an emphasis on conversion. But when it comes to the intellect and education, Puritanism and evangelicalism are nearly polar opposites. If, as Smart suggested, you can differentiate one member of the religion family from another by the religious dimensions it most comfortably occupies, Puritanism and evangelicalism are distant relatives. Puritans went to great lengths to spread religious literacy. So did the evangelicals who populated the Bible, tract, and Sunday school organizations of the Benevolent Empire. But over the course of the nineteenth century evangelicals learned to ignore religious learning. Evangelicals did more than that, however. In the name of heartfelt faith, unmediated experience, and Jesus himself, they actively discouraged religious learning. To evangelicalism, therefore, we owe both the vitality of religion in contemporary America and our impoverished understanding of it. Here evangelicalism was assisted, however, by liberal Protestantism, a movement that sought to accommodate Christianity to modern circumstances. Although liberal Protestants disagreed with evangelicals on such matters as the inspiration of the Bible, they shared with their antagonists an emphasis on morality and experience that also tended to shut doctrine out.

There are many ways to tell this story of Americans' descent into pious ignorance. Here I focus, first, on schools and colleges and, second, on churches. Between the Second Great Awakening and World War I, schools and colleges learned to forget about religion. As educational institutions secularized their curricula, the burden of disseminating knowledge about religion fell on the churches. But this burden shifted just as American Protestants were moving away from Christianity's doctrinal dimension, emphasizing experience and ethics instead.

Nonsectarianism and the Public Schools

Today Americans often think of public schools as bereft of religious influences. But when public schools spread throughout New England during the late eighteenth century and across the nation over the course of the nineteenth, religion was a daily presence. Dutch Reformed schools in New York, Presbyterian schools in the Carolinas, and Quaker and Lutheran schools in Pennsylvania were religious through and through; the Bible was their core text. But public schools emphasized faith too. Early superintendents were typically Protestant ministers, as were many pioneering advocates of public education. Their schools promulgated, in the words of historian Lawrence Cremin, "a Christian *paideia* that united the symbols of Protestantism, the values of the Old and New Testaments, *Poor Richard's Almanack,* and the *Federalist* papers."[163]

From the beginning, however, reformers struggled over how to make "common schools" truly common in a country that was so religiously diverse. The goal of public education was to produce good citizens. Because it was widely believed that morality depended on religion, it was assumed that the schoolhouse would have to stand on a religious foundation to accomplish this aim. But what might such a foundation look like in a nation with so many different kinds of Protestants, to say nothing of a burgeoning Catholic population? How to inculcate religion without dividing religious groups against one another and thereby undermining the unifying purpose of these "common schools," their charge to transform children of all religions and ethnicities into Americans—to make *e pluribus unum,* "out of many, one"?

The solution that emerged, early in Massachusetts and Ohio and eventually nationwide, centered on the concept of generic religion, which was variously described as "nonsectarianism" or "nondenominationalism." This solution, which is now widely (and erroneously) used in Supreme Court decisions, rests on one core conceit, namely, that lurking inside the particular expressions of different religious groups was what education reformer John Dewey would later call a "common faith." Drawing on this concept, public school advocates argued that though the First Amendment prevented them from preaching any particular form of Protestantism—Methodism, for example, or the Calvinism of the *New England Primer*—it did not prohibit them from inculcating Protestantism in general. As long as the schoolhouse faith they were preaching was "nonsectarian," public school teachers could preach it unimpeded. This ideal first became a reality in 1827, when Massachusetts passed a law prohibiting use of public funds to buy any schoolbooks "which are calculated to favour any particular religious sect or tenet." This law was the nation's first to restrict public support for sectarian religious instruction, and it was intended, it should be emphasized, not to kill the teaching of religion in public schools but to preserve it.[164]

Two contradictory impulses fueled this nonsectarian ideal. The first was tolerance, more specifically the desire of Protestants of competing denominations to get along with one another in order to pursue common projects. As has been noted, most of the voluntary associations of the Benevolent Empire were not affiliated with any one denomination. Inside these interdenominational groups, Protestants downplayed doctrinal differences in order to work together for abolitionism or temperance or missions. Tolerance, in short, would get things done.

The second impulse behind the nonsectarian ideal was intolerance, since the comity in these circles was by no means extended to Roman Catholics. In fact, one of the main motivations underlying the evangelicals' nondenominational efforts was the desire to present a united front against what many saw as a worrying wave of Roman Catholic immigration. Protestant leaders routinely described Catholicism as a form of brainwashing incompatible with liberty, insisting that the Vatican's refusal to allow Catholics to interpret the Bible and church teachings for themselves amounted to spiritual tyranny. How better to do battle with the Catholic menace and uphold the principle of freedom of conscience than to speak in one voice against the "malignant, social, anti-Christian poison" that was popery?[165]

The key figure behind the nondenominational or nonsectarian solution to the problem of religion in public education was Horace Mann, the education reformer (and, not coincidentally, Unitarian) who served as the secretary of the Massachusetts Board of Education from its founding in 1837 until 1848. More than anyone else, Mann determined the role religion would play in the nation's public schools.

Mann's approach to universal education (which now included girls as well as boys) focused on the common school—the "sacred temple of education," as he called it—and featured five interlocking elements. The first was to teach piety, which in his view was necessary for cultivating virtue, which was in turn necessary for preserving social order and safeguarding democracy. The second was to limit religious education to those doctrines on which all Christians could agree, "leaving to the family, the pulpit, and the Sabbath School, that more full doctrinal instruction which parents may desire." This meant excluding from public schools texts that took a specific position on controversial theological questions. "In every course of studies, all the practical and perceptive parts of the Gospel should be sacredly included," Mann wrote, "and all dogmatical theology and sectarianism sacredly excluded." The third was to locate this classroom piety in the moral (as opposed to the doctrinal) truths of the Christian tradition—to teach what sociologist Nancy Ammerman would later describe as "Golden Rule Christianity." The fourth was to ground this shared morality in the King James Bible, which was to be read in public schools (as it had been published by the American Bible Society) "without note or comment." The fifth was to provide some cover for what might otherwise be seen as secular drift by allowing for three religious rituals in the public schools: prayer, hymn singing, and devotional Bible reading.[166]

Some of the problems with this approach will be immediately apparent to twenty-first-century readers. The most obvious is that this ostensibly generic schoolhouse faith is nothing of the sort. What Mann called "the religion of heaven" and "the religion of the Bible" is plainly Christian.[167] Teachers taught the Bible, after all, not the Quran or the Tao Te Ching. So this supposedly common faith excluded on the face of it Muslims, Hindus, and Buddhists, to say nothing of agnostics and atheists. Another problem, apparent to many nineteenth-century observers, was that Mann-style nonsectarianism also excluded Roman Catholics and Jews and, as we shall see, many evangelicals too.

Bible Wars

Roman Catholic opposition to this schoolhouse piety took many forms, including protests against the anti-Catholic diatribes printed in many popular schoolbooks. But Catholic protests homed in on the Bible. The article *the* here is instructive, since Mann's approach assumed that there was one Bible rather than many (or that Christians could at least agree on which one their children should read). Neither assumption was true. By the 1830s there were already many Protestant Bibles, though popular devotion to the King James Version largely masked that problem. The real rub was that Catholics had their own version, the Douay-Rheims, which was based not on ancient Hebrew and Greek manuscripts (as Protestant Bibles were) but on the Latin Vulgate translation of the fourth and fifth centuries. Catholics also maintained, then as today, that scripture must be read communally—in the light of church traditions. So their translation included doctrinal guidance in the form of footnotes and commentaries. No wonder Catholics viewed the insistence that the Bible be read "without note or comment" as anything but neutral.

These tensions simmered before exploding in the Bible wars of the midnineteenth century. The most visible battlefield in these early culture wars was Philadelphia, where Protestant-Catholic riots over whose Bible would be read in public schools left over a dozen people dead and Catholic churches burned to the ground in 1844. But some of the best arguments on both sides of the question came from New York City's public school controversy of the early 1840s.[168] There a privately run, nondenominational Protestant organization called the Public School Society ruled the roost, doling out public funds and, in keeping with its mandate "to inculcate the sublime truths of religion and morality contained in the Holy Scriptures," seeing to it that students in its city's schools were reading a Protestant Bible, reciting Protestant prayers, and singing Protestant hymns.[169]

Buoyed by a call from Governor William Seward for the "establishment of schools in which [children] may be instructed by teachers speaking the same language with themselves and professing the same faith," Catholics requested funds from the Public School Society for precisely that purpose. After their request was denied, Catholic bishop John Hughes argued that the city's supposedly nonsectarian schools were actually Protestant and anti-Catholic. According to Hughes, the King James Bible used as a reader in these schools was a sectarian book, and popular history textbooks slandered Catholicism as tyrannical. The American Bible Society responded with a petition insisting that the Bible "is a book peculiarly appropriate for use in common schools, and cannot be excluded from them without hazard both to our civil and religious liberties." *American Protestant Vindicator,* a nativist newspaper, found the Catholic position preposterous. Catholics, it editorialized, "demand of republicans to give them funds to train up their children to worship a ghostly monarchy of vicars, bishops, archbishops, cardinals, and Popes!"[170]

After it became plain that public funds for Roman Catholic parochial schools would not be forthcoming—to do so, the Public School Society determined, would create an "unholy alliance" between church and state—Hughes changed his tack, arguing (with the support of New York City's Jewish leaders) for legislation that would mandate completely secular, Bible-free public education.[171]

Soon many evangelical Protestants were sailing the same course. While Catholics attacked "nonsectarian" religion in the schools as too specific, these Protestants saw Mann-style faith as too generic—the sort of watered-down religion "that infidels might believe, and sensualists applaud." The best plan was to teach children the one true faith, but if that was not legally permissible or politically feasible then it was better to secularize the public schools than to let Mann's Unitarianism prevail. In this way, as legal scholar Philip Hamburger argued, "the idea of separation of church and state first attracted widespread support and even national attention."[172]

The real mistake Mann and his supporters made was assuming that religion could be made generic. It cannot. Just as it is not possible to speak language in general (at any given moment, you have to pick one), it is not possible to inculcate religion in general. That is because religion in general does not exist; all that we have are specific religious expressions.

To put the matter more concretely, those who want to teach about religion have to decide which scripture(s), if any, students are going to read, in which translation(s), and with (or without) which commentary. Mann's Catholic critics understood this. So did many Protestants. In fact, some of Mann's angriest opponents were evangelicals who saw no difference between Mann's Unitarianism and his ostensibly generic schoolhouse faith. What sort of Christianity, one critic asked, does not teach the "supernatural scheme of salvation," including "the doctrines of election and predestination" and the "perseverance of the saints"? Or, as another put it, religious instruction in the public schools was being reduced under Mann to "the vague transcendentalism of our poetical moralists." You cannot simultaneously keep real religion in the public schools, these critics argued, and keep sectarianism out of it.[173]

In 1869 and 1870 Cincinnati's board of education voted to outlaw hymn singing, Bible reading, and religious education from its public schools. By this time Roman Catholics were America's largest denomination, and once again high dudgeon ensued. Most Protestants argued the old saw of a common religion for the common schools; in a *Harper's Weekly* cartoon dated March 19, 1870, Thomas Nast depicted Pope Pius and his Catholic clerics firing an "ecclesiastical canon" at a public school. Meanwhile, a coalition of Jews, freethinkers, Catholics, and a few evangelicals insisted (as Hughes had earlier) that nonsectarian religion was a chimera—that, in a city as diverse as this commercial hub of the West, inculcating religion in public school students could only undermine the public schools' mission to unify the populace.[174] In the end the Cincinnati school board withdrew the King James Bible from the curriculum and the secular model triumphed.

Godless Schools

Bible wars in Philadelphia, New York, Cincinnati, and other cities produced four important results. The first was that it became nearly impossible to discuss religion in most public schools. Increasingly, superintendents and school committees came under pressure to cede the topic of religion to Sunday schools, and increasingly teachers and administrators succumbed to that pressure. As early as the 1840s the General Assembly of the Presbyterian Church was reporting that "the common school system is rapidly assuming not a mere negative, but a positively anti-Christian character." By the start of the Civil War public schools were not quite "as godless as a steam engine" (as one wag in Cincinnati quipped), but the subject of religion had largely vanished from public school curricula.[175]

In 1875 James Blaine, a Republican congressman from Maine, inspired by an 1855 Massachusetts law banning state support for sectarian (read: Roman Catholic) schools, introduced a constitutional amendment to outlaw the flow of tax dollars to schools "under the control of any religious sect."[176] The Blaine Amendment, as it came to be called, was a stealth attempt to preserve Protestantism in the public schools. It passed overwhelmingly in the House but lost by a few votes in the Senate. It lived on, however, in the laws and constitutions of dozens of other states, which passed Blaine-style language banning state funding for sectarian textbooks, sectarian instruction, and sectarian schools.

Some schoolbooks, such as the popular McGuffey readers, continued to reprint Bible passages, but schoolbooks for the most part lost their theological swagger. References to animals and children, eagles and flags displaced references to Old Testament prophets and New Testament evangelists. Coverage of such subjects as bookkeeping, sewing, and science edged out theology, which when it did survive became vaguer and vaguer. Later editions of Webster's speller dropped its famous first lesson ("No man may put off the law of God ..."). The McGuffey readers were secularized too, bowing to the new gods of patriotism and practicality. While about a third of the lessons in McGuffey's fourth reader in the late 1830s and early 1840s were religious, little religious content remained after 1850, and the 1879 editions featured only two Bible passages: the Lord's Prayer and the Sermon on the Mount. By the late nineteenth century a new Catholic archbishop, John Ireland of St. Paul, Minnesota, was lamenting that intramural squabbles between Catholics and Protestants had placed "the nursery of thought," that is, the public schools, "into the hands of unbelievers and secularists." And by the early twentieth century historians were writing books with such titles as *The Secularization of American Education* (1912), which concluded that "a gradual but widespread elimination of religious and church influences from public education" had been afoot "for somewhat over a century."[177]

Compensating for this loss was the second outcome of the Bible wars of the midnineteenth century: the consolidation in the public schools of largely vestigial civic rites—hymn singing, praying, Bible reading—that under the newly nonsectarian public school regime had the trappings of religious significance with little actual piety. Because these empty ceremonials were typically performed before the start of the school day, they were, as historian R. Laurence Moore observed, literally "extracurricular."[178] And they were intended not so much to transmit religious knowledge as to foster religious feeling. In all likelihood, however, these formalities did little of either. They amounted to little more than a fig leaf covering collective embarrassment over a system that was abandoning religion as a subject of instruction.

The third outcome of these Bible controversies was the substitution of morality for religion. At least in the nineteenth century, educators did not give up explicitly on the long-standing conviction that morality needed to stand on the rock of religion in order to be secure. But Americans gradually confused religion with morality and subsumed the former into the latter. The lowest-common-denominator Protestantism once preached in public schools morphed into generic Christianity, then into generic moralism. Shortly after the Civil War the Congregational minister Henry Ward Beecher, the most popular liberal Protestant preacher of his era, said that public schools no longer needed to preach "technical" religion; preaching "morality and true virtue" and "fellowship and common feeling" would suffice. In postbellum McGuffey readers, the Calvinist theology of sin and salvation that pervaded early editions gave way to bland lessons on "a morality of industry, self-denial, sobriety, thrift, propriety, persistence, modesty, punctuality, conformity, and submission to authority." And such virtues were said to beget not so much salvation as prosperity. Other schoolbooks dumped theology too. "As systematized theology," historian Ruth Miller Elson wrote in her exhaustive survey of nineteenth-century schoolbooks, "religion almost disappears from the later books, but it always maintains a prominent place with regard to man's moral behavior. It has become a religion of ethics rather than one of theology."[179]

A fourth outcome of the Bible wars was rapid growth in parochial education among Catholics, who continued to insist, first, that education was a parental obligation rather than a state prerogative and, second, that Catholic parents who sent children to public schools were abrogating their sacred duty to raise their children in the one true church. In 1884 a gathering of American Catholic bishops decreed that every Catholic parish support at least one parochial school. By 1895 over 750,000 Catholics were enrolled in some four thousand Catholic schools.[180]

All this happened during the heyday of the public school movement, as public schooling was migrating out of New England toward the South and the Midwest, and as nationwide enrollment rates were skyrocketing—from just 38 percent of all white children in 1840 to close to 61 percent in 1870. It happened while what education reformer Booker T. Washington called a "veritable fever" for learning was seizing African Americans after the Civil War. To put it another way, just as America's current system of nationwide public schooling was replacing a patchwork of privately funded dame schools, charity schools, parochial schools, and academies, the focus of education shifted from teaching religious doctrines to inculcating moral character. The great exodus of religion from the minds of American citizens was under way.[181]

The effects of this exodus remain with us today, notably in our collapsing of religion into "values" and "values" into sexual morality, which in turn functions via an odd sort of circular reasoning as a proxy for religiosity. At least in popular parlance, what makes religious folks religious today is not so much that they believe in Jesus' divinity or Buddhism's Four Noble Truths but that they hold certain moral positions on bedroom issues such as premarital sex, homosexuality, and abortion.

Nonsectarianism and Higher Education

Also contributing to religious illiteracy were developments in higher education that paralleled those in public schools. Here too the nondenominational ideal and the fiction of generic religion chipped away at religious literacy. Here too teaching doctrine yielded to inculcating character. And once again the culprits were not secularists but believers. Higher education resisted secularization longer than the public schools, however, since here the key transformation occurred at the end rather than in the middle of the nineteenth century. In fact, this transformation was not complete until the early twentieth century, when faculty and administrators finally became convinced that it was possible to teach morality quite apart from religion.

Historians of higher education have often interpreted these changes as a revolution in which the secular university overthrew the denominational college. For present purposes, however, the site of this shift matters less than its inner workings, which saw (in colleges and universities alike) such values as utility, research, specialization, and professionalization trump the pious preoccupations of the prior model—"its traditionalism, authoritarianism, paternalism." Perhaps the most important innovation of the new paradigm was the idea that knowledge was something to create rather than something to preserve—that scholarship was about "searching" rather than "conserving."[182]

As early as the 1820s critics of the colleges' fixed curriculum were arguing that courses of study top-heavy in Latin, Greek, and Hebrew had to make room for such subjects as the natural sciences, history, engineering, and agriculture. Real change on this score waited, however, until the passage of the Morrill Act of 1862 provided financial incentives for higher education in agriculture and other practical subjects, and the Civil War made palpable the importance of science and technology. Initially, college presidents shuffled these subjects off to new schools of their own (agricultural schools, schools of engineering, and so on), but in the last decades of the nineteenth century new topics stampeded into college curricula as electives, and the dusty fixed curriculum was no more.

Over the course of the late nineteenth century, faculty fiat gave way to student choice, and the old emphasis on learning content (covering it all) yielded to acquiring certain skills. Some have argued that during this postbellum era, which also saw research emerge as a key mission of the university and specialization as a key characteristic of that mission, science displaced theology as the central discipline in most American universities. According to this view, as freedom of thought became the sine qua non of university life and religious orthodoxy came to be seen as an enemy of that freedom, the study of religion receded so science could proceed. This narrative is not quite right, since character building remained a key aim of American universities and religion remained character's prerequisite. What really happened on the religion front was a shift from denominational to nondenominational Protestantism; higher education had its Horace Manns too.

One such Mann was Charles Eliot, who served as the president of Harvard from 1869 until 1909. Eliot, also a committed Unitarian, instituted a wide-ranging elective system for Harvard undergraduates, which he described as both "an outcome of the spirit of the Protestant Reformation" and "an outcome of the spirit of political liberty." Eliot believed that "the whole work of a university is uplifting, refining, and spiritualizing," but he wanted to accomplish that spiritual uplift through electives in literature, science, and the arts rather than mandatory theological instruction.[183]

Eliot changed Harvard's motto from *In Christi Gloriam* ("To the Glory of Christ") to *Veritas* ("Truth") in 1884 and put an end to compulsory chapel in 1886—two reasons evangelist Billy Sunday called him "so low-down he would need an aeroplane to get into hell." But Eliot ought to be remembered not for trying to kill religion at Harvard but for trying to save it. Like Mann, he was a liberal Protestant rather than a secularist. "A university cannot be built upon a sect," he once wrote, and, according to historian Julie Reuben, "Eliot's notion of the unsectarian university triumphed" nationwide. "Unsectarianism" became, according to Cornell University's first president, Andrew Dickson White, the "guiding idea" of higher education reform. During the late nineteenth century Johns Hopkins and Stanford were established on an "unsectarian" basis, and all the great public Midwestern universities—Michigan, Wisconsin, Indiana, Illinois, among them—also began as nonsectarian Protestant institutions. Many colleges founded to train ministers farmed out theological instruction to separate divinity schools and then, in the name of tolerance and pluralism, wriggled away from their roots in Episcopalianism or Congregationalism. Required courses in natural theology and evidences of Christianity were retired. Mandatory chapel services showcased singing over sermonizing before becoming electives themselves. A particularly hard blow to denominational particularity in higher education came in the form of a 1906 decision by the Carnegie Foundation to restrict a generous pension program for faculty to nondenominational institutions. Within a few years of that decision, the denominational college paradigm was dead.[184]

Establishing Unbelief

The modern secular university did not entirely neglect religion as a subject of inquiry; it just turned that subject into one specialization among many—a field that would come to be known as religious studies. As early as the 1850s Bible courses were popping up at American colleges, and they were commonplace by century's end. This may seem to be a positive trend for partisans of religious literacy, but Bible courses multiplied only because religion was being banished from virtually every other discipline. Under the earlier one-size-fits-all curriculum, all manner of courses with religious content were required of every student. To get a college degree, it was agreed, you needed to be religiously literate. But with the rise of the electives system after the Civil War, learning about the Bible became a take-it-or-leave-it proposition.

By the start of the twentieth century the term *humanities* had acquired its current sense as the home of such humane disciplines as philosophy, art history, classics, and literature (though, it should be noted, not the study of religion). In the process the humanities, which previously had referred more narrowly to the study of Latin and Greek, acquired a new burden: inculcating character in college students. The old capstone courses on moral philosophy gave way to introductory courses in Western civilization, literature replaced classics as the "backbone of the humanities," and the humanities themselves were increasingly described in quasi-religious terms—as carriers of common moral and spiritual sensibilities from generation to generation.[185]

Whereas the rise of the humanities helped to collapse religion into what we now call spirituality, the key development in this era of the emergent university was the collapse of religion into morality. This had happened earlier in the public schools, when Mann and his minions, determined to make a place for religion in the curriculum, decided that the only religion the common school could abide was a vaguely spiritual morality. In the late nineteenth and early twentieth centuries the lords of higher education came to the same conclusion. As enrollments skyrocketed and the United States became a "land of colleges," far more Catholics and Jews matriculated than ever before, and higher education was confronted with the challenge of religious diversity. Presidents responded to this challenge as school superintendents had decades before—not by banishing religion from their environs but by trying to make it generic. College chaplains jettisoned biblical exegesis for inoffensive homilies on the moral life—all in an effort, in the words of Harvard philosopher William Ernest Hocking, "to shear the sermon of its possibilities of mischief." College courses too reduced religion to morality. "Religion," Clyde Votaw of the University of Chicago wrote in 1906, "means reverence, trust, obedience, faithfulness, industry, sincerity, honesty, truthfulness, righteousness, justice, purity, honor, kindness, sympathy, helpfulness, health, and happiness." Earlier definitions would have mentioned truth. But by the early twentieth century both secondary and higher education had largely done away with the doctrinal dimension of religion on the grounds that it was just too mischievous. In colleges and universities, as in public schools, deeds had triumphed over creeds; religion had been reduced to doing good.[186]

The secularization of higher education—what church historian George Marsden has referred to as "a virtual establishment of nonbelief"—proceeded more slowly in the South; South Carolina's lawmakers passed an act in 1890 ruling that the president of the University of South Carolina could not be an infidel or an atheist. Catholic colleges, where the nondenominational ideal was always rightly reckoned as Protestant, retained something of their sectarian identity (including mandatory theology courses). So did many Presbyterian colleges. But "by the early 1920s," Marsden writes, "studies of religious subjects had become only a minute part of the curriculum" nationwide. With the exception of a Bible course here and there, the study of religion was outsourced to theological schools. The subject of religion would not return in force to the college curriculum until the 1950s and 1960s, when the academic study of religion as we know it today would gain acceptance, first in denominational colleges, then in private colleges and universities, and finally in state schools.[187]

From the Head to the Heart

The rising tide of religious ignorance in public schools and higher education might have been stemmed by the churches, which saw explosive growth over the course of the nineteenth and early twentieth centuries.[188] But many of the same trends that led public school teachers and college professors to marginalize and trivialize religion paralyzed the churches too, turning the evangelical century of the Great Awakening and the Benevolent Empire into the century in which religious literacy lost its way.

Many trends transformed Christian congregations and voluntary associations into aiders and abetters of religious amnesia. The most important of these shifts were: from the intellect to the emotions, from doctrine to storytelling, from the Bible to Jesus, and from theology to morality. In each case a new approach to religion was offered to Americans with all the seduction of the serpent in the Garden of Eden. In each case Americans succumbed to the temptation. This time, however, knowledge was lost rather than gained.

As historian Richard Hofstadter observed in *Anti-Intellectualism in American Life* (1963), learning was highly prized in the colonies and the early republic. Puritan clergy were "the first class of American intellectuals," and the nation's founders were "sages, scientists, men of broad cultivation, many of them apt in classical learning." Gradually, however, the demands of democracy, romanticism, and commercial capitalism produced a "widespread belief in the superiority of inborn, intuitive, folk wisdom over the cultivated, oversophisticated, and self-interested knowledge of the literati and the well-to-do." The 1828 election of Andrew Jackson as president (not to mention the apotheosis of Davy Crockett) marked this monumental shift from a nation in which learning was a source of pride to one in which learning was the butt of a joke.[189]

Nowhere was this shift from learning to feeling more palpable than in religion. While the Puritans had held the head and the heart in a creative tension, criticizing both "rationalists," who made the brain the essential religious organ, and "enthusiasts," who subordinated reason to the affections, evangelicals made a virtue of their ignorance. Possessed by the antiauthoritarian and antiaristocratic spirit of the War of Independence, they scorned the learned clergy of Harvard and Yale and romanticized graduates of the school of hard knocks. They came to believe, as one Sunday school leader wrote, that "the efficacy of moral and religious instruction consists more in what our children are brought to feel, than what they are taught to know." In short, they exhibited all the hallmarks that Hofstadter associated with American anti-intellectualism: "the feeling that ideas should above all be made to work, the disdain for doctrine and for refinements in ideas, the subordination of men of ideas to men of emotional power."

Many Congregationalists and Presbyterians resisted these developments, but the Methodists and Baptists who seized control of Christianity in the early republic made sport of criticizing those who valued scholarship at the expense of the spirit. To borrow an image from *The Wizard of Oz,* they saw Calvinism as a Tin Man faith, devoid of the heartfelt piety of genuine religion. Evangelicals practiced instead a Scarecrow faith bereft of a brain (though in this case proud of it). The road to hell was paved in their view with logic and learning; the path to salvation ran through the heart. If, as Hofstadter has argued, colonial New England was "a thinking community," evangelical America was a feeling community, and its feelings grew more intense as it ventured farther south and west.[190]

One of the big stories of early American history was the emergence of what historian Nathan Hatch has described as "religious populism." According to Hatch, during the Second Great Awakening a series of firebrands (many of them untrained and illiterate) effected a second American revolution by snatching religious authority from elites. Like the patriots of 1776, they opposed authority, aristocracy, and tradition, but they did so in the realm of religion rather than politics. For these "populist preachers" and their "sovereign audience," rational debates about doctrine were beside the point and theological education was useless. The urgencies of the age were feeling and acting: a heartfelt relationship with Jesus and practical action to reform sinners, missionize the heathen, and otherwise save the world. Like the bishop boasting of his pious ignorance in Martin Marty's story, Cartwright bragged in his autobiography about his own lack of education. Worried that his beloved Methodist upstarts were beginning to follow other denominations down the road to respectability (and ruin), he called theological training for ministers "a perfect failure." His reasoning was pragmatic: "Perhaps, among the thousands of local preachers employed and engaged in this glorious work of saving souls, and building up the Methodist Church,... not one of them was ever trained in a theological school or Biblical institute, and yet hundreds of them preached the Gospel with more success and had more seals to their ministry than all the sapient, downy D.D.'s in modern times."[191]

This lowbrow anti-intellectualism found a highbrow analog—what historian Christopher Lasch later called "the anti-intellectualism of the intellectuals"—in such liberals as the Transcendentalist sage Ralph Waldo Emerson and the poet of democracy Walt Whitman. Both of these men labored to make religion more personal and less abstract, to free it from both doctrine and dispute. Emerson was an heir of the Puritans, but he was as dismissive as any camp meeting preacher of the Christian creeds. "We can never see Christianity from the catechism," he wrote, preferring the purview "from the pastures, from a boat in the pond, from amidst the songs of wood-birds." Echoing Emerson, Whitman sneered at Christianity's doctrinal dimensions in favor of a more experiential faith. "The true Christian religion," he wrote, "consists neither in rites or Bibles or sermons or Sundays—but in noiseless secret ecstasy and unremitted aspiration."[192]

This spiritual anti-intellectualism—both highbrow and lowbrow, liberal and evangelical—drove a wedge into the Puritan synthesis of head and heart, forcing many Americans to make a Solomonic choice between the intellect and the emotions. There is an impression, a minister wrote in 1853, "that an intellectual clergyman is deficient in piety, and that an eminently pious minister is deficient in intellect."[193] As time went on, Americans by the millions would choose piety and check their intellects at the churchhouse door. They would endeavor not to know Jesus but to feel him. Indeed, this is the aim of much of American Christianity today, and it is with us every time, in Sunday schools and public schools alike, children pretend they don't know something in order to be cool.

From Doctrine to Storytelling

Changes in the American sermon also contributed to the decline in religious literacy. In colonial America sermons typically foreswore personal narratives and commonplace illustrations in favor of biblical exegesis and doctrinal exposition, so parishioners received from the pulpit a thorough education in both the Bible and the teachings of their denominations. "From the landing of the *Mayflower* through the Revolution," writes one historian of the homily, "the regular Sunday sermons continued to be about the great classical themes of Calvinist Christianity: sin, salvation, and service." These sermons, adds another scholar, were typically "doctrinal lectures such as one might hear in a theological classroom, usually of abstract exposition." This model was challenged during the Great Awakening of the early eighteenth century by the impassioned extemporaneous sermons of Whitefield and, to a lesser extent, by settled Congregationalist pastors such as Edwards, who injected some drama and everyday metaphors—most memorably, the spider and its web—into his preaching. In the early nineteenth century, however, the old-fashioned sermon came under attack for being dry, dull, dead, and dogmatic. Emerson authored the most oft-quoted critique when he quipped that the preaching of his minister, Barzillai Frost, befitted his name. ("Corpse-cold," Emerson called it.) Other American writers also made sport of criticizing pastors for failing to liven up what Mark Twain once called "the drowsy pulpit." In *The Gates Ajar* (1868) Elizabeth Stuart Phelps wrote that the traditional preaching of her pastor "Dr. Bland" made her heroine Mary shiver.[194]

In the days when towns paid their salaries, ministers responded to such criticisms with little more than a shrug. But the First Amendment produced a spiritual marketplace in which believers voted for churches and ministers alike with their feet. In this new religious economy the minister learned to give his parishioners what they wanted, and what they wanted was to be entertained. As hoary Puritan strictures against religious fiction—indeed, any swoon into the imagination—fell away and religious novels such as Susan Warner's *The Wide, Wide World* (1850) and Harriett Beecher Stowe's *Uncle Tom's Cabin* (1852) became best sellers, ministers adopted many of the techniques of these "scribbling women" (as writer Nathaniel Hawthorne once called them).

Stowe wrote in 1872 that the world was "running mad for Stories," adding, "Soon it will be necessary that every leading clergyman shall embody his theology in a serial story, to be delivered from the pulpit Sunday after Sunday." The trend never became quite that universal, but long before Stowe ventured this prophecy many ministers—on both the theological left and the theological right—had largely surrendered the old-fashioned doctrinal sermon in favor of the sort of thing American churchgoers hear today: colloquial sermons peppered with personal stories about friends dying and giving birth, salted with entertaining anecdotes about farms and factories, and light on both biblical exegesis and Christian doctrine. Whereas their predecessors had offered their congregations Calvinism or Unitarianism, these ministers served up the theology of everyday life, subordinating biblical teaching to literary flourishes. Their entertaining sermons "employed daring pulpit storytelling, no-holds-barred appeals, overt humor, strident attack, graphic application, and intimate personal experience." Ministers embraced story sermons because theologian Horace Bushnell had convinced them that Christian language was more about poetry than propositions and because they increasingly (and correctly) understood themselves to be in competition not only with peers in nearby pulpits but also with secular entertainments, including newspapers, plays, and novels.[195]

American ministers became storytellers because Bushnell had a point—because the Bible is at least as much about poetry as about propositions, because some believers have always found it easier to find God in stories than in dogmas. But the main reason many preachers fled, as historian Ann Douglas put it, "from dispute, doctrine, and scholarship" to sentimentalism, sensationalism, and stories is that the narrative sermon worked. It produced conversions. It filled the churches. It also had something of a pedigree in the parables of Jesus. The revolution wrought on the American pulpit was not total, however; revolutions never are. As literary critic David Reynolds has noted, Christian Scientists kept personal reflections out of their services by mandating the reading during Sunday services of lesson sermons; Mormons continued to insist on exegesis of the Bible and the Book of Mormon; and some confessional Christians, particularly of the Presbyterian, Episcopalian, and Lutheran varieties, kept doctrine alive too. By the postbellum era of Henry Ward Beecher and other "Princes of the Pulpit," however, the story sermon had become the norm among liberal and evangelical Protestants alike. T. DeWitt Talmage titillated his parishioners with risqué tales of bars, brothels, and other "spicery," while other preachers not only ignored theology but bragged about doing so. When a woman objected to the theology of popular revivalist Dwight L. Moody, he quipped, "My theology! I didn't know I had any." Sam Jones—dubbed the "Moody of the South" because of his prowess as an evangelist and his penchant for homespun preaching—boasted, "If I had a creed, I would sell it to a museum."[196]

Many have remarked on what was gained when doctrine became antiquarian. As preachers spiced up their sermons with stories, converts crowded into the pews, particularly in denominations such as the Baptists and the Methodists that embraced wholeheartedly this new homiletic style. But what was lost in the bargain is not often noticed. Whereas the pulpit had served as a key link in the chain of memory binding American

Protestants to their religious past, by the end of the Civil War few preachers were offering robust religious instruction. Or, as historian Henry Steele Commager put it, "Religion prospered while theology slowly went bankrupt." Once upon a time, the sermon had educated parishioners about such Christian staples as the Trinity and the Ten Commandments, and the stories ministers told from the pulpit were restricted to the grand biblical narratives of Moses, Abraham, Sarah, Jesus, and Mary. Over the course of the nineteenth century, however, the sermon descended, as Hofstadter put it, "from the vernacular to the vulgar"; the pew became a place where you could hear the likes of Moody fuming that "an educated rascal is the meanest kind of rascal" and Jones referring to "literary preachers" as "A. B.'s, Ph.D.'s, D.D.'s, LL.D's, and A.S.S.'s."[197]

This legacy is with us today in the narrative preaching style, which according to one historian of the sermon now aims "to achieve a happening rather than an understanding." It is with us as well in "seeker-sensitive" megachurches, many of which have decided to stop preaching the basic teachings of the Christian tradition because marketing research has indicated that "seekers" find that kind of thing to be a turnoff.[198]

From the Bible to Jesus

A third temptation that undermined religious literacy in nineteenth-century America was Jesus himself. As has been noted, one of the mantras of the Protestant Reformation was *sola scriptura,* the view that the Bible should serve as the sole authority in matters of Christian faith and practice. This mantra motivated generations of American Protestants to learn to read and to read the Bible. Biblical inspiration came under attack, however, over the course of the nineteenth century. Advances in geology challenged the conventional wisdom that the world was only six thousand years old. Darwin's evolutionary theories seemed to put human beings on a continuum with apes. And the rise of biblical studies called into question Moses's authorship of the Pentateuch and Paul's authorship of some of the "Pauline" epistles.

After the Civil War evangelical and liberal Protestants increasingly distinguished themselves from one another. Evangelicals responded to these challenges by reasserting the divine authority of the Bible. Liberals responded by pledging their allegiance to Jesus, substituting the old *sola scriptura* slogan with *solus Jesus* ("Jesus alone"). But liberal Protestants were not the only Christians who made this move to Jesus-onlyism. Evangelicals did too. Each camp increasingly saw the Christian life as an encounter not with a book but with a person. What made you a Christian, both conservatives and liberal Protestants argued, was not affirming a particular catechism or knowing certain Bible stories; rather, what made you a Christian was having a relationship with an astonishingly malleable Jesus—an American Jesus buffeted here and there by the shifting winds of the nation's social and cultural preoccupations. Liberals looked at Jesus largely as a moral exemplar while conservatives accepted him as a bosom friend, but each camp was giving up on approaching him through the traditional creeds and confessions of Christendom.[199]

Phillips Brooks, rector at Boston's Trinity Church and the most influential Episcopalian preacher of the nineteenth century, once defined preaching as "the bringing to truth through personality." Brooks, a liberal whose belief in the goodness of humanity was outweighed only by his conviction of the goodness of God, was referring principally to the personality of the preacher. The sermon, he believed, should familiarize its listeners with the preacher's life—his everyday deaths and resurrections. But this oft-quoted formula also refers to the life of Jesus. "Beware of the tendency to preach about Christianity," Brooks wrote in a popular homiletics manual, "and try to preach Christ." The trouble with this approach, of course, is that it makes church teachings about Jesus optional, and wherever church teachings are optional there is the temptation to forget them altogether.[200]

From Theology to Morality

Of all the forces undermining religious literacy in nineteenth-century America, the most important was the shift from theology to morality. Historians disagree about when this transformation took place in the churches.[201] Some trace its beginnings to the colonial period. It was during the nineteenth century, however, when Americans of all stripes became moralists. One cause of this shift was the rise of nondenominationalism, which operated inside churches and voluntary associations much as "nonsectarianism" and "unsectarianism" did in public schools and universities. As Protestants vowed to work together to Christianize the nation and vanquish the Catholic menace, they had to find a foundation on which this cooperation might proceed. Doctrine was a nonstarter, since Baptists and Episcopalians disagreed on the propriety of infant baptism, Lutherans and Quakers disagreed on the sacramental nature of Holy Communion, and Universalists (who believed that hell was empty) disagreed with most of their coreligionists on the afterlife. So Protestants found their basis for cooperation in the moral realm—with an ethic that combined Christianity, republicanism, and capitalism.

Liberal and evangelical Protestants mixed this concoction in different measures. As these two camps defined their boundaries after the Civil War, the spiritual left gravitated toward the Social Gospel, which saw sin and salvation as social; liberal Protestant theologians such as Walter Rauschenbusch, a Baptist minister from Manhattan's "Hell's Kitchen" and the leading light of the Social Gospel movement, argued that it was more important to care for the poor than to memorize the Apostles' Creed. Evangelicals focused their inquiry on individual behavior rather than social structures, but they too asked themselves, "What would Jesus do?" Despite all that divided liberal and conservative Christians (Catholics included), both camps were well on their way to reducing religion to morality. As strange as it may sound, the vast majority of American Christians were coming to affirm the heart of the creed of Deist Thomas Paine, who once wrote that "my religion is to do good."[202]

The Judeo-Christian Tradition

Religious illiteracy today is a product of the Second Great Awakening. It is also a product of the postwar revival of the 1940s and 1950s, which saw attendance and membership rates at houses of worship hit all-time highs and witnessed an unprecedented boom in church and synagogue construction. Under the influence of President Dwight Eisenhower, who became the first US chief executive to be baptized in office when he took the plunge on February 1, 1953, piety went public in postwar politics: "under God" was written into the Pledge of Allegiance in 1954, and "In God We Trust" became the nation's official motto in 1956. But once again this fervor was not free. As Protestants, Catholics, and Jews came together to fight godless Communism—just as Baptists, Methodists, and other evangelicals had united to fight popery a century earlier—believers again jettisoned content in order to find common ground.

During the nineteenth century Protestants had been able to agree at least on the broad outlines of the Christian story of sin and salvation, but as Catholics and Jews were integrated into mainstream religious life, lowest-common-denominator Protestantism had to be dropped in the name of a broader pluralism. What had been a Protestant culture was reconceived in the chill of the Cold War as a Judeo-Christian nation. Increasingly Protestants, Catholics, and Jews saw themselves as adherents to a common faith that Eisenhower referred to as "the Judeo-Christian concept." This concept was defined more by what it opposed than by what it denied; in a world of Nazis, Fascists, and Communists, the Judeo-Christians were the other guys. But Judeo-Christianity, while a broad sea, was not infinitely shallow. At least in its public guise as "civil religion," it no longer affirmed the divinity of Jesus, since that would have excluded Jews. But it did affirm one God who was Creator, Lawgiver, and Judge, who inspired the Bible, acted in history, and adopted Americans as a chosen people of sorts. In many hands, however, even that minimal content evaporated.[203]

In the classic statement of "piety on the Potomac," Eisenhower said in a December 1952 meeting with a Soviet official that "our form of government has no sense unless it is founded in a deeply felt religious faith, and I don't care what it is." "Faith in faith" is what sociologist Will Herberg called this strange brew of devotion to religion and insouciance as to its content. As a Jew, Herberg welcomed a "triple melting pot," which saw Protestants, Catholics, and Jews as "three diverse, but equally legitimate, equally American, expressions of an over-all American religion, standing for essentially the same 'moral ideals' and 'spiritual values.'" He was disturbed, however, to see that many Americans seemed more devoted to "the American Way of Life" than to the God of Abraham, Isaac, and Jacob. Surveying the American scene in the mid-1950s, Herberg saw "pervasive secularism amid mounting religiosity": "Christians flocking to church, yet forgetting all about Christ when it comes to naming the most significant events in history; men and women valuing the Bible as revelation, purchasing and distributing it by the millions, yet apparently seldom reading it themselves."[204]

Herberg was wrong to equate Ike-like piety with secularism, but he was right to see how vapid this "faith in faith" had become among religious liberals and conservatives alike. The religious best sellers of the day—*The Power of Positive Thinking* (1952) by the liberal Norman Vincent Peale and *Secret of Happiness* (1955) by the evangelical Billy Graham—preached therapy more than theology, happiness rather than salvation. Then, as today, debating (or even discussing) religious doctrines was considered ill-mannered, a violation of the cherished civic ideal of tolerance, so it was difficult for children to learn or for adults to articulate what set their religious traditions apart from others. More important than even God, it seemed, was keeping the "placid decade" peaceful.

During the 1940s and 1950s there were only three socially acceptable American religions. Military dog tags came with three and only three religious preferences: *P* for Protestant, *C* for Catholic, and *H* for Jew

(Hebrew). To call oneself "a Buddhist, a Muslim, or anything but a Protestant, Catholic, or Jew," Herberg wrote, was "somehow not to be an American." That changed, of course, in the 1960s, which among other things witnessed the demise of the cult of commonality at the hands of the cult of particularity. As civil rights gave way to Black Power and the man in the gray flannel suit to the hippie, *assimilation* and *conformity* became bad words. Individuals clamored to be understood not as generic human beings or even generic Americans but as the unique women, blacks, Native Americans, Latinos, Buddhists, or lesbians that they were. In this climate the Judeo-Christian concept came under attack from many quarters. Calling Protestantism, Catholicism, and Judaism "radically different" religions, Catholic theologian John Courtney Murray wondered in 1960 whether they were comparable, much less indistinguishable. Arthur A. Cohen said the sort of things you might expect someone would say in a book called *The Myth of the Judeo-Christian Tradition* (1969). By the early 1970s, writes Silk, "the Judeo-Christian tradition had lost its charm."[205]

Nonetheless, the Moral Majority proceeded during the 1980s and 1990s on a Judeo-Christian basis, opening its doors (if not its arms) to conservative Catholics and Orthodox Jews committed to reversing America's moral degradation in the name of God and the Good. In the process the Religious Right politicized Judeo-Christianity, using it to attack not just godless Communists (as Eisenhower had done) but liberal Democrats too. And so the Judeo-Christian tradition morphed into the "Judeo-Christian ethic," which was eventually conflated with "family values." This new political theology helped religious conservatives gain political power, but this power came at a price since, under the gentleman's agreement struck by the Moral Majority with culturally conservative Catholics and Jews, anything specifically Protestant, Catholic, or Jewish had to be checked at the door.

Today the Christian Coalition, which superseded the Moral Majority in the 1990s, works on a more explicitly evangelical basis. But most politically active evangelicals—"values evangelicals," in the neologism of NYU law professor Noah Feldman—are Judeo-Christians when it comes to politics. As Feldman observes, "Values evangelicals understand that they cannot get bogged down in doctrinal disagreement when identifying shared values." Like the "nonsectarian" Protestants of the early public school movement, values evangelicals find they have to "paper over real theological differences" and "water down the traditions to which they belong in order to find common ground."[206]

Abrahamic America

Today the "triple melting pot" is widely seen as a myth, and Americans are flirting with more cosmopolitan conceptions of their nation's religious identity than Judeo-Christianity. One such alternative, Judeo-Christian-Islamic America, seemed to emerge fully formed from the smoke of September 11, 2001, but Muslim groups were referring to "a Judeo-Christian-Muslim society" in the late 1980s and scholars of Islam were using the phrase "Judeo-Christian-Islamic" in the early 1990s. "It's now official," William Safire wrote in his "On Language" column in the *New York Times* in 1995. "Ours is a Judeo-Christian-Islamic heritage." According to this "Abrahamic" model Judaism, Christianity, and Islam are the new holy trinity of American religions. Jews, Christians, and Muslims are all "people of the book" who share, in addition to a common ancestry in Abraham, the conviction that there is one God who speaks through prophets, acts in history, and will judge human beings in the last days.[207]

While postwar American presidents who wanted to discuss religious congregations initially referred to churches and synagogues, both President Bill Clinton and Vice President Al Gore spoke repeatedly of America's churches, synagogues, *and* mosques. As mindful as the Democrats of the rising political clout of American Muslims (particularly in the battleground state of Michigan), President George W. Bush referred in his January 2001 inaugural address to "church and charity, synagogue and mosque." After 9/11 Muslim imams became a requirement for any interfaith gathering, and *National Geographic* ran a cover story on "Abraham: Father of Three Faiths."[208]

Although this new Abrahamic model describes America's current religious landscape more accurately than the old Judeo-Christian model, it too sacrifices religious literacy at the altar of tolerance. Just as the shift from a Protestant to a Judeo-Christian conception of the nation required Americans to jettison particulars of the Christian story, the shift from the Judeo-Christian tradition to the Abrahamic tradition requires them to jettison particulars of both Christianity and Judaism. So it should not be surprising that some have resisted this recasting of Herberg's "triple melting pot." The American Jewish Committee, concerned that Jews might lose their status as the nation's most important religious minority, commissioned a 2001 study, which concluded that the US Muslim population was not growing as quickly as many imagined. Meanwhile, some evangelicals tried to resuscitate the Christian America model, and conservative Catholic Richard John Neuhaus insisted that Americans draw a line in the sand at Judeo-Christianity. Otherwise, Neuhaus wrote in his magazine, *First Things,* we will be soon be referring to the United States as a "Judeo-Christian-Buddhist-Hindu-Islamic-Agnostic-Atheist society."[209]

That is a fairly accurate description of what Supreme Court Justice Tom Clark was doing when he referred in 1965 to the United States as "a nation of Buddhists, Confucianists, and Taoists, as well as Christians." But this vision of a "multireligious America" has been articulated most forcefully by Harvard's Diana Eck, a self-described "Christian pluralist" who argues in *A New Religious America* (2001) and on her Pluralism Project Web site that the United States is a religiously diverse nation under many different gods. This approach to the religious identity of the nation sees the United States as a shining city on a hill. But in this case America's destiny is not to showcase Judeo-Christianity but to serve as the example *par excellence* of religious pluralism.[210]

The most natural constituency of this "multireligious America" perspective is the "spiritual but not religious" demographic, whose first principle seems to be disdain for so-called organized religion. Harking back to Thomas Jefferson and his animadversions against "the metaphysical abstractions" and "the maniac ravings" of "religion-builders," twenty-first-century spiritual folk believe that authentic piety is fundamentally a matter of practice, not belief.[211] To them, dogma is always stolid and ritual always empty. Real religion—which is to say spirituality—happens not when some authority tells you what to think but when you discover in your own experience some sliver of the ineffable Something. Spirituality, in short, is religion stripped down to its experiential dimension. More than do-it-yourself-religion, spirituality is do-without-religion, a form of faith that denies its connections to the institutions, stories, and doctrines that gave it birth—religion without memory.

Current interest in contemplative practice has caused "spiritual but not religious" folks to rediscover such neglected resources inside Christianity and Judaism as centering prayer and Kabbalah. But it has also led them to Buddhism, Hinduism, Taoism, and other Asian religions in search of various forms of meditation, yoga, and tai chi. With this quest has come renewed awareness of Asian religions since some yoga teachers, for example, initiate their students not only into the health benefits of yoga but also into the philosophies and myths that developed and sustained its techniques and practices through the ages. Here too, however, the trend is toward religion stripped down to its "essentials"—essentials that in this case are confined almost entirely to the experiential or moral dimensions. This development is well advanced in the American Buddhist community, where some have argued that Buddhism can get along just fine without such staples as karma and reincarnation. "Buddhism Without Beliefs," as this movement has been called, aims to distill the Buddhist life down to nothing more than one's favorite sitting or chanting practice, and then to put that practice at the service of such American preoccupations as happiness.[212]

The tendency to shirk from doctrine is particularly pronounced in the "multireligious America" camp. Here even the minimal monotheism of the Judeo-Christian-Islamic model must be sacrificed since many Buddhists don't believe in God and many Hindus believe in more than one. The only common ground here seems to be tolerance itself. When pluralists gather for interreligious dialogue, their discussions always seem to circle back to ethics. The common statement that came out of the Parliament of the World's Religions—an interreligious event held in Chicago in 1993 to commemorate the original World's Parliament of Religions, convened in that same city a century earlier—was called "Toward a Declaration of a Global Ethic." It affirmed the Golden Rule along with peace and justice, but it offered not a whisper about theology. The psychologist of religion William James once described the United States as an "intellectual republic"; we live today in a moral one instead.[213]

Fundamentalists and Other Intellectuals

This multigenerational exodus away from religious literacy—an exodus through the wilderness of the Second Great Awakening, the Eisenhower revival, 9/11, and the recent spirituality vogue—implicated evangelicals and liberal Protestants alike and, closer to our time, Catholics and Jews as well. Nonetheless, it met resistance. During the Second Great Awakening the German Reformed theologian John W. Nevin denounced revivals as places where "a taste for noise and rant supersedes all desire for solid knowledge" and "no room is found either for instruction or reflection." His Mercersburg Theology (so called because he taught at the German Reformed Seminary in Mercersburg, Pennsylvania) accented liturgical literacy, insisting that Christians come to know Jesus through Holy Communion. The Transcendentalist turned Catholic Orestes Brownson took a similar tack, denouncing revivalism as "one grand imposture and scheme of charlatanism," which, after agitating the emotions but leaving the brain with nothing to do, led more often than not to "skepticism, indifferentism, irreligion, and sometimes positive infidelity."[214]

Many Presbyterians dissented from evangelical anti-intellectualism too. While revivalists traded in Calvinism for Arminianism, Presbyterians continued to affirm the distinctive theology bequeathed to them by Geneva's John Calvin, Scotland's John Knox, and the Westminster Confession (which Presbyterians adopted in 1729). Moreover, they taught this theology to their children in sermons, Sunday schools, and parochial schools. Unlike the Methodists, who wrung their hands for generations about whether to found divinity schools, Presbyterians established many such schools, beginning in 1812 with Princeton Theological Seminary, an institution that emphasized the truths of the Bible alongside the love of Jesus.

At least until the 1960s, when Vatican II squeezed much of the content from Catholic religious education, Catholics were resisters too. Children memorized the Baltimore Catechism, which taught them the creeds, commandments, and sacraments of their tradition. "Who made us? God made us," that catechism began, and it did not stop until it had instructed young Catholics in distinctly Catholic ways of thinking about baptism, confirmation, confession, marriage, sin, redemption, saints, relics, the Trinity, the Blessed Virgin Mary, papal infallibility, and purgatory. The Catholic writer Garry Wills remembers his pre–Vatican II childhood as "a vast set of intermeshed childhood habits—prayers offered, heads ducked in unison, crossings, chants, christenings, grace at meals; beads, altar incense, candles, nuns in the classroom, alternately too sweet and too severe, priests garbed black on the street and brilliant at the altar; churches lit and darkened, clothed and stripped, to the rhythm of liturgical recurrences ... all things going to a rhythm, memorized, old things always returning, eternal in that sense, no matter how transitory." What lends pathos to this passage, and to hundreds of similar recollections of a bygone Catholic childhood, is that all this education *was* transitory. After Vatican II American Catholics largely gave up on cultivating doctrinal and liturgical literacy, the habits of body and mind learned by Wills and prior American Catholic generations almost by osmosis. But for as long as Catholics remained religious outsiders, which is to say until around the time John Kennedy became our first Catholic president, they resisted our descent into religious ignorance too.[215]

Fundamentalists, however, may have been the quintessential resisters. The stereotype of fundamentalists—born in the acerbities of journalist H. L. Mencken (who vilified the Scopes Trial plaintiffs as "anthropoid rabble" engaged in "simian gabble") and nurtured by such popular fare as the novel *Elmer Gantry* (1927) and the Broadway play *Inherit the Wind* (1955)—is that they are uneducated country bumpkins. In reality fundamentalism from its inception was at least as popular in cities as it was in rural areas, and today fundamentalists, who trace their intellectual roots to such movements as dispensational premillennialism, Princeton theology, and Scottish commonsense realism, are one of the very few American Protestant groups that still take doctrine seriously. Fundamentalists first announced their presence with a series of theological tracts called *The Fundamentals* published between 1910 and 1915. These pamphlets have typically been read as broadsides against liberal Protestants, who from the fundamentalist perspective wrongly emphasized social amelioration in this world over individual salvation in the next. But *The Fundamentals* were addressed as well to the lack of attention among evangelicals to what fundamentalists saw as the plain facts of the Bible. This legacy is visible today in works such as *No Place for Truth, or, Whatever Happened to Evangelical Theology?* (1993) by theologian David F. Wells, who blasts evangelicals for trading in "historic Protestant orthodoxy" for "vacuous worship" and "paper-thin piety."[216]

Confessionalists-Experientialists-Moralists

It is now common to divide American Christianity not so much into denominations as into liberal and conservative camps. As sociologist Robert Wuthnow has argued, liberal Protestants today share more with liberal Catholics than they do with conservative Protestants, and conservative Catholics share more with evangelicals and fundamentalists than they do with liberal Catholics. Believers don't disagree on theology much because theology has ceased to be remembered. They disagree instead on cultural politics—on "family values."[217] This fault line, however, does little to illuminate Americans' fall from religious literacy since in this story both liberals and conservatives partook of the forbidden fruit.

A more relevant fault line for this story divides American Christians into three groups: confessionalists, who emphasize above all else Christianity's doctrinal dimension (and encounter God via reason); experientialists, who emphasize its experiential dimension (encountering God via the emotions); and moralists, who emphasize its ethical dimension (encountering God via the will).[218] Many Christians, of course, are a mixture of these things. But over the course of the last two centuries American Protestants and Catholics alike have migrated away from confessionalism to some combination of experience and morality, and in recent years the moralists have triumphed.

One episode that captures this collapse of religion into morality is the 2003 election of New Hampshire's Gene Robinson as the first openly gay bishop in the Episcopal Church. This bitterly contested action, which some believe could tear in two not only the Episcopal Church but also the global Anglican communion of which it is a part, can be read, in keeping with Wuthnow's thesis, as a skirmish in the ongoing culture wars. But what is most striking about the two sides in this debate is not how angry they are with one another but how much they have in common. Both camps seem to see sex as a matter of ultimate concern, as if Christianity had nothing more important to do than opine on our moral lives, as if Jesus came into the world not to save human beings from their sins but to save them from either homophobia or sexual licentiousness. Both sides, in short, have collapsed religion almost entirely into its moral dimension.[219]

The voices of confessional Christians have not been entirely drowned out, however. A group named the Alliance of Confessing Evangelicals issued a manifesto in the 1990s calling for evangelicals to confess their "unfaithfulness" to the historic teachings of the church. "Historic evangelicalism was confessional," that declaration reads. But today "the essential truths of Christianity ... have faded from Christian consciousness." Confessional Christians, however, seem to be a voice crying in the wilderness. As the nation has migrated from understanding itself as Protestant to understanding itself as Christian, then Judeo-Christian, and then Abrahamic, many have jettisoned (in the name of tolerance) the great teachings and stories of the Christian tradition. The recent vogue of spirituality has piqued interest in Asian religious traditions but only in the vaguest sort of way. Yoga, for example, has been scandalously secularized, stripped in the name of the high god of fitness of its ancient roots in Hindu techniques for immortality. Most Americans, in short, remain far more committed to respecting other religions than to learning about them.[220]

Reversing these trends will be difficult since with each passing generation, more and more of our collective memory of religion withers away. Still, there are reasons for hope. With the return in the last few decades of the cult of particularity has come renewed interest in the particularities of the world's religions. It is no longer the case, as it was in the 1950s, that being a Buddhist or a Hindu somehow marks you as un-American. As recently as the 1980s many popular textbooks on the world's religions pretended in the name of pluralism that all religions were different paths up the same mountain, and that view persists in popular books by Huston Smith and Karen Armstrong, among others. But this trend has been reversed, at least in higher education, where even introductory religious studies courses typically recognize the fact that the world's religions, which address very different problems through different techniques and to different ends, aren't even climbing the same mountain. Moreover, we may be at a tipping point where we are realizing that you cannot really respect a religion that you do not understand and that understanding a foreign religious tradition means wrestling with ways in which that religion is fundamentally different from your own.

The Fall into religious ignorance is reversible. Admittedly, we cannot go back to the Protestant "paradise" of the *New England Primer* and the early McGuffey readers. Even if we could, few Americans (including me) would want to do so, not least because we rightly demand a far greater measure of religious tolerance than the Puritans were willing to mete out. But perhaps redemption of a different sort is still possible.

The Proposal

Part 3

The Proposal

Five

Redemption (What to Do?)

Many American churches have annual Bible Sundays, when they present to children copies of the Bible. In 2006 my eight-year-old daughter received a Bible at the Lutheran church that we attend (fairly irregularly, I must confess). Before the presentation the minister called the children and their parents up near the altar and handed Bibles to the grown-ups. He then read from the words of the Lutheran baptismal liturgy, reminding parents of their prior vow to "teach [their children] the Lord's Prayer, the Creed, and the Ten Commandments" and to "place in their hands the Holy Scriptures."[221] So charged, I made good on at least a portion of that promise, placing in my daughter's hands a shiny new copy of the New International Version Children's Edition, with a smiling Jesus on the cover and a cute little lamb in his arms.

After the service I decided a short quiz was in order. So I asked my daughter to name a book in the Bible. No response. "How about a Bible character," I asked somewhat desperately, "other than Jesus?" To which, after giving the matter considerable thought, she responded, "Tom."

Now "Tom" is, I must admit, a correct answer, assuming of course that you are on sufficiently friendly terms with your Bible heroes and heroines. Thomas was one of Jesus' twelve apostles—the one who said he wouldn't believe that his Lord had risen from the dead unless he could thrust his own hand into Jesus' wounded side. And while he is known today as "Doubting Thomas," I suppose he might have been "Tom" to his friends. Still, I must admit to some embarrassment over how little my daughter seemed to know that Bible Sunday about the Good Book.

In her defense (and my own) I must add that on a prior occasion she was able to go on and on about Moses. "He's the guy," she proudly informed me after I asked her what she had learned one day in Sunday school, "who took a bunch of people into the desert and when they ran out of food and got really, really thirsty God told him to whack a rock with a stick and he did and the water came spurting out!" Alas, my older daughter (who, I should add, was able on Bible Sunday to name five biblical books—Matthew, Mark, Luke, John, and Genesis—but no more) did not have any Moses stories close at hand, since on the day her sixth-grade Sunday school class covered Moses and the rock they focused, as any self-respecting modern American Protestant might, on the myriad problems of water as a scarce world resource. (Perhaps she would have done better if she had seen the Disney film *The Prince of Egypt;* then again, maybe not.)

As this tale of woe illustrates, families and religious congregations can do a better job of teaching young people about religion. For generations the church and the family were the dominant educational institutions in North America, and there is no reason why they should abrogate their teaching responsibilities today. True, America's marketplace of religion puts pressure on preachers to entertain their parishioners, who on any given Sunday are free to go elsewhere. But if schools can go "back to basics," why can't religious congregations do the same—preach more regularly from their scriptures and teach their groups' distinctive doctrines in Sunday schools, Sabbath schools, and religious camps? Parents could also do a better job teaching their children about their religious traditions. Some friends tell me that they don't bring their sons and daughters to worship services or talk with them about their faith because they want their children to be free to choose a religion for themselves. This is foolhardy, not unlike saying that you will not read anything to your daughter because you don't want to enslave her to any one language. The fact of the matter is that you cannot avoid teaching religion to your kids; if you offer them nothing, you are telling them that religion counts for nothing.

The media could do a better job also. When the popular press took off in the early nineteenth century, newspaper and magazine editors took seriously their responsibility to inform the citizenry. But they also took seriously the imperative to make money, and over time the straightest path to that goal proved to be entertainment rather than education. Even if the media were committed to educating Americans for citizenship, however, they are not committed to covering religion. The Religion Newswriters' Association works hard to educate its members about religions, and there is an excellent joint master's program in religion and journalism at Columbia University. But coverage of religion remains superficial, oscillating back and forth between exposés of religious hypocrites and fluff pieces on exotic faiths. According to journalist Jeffrey Sharlet, "Religion, in the true broad sense, underlies, controls, permeates at least half the stories in the news, probably a lot more." Iran, Iraq, and Israel, he notes, are all religion stories. But it's a rare reporter who captures that reality, in part because the average reporter is no more informed about religion than the average American.[222]

Individuals, of course, can educate themselves by picking up and reading a Bible or a Quran (or both), by attending a book group that focuses on spiritual matters, or by forming a local salon devoted to religious conversation. They can also turn to the next chapter of this book and review its Dictionary of Religious Literacy. Making an effort to learn basic information about Christianity can help you decode the code words politicians use when communicating to religious communities. Learning about Islam can make you less reliant on so-called experts on the Middle East, most of whom have a political or theological ax to grind.

Still, it must be admitted that the dominant venues for education in the United States today are schools, colleges, and universities. So we should concentrate our religious literacy efforts here. Despite the 2002 Supreme Court ruling that found vouchers for private religious schools constitutional, nearly nine out of every ten American schoolchildren attend a public school. (Another 8 percent go to religious schools, 2 percent to independent private schools, and 2 percent to home schools.) So plainly the place to start is public education. And here the situation is grim. Religion is rarely taught in public schools—a Department of Education survey from the 1980s found that only 640 out of the nation's 15,000 high schools offered a stand-alone course in religious studies—and when students bring this subject up it typically makes teachers very nervous. A colleague who teaches in the School of Education at Fairleigh Dickinson University in New Jersey reports that the public school teachers she encounters are not merely afraid to include religion in their lesson plans, they are "scared to death" even to mention the subject at all. When students ask them about Islam or Christianity, they awkwardly change the subject. It is time for all this to change.[223]

Is It Constitutional?

The question of religious studies in the public schools is frequently entangled with related concerns about religion and public education. The literature in this area is voluminous, and the questions are legion.[224] Do schoolchildren have the right to say grace before lunch? Are student religious clubs lawful? May student speakers at graduation hold forth on their religious beliefs? May music teachers lead students in Christmas carols? Should schools commemorate Hanukkah or Kwanzaa? May teachers wear religious garb? How about students? May students express their religious convictions in writing assignments? Should governments offer parents vouchers to pay for tuition at religious schools? May students be granted release time out of the school day in order to receive religious instruction off campus? May students distribute Bibles and other religious literature on public school grounds? May students opt out of biology lessons on evolution for religious reasons? These are all important questions, and answers to many of them remain up in the air, awaiting definitive rulings from the courts.

For our purposes, however, it is important to disentangle these matters from our core question, on which the Supreme Court has made its position plain. That question is whether it is constitutional to teach about religion in the public schools, and the answer is an unequivocal yes. All too frequently public school administrators, teachers, and parents have misinterpreted landmark Supreme Court decisions on prayer and devotional Bible reading in the public schools as rulings against teaching about religion. So teachers act as if even mentioning God or Allah or Jesus or the Quran will land them in jail. Nothing could be farther from the truth.

In *McCollum v. Board of Education* (1948), Supreme Court Justice Robert Jackson voted with the majority to outlaw Sunday-school-style religious instruction—the "teaching of creed and catechism and ceremonial"—in public schools. But he worried about leaving "public education in shreds" if all references to God were ruled out of bounds in the classroom. "Music without sacred music, architecture minus the cathedral, or painting without the scriptural themes would be eccentric and incomplete, even from a secular point of view," Jackson wrote. "Certainly a course in English literature that omitted the Bible and other powerful uses of our mother tongue for religious ends would be pretty barren. And I should suppose it is a proper, if not an indispensable, part of preparation for a worldly life to know the roles that religion and religions have played in the tragic story of mankind." Admitting that it can be difficult to determine precisely when teaching tips over into preaching, Jackson insisted nonetheless on keeping the study of religion in the public schools. "The fact is," he concluded, "that, for good or for ill, nearly everything in our culture worth transmitting, everything which gives meaning to life, is saturated with religious influences."[225]

In *Abington v. Schempp* (1963), which outlawed devotional Bible reading in the public schools, the Supreme Court again gave a constitutional seal of approval to the academic study of religion. Speaking for the majority, Justice Thomas Clark wrote:

> [I]t might well be said that one's education is not complete without a study of comparative religion or the history of religion and its relationship to the advancement of civilization. It certainly may be said that the Bible is worthy of study for its literary and historic qualities. Nothing we have said here indicates that such study of the Bible or of religion, when presented objectively as part of a secular program of education, may not be effected consistent with the First Amendment.

Justice William Brennan, in a concurring opinion in the same case, echoed Clark:

> The holding of the Court today plainly does not foreclose teaching *about* the Holy Scriptures or about the differences between religious sects in classes in literature or history. Indeed, whether or not the Bible is involved, it would be impossible to teach meaningfully many subjects in the social sciences or the humanities without some mention of religion.[226]

In *Stone v. Graham* (1980), which overturned a law requiring that the Ten Commandments be posted in Kentucky's public schools, the Supreme Court again went out of its way to affirm that "the Bible may constitutionally be used in an appropriate study of history, civilization, ethics, comparative religion, or the like." And in *Edwards v. Aguillard* (1987), a case invalidating Louisiana's "Creationism Act," Justice Lewis Powell wrote, "Courses in comparative religion of course are customary and constitutionally appropriate."[227]

Teaching Around Religion

Unfortunately, such courses are far from customary. Few school administrators understand the crucial distinction that these justices have repeatedly made between studying the Bible academically (which is constitutional) and reading it devotionally (which is not). Few schools of education instruct future teachers about the distinction Justice Goldberg made between "teaching about religion" (objectively) and "the teaching of religion" (confessionally) so many public school teachers simply avoid the subject altogether. Rather than teaching "about religion," these instructors teach, as historian Martin Marty once put it, "around religion." When it comes to religion, silence is their métier.[228]

Silence can lie as well as words, of course, and in this case the lie is that religion doesn't matter: it has no social, political, or historical force so students can get along just fine without knowing anything about it. This approach flies in the face of decades of Supreme Court rulings. It also lends credibility to the complaint, common in conservative Christian circles, that public schools, far from being religiously neutral, are actively promoting a "culture of disbelief."[229]

The Supreme Court has repeatedly ruled that the First Amendment requires of state governments not just neutrality among religions but also neutrality between religion and irreligion. The current strategy of obeying the law by avoiding religion may well be violating the Constitution, by indoctrinating students into a secular view of the world. At a minimum, this tendency is fueling the self-identity of many evangelicals as a besieged minority. This self-identity is fueling in turn an enrollment boom in conservative Protestant private schools, which soon will pass Roman Catholic institutions (if they have not done so already) as the most popular parochial schools in the nation. The neglect of religion in public schools may also be contributing to a parallel boom in Muslim private schools, which jumped from about 50 in 1987 to some 220 in 2005. To students who remain in public schools, this misguided approach offers, as philosopher Warren Nord has argued, "an illiberal education." It also fails to prepare students for citizenship in a world in which religion matters.[230]

New Consensus

Happily, however, a new consensus concerning religious studies in the public schools has emerged among education activists on both the left and the right. This new consensus, which understands teaching about religion to be both constitutional and imperative, steers deftly between two extremes: a religious extreme (the "sacred public school"), which sees the public school as a place to preach conservative Christianity, and a secular extreme (the "naked public school"), which sees the public school as a place where any mention of religion is out of bounds. The *via media* here is the "civic public school," which fosters objective teaching about religion while avoiding either denigrating or promoting it.[231]

In April 1995 thirty-five very different groups, including the National Association of Evangelicals, the American Muslim Council, and the American Humanist Association, signed on to "Religion in the Public Schools: A Joint Statement of Current Law," which specifically endorsed teaching about religion in the public schools. In 1999 President Clinton's Department of Education sent a memo to every principal in the country stating, "Public schools may teach about religion—for example, in classes on history, music, the arts, or comparative religion, the Bible (or other scripture)-as-literature, the role of religion in history—but public schools may not provide religious instruction." Also in 1999 a document called *The Bible and Public Schools: A First Amendment Guide* was endorsed by a wide variety of educational, religious, and political groups, including (on the left) the People for the American Way Foundation and the Anti-Defamation League and (on the right) the National Association of Evangelicals and the Christian Legal Society. "Educators widely agree," that document read, "that study *about* religion, where appropriate, is an important part of a complete education. Part of that study includes learning about the Bible ... [which] contributes to our understanding of literature, history, law, art, and contemporary society."[232]

Many states and school districts now have standards and policies that, at least in theory, carve out a place for religion in public school curricula. Moreover, significant gains have been made in teacher training and certification in religious studies, notably in California and Utah, where religious studies scholars at colleges and universities have teamed up with local school districts for that purpose.[233] Harvard Divinity School's Program in Religion and Secondary Education offers master's students an extensive program that focuses on integrating the study of religion into courses in English, history, and social studies, and culminates in a teacher's license. Some schools of education offer courses on religion in public education. A one-semester course at California State University, Chico—for undergraduates pursuing teaching certificates—covers First Amendment issues and the world's religions.

Over the last decade newspapers have also endorsed teaching about the Bible in public high schools. The *Chicago Tribune* wrote in a 2005 editorial that "trying to understand American literature and history without some knowledge of the Bible is like trying to make sense of the ocean despite a complete ignorance of fish." Its editors continued, "Public schools have no business using Bible instruction to advance a religious agenda. But when they decline to impart knowledge about such an important subject, they are not doing anything to preserve the separation of church and state. They are merely failing their students."[234]

Given this consensus, the question is turning from *whether* to teach about religion to *how*. And plainly the way to do that is to steer clear of both advocating religion and impugning it while at the same time communicating that individual religious convictions are to be treated, as a matter of both law and civility, with respect.[235]

Bible 101

When asked in a 1986 survey what book they would like to see their first-year students read, college English professors chose the Bible. Yet a 2005 study found that only 8 percent of public high school students have access to an elective Bible course in their schools. As a result an entire generation of Americans is growing up ignorant of the most influential book in world history, unable to understand biblical allusions in fictional works by Herman Melville, Mark Twain, and Toni Morrison, not to mention the 1,300 biblical allusions in Shakespeare or the prominence of Ezekiel 25:17—"You will know I am the Lord when I lay my vengeance upon you"—in the film *Pulp Fiction*. "Twenty-five years ago," an English teacher interviewed in the 2005 study said, "I could count on more students knowing the Cain and Abel story. Knowing the Abraham and Isaac story. And knowing other allusions. For example, in *All the King's Men*, there's a reference to Saul on the road to Damascus. Now I'm lucky if one student knows it." Or, as another put it: "I'll make comparisons, you know, I'll say: 'You know, like Noah and the ark or like Moses ... and I'll have kids kind of look at me: 'Who's Noah?' or 'Who's Moses?' and then you have to step back."[236]

But biblical illiteracy does not just put a crimp in your SAT scores or your lesson plans. It is a civic problem too. After President George W. Bush pledged in his first inaugural address, "When we see that wounded traveler on the road to Jericho, we will not pass to the other side," few Americans understood that he was alluding to the New Testament story of the Good Samaritan. And when they hear politicians refer to "Sodom and Gomorrah" (in the context of gay marriage) or "an eye for an eye" (in the context of capital punishment), they are often, in the words of one teacher included in the 2005 poll, "clueless." If presidents quote in their inaugural addresses from the biblical books of Micah (as Jimmy Carter did) or Galatians (as Bill Clinton did), shouldn't the people whose votes put them in office be able to understand what their elected officials are saying, to evaluate whether they are reading the Bible correctly or abusing it for partisan political purposes?[237]

Public schools should include one required course on the Bible for all high school students. The Bible should be taught in other courses wherever it is relevant, but "natural inclusion" of biblical topics in history and literature courses is not enough. Public school students should not learn about this classic only in passing. They need at least one course dedicated entirely to the Bible.

The Bible courses schoolchildren need are not Sunday school fare. A Bible curriculum used for over fifty years in elementary schools in Rhea County, Tennessee (home of the Scopes Trial), was rightly outlawed in 2002 by a US District Court judge who ruled that this curriculum unlawfully aimed to "endorse and advance religion" by, among other things, teaching children to sing "Jesus Loves Me" and "My God Is So Great." Curricular materials offered by the National Council on Bible Curriculum in Public Schools (NCBCPS) probably will not pass constitutional muster either. Although these materials have according to the group's Web site been adopted in over 353 school districts in 37 states, they are heavily slanted toward conservative Protestant theology and the "Christian America" perspective. They also presuppose a Christian audience (for example, by referring to Jesus as "our high priest") and repeatedly depict Jesus as fulfilling "Old Testament" prophecies. In 1998 a federal judge granted an injunction against a New Testament course in Fort Myers, Florida, based on these materials.[238]

If the Bible courses proposed here should not preach the Bible, neither should they debunk it, since attacking scripture as a fool's errand is unconstitutional too. Public school Bible courses should not focus on biblical criticism. They should not try to prove that Moses did not write the first five books of the Hebrew Bible or that the Gospel of Matthew contradicts the Gospel of John. They need to avoid the pitfalls of both proselytizing for Christianity and crusading against it. They should neither bolster nor undermine the convictions of students who believe that the Bible is the Word of God. Although they are about religion, these courses should not be religious (or irreligious) themselves.

The Bible courses envisioned here would include but would not be limited to teaching about the Bible as literature. Many advocates for religious studies in the public schools—including the people at the Virginia-based Bible Literacy Project behind a textbook called *The Bible and Its Influence* (2005)—have stressed the Bible-as-literature approach, in part because it is relatively uncontroversial. Who can deny that the Bible has had a greater influence on American and world literature than any other book, or that ignorance of the Bible makes it difficult to understand great literature? But public school students deserve more than Bible-as-literature courses. They should learn the afterlife of the Bible too. They need to be told about the historical influence of biblical characters and stories on politics and economics, music and film. The Bible cannot be taught as if it is a repository of historical and scientific facts. But neither should teachers and students approach it as literature alone, as if its words have resonated over the centuries solely in the imaginations of poets and playwrights. Students must understand the historical force of the Bible—how its words have beckoned adventurers to new lands and motivated politicians to create new governments. This appears to be the approach of a bill signed into law in 2006 in Georgia requiring elective Bible courses statewide, and of the Bible Literacy Project's new textbook.

Finally, these courses need to familiarize students with the Bible itself—its key phrases, stories, and characters. At a minimum, students in public school Bible courses should read all of Genesis and the Gospel of Matthew. They should learn that the Protestants' Bible has sixty-six books whereas the Catholic Bible has seventy-three. They should learn that the Old Testament is a Christian name for the Hebrew Bible and not a title that Jews use themselves. They should also learn something about different translations of the Bible. In fact, students might be encouraged to bring to school Bible translations of their own choosing since the presence of different Bibles in the classroom will prompt useful discussions about canonization and translation.

Some have argued against Bible courses in the public schools on the grounds that they somehow "establish" Judeo-Christianity. For these courses to be fair, this argument goes, teachers need to give equal time to all the world's scriptures, treating the Bible as one sacred text among many. This is absurd and impractical. Of course, students can learn much from reading the Quran and the Tao Te Ching. But the Bible, which the Supreme Court has described as "the world's all-time best seller," is of sufficient importance in Western civilization to merit its own course.[239] Treating it no differently from, say, the Zend Avesta of the Zoroastrians or Scientology's Dianetics makes no educational sense. (And what teacher has the hours—or the training—to give "equal time" to *all* the world's scriptures?)

Public school Bible courses are open to many other objections. From the left, the most common is that public schools need to be entirely shorn of religion—that any mention of religion amounts to an unconstitutional breach of the wall of separation between church and state. This view has been rightly rejected both by President Clinton, who noted in a 1995 speech that "the First Amendment ... does not convert our schools into religion-free zones," and by Supreme Court Justice Robert Jackson, who argued in his *McCollum* opinion that "one can hardly respect a system of education that would leave the student wholly ignorant of the currents of religious thought that move the world society."[240]

On the right, some conservative Christians argue that to study the Bible *as* literature or *in* history distorts scripture beyond recognition since the Bible's real meaning is and always shall be religious. Studying the Bible objectively and academically, in short, reduces "The Book" to "a book." One powerful reply to this objection comes from Charles Colson, the Watergate criminal turned evangelical spokesman. "Some critics fear that merely studying the Bible's role in history, or as literature diminishes it," writes Colson. But such a course, he argues, does not prevent Christians from taking the "next step" and trying to convert young people to Christianity. As Colson recognizes, however, spurring young people to take this "next step" cannot be the job of public schools. "Can people be good citizens," Colson asks, "if they don't know their own history?" The answer, of course, is no. And they can't be effective citizens (or neighbors) if they don't know something about the Bible.[241]

World Religion 101

Of course, knowing about the Bible is not enough in a country with over 1,200 mosques and more Hindu temples than any country outside India. So in addition to a required Bible course for every US public high school student, we need a mandatory course in the religions of the world. This is the place for middle school or high school students to encounter such scriptures as the Quran and the Bhagavad Gita and to learn about how the Jain ideal of *ahimsa* (nonviolence) inspired Gandhi's program of nonviolent direct action, how the Protestant Reformation changed the face of Europe, and what the US Supreme Court has said about the religious rights of Native Americans.

It is now commonplace to observe that we live in a global world, and the cliché has been a long time coming. Over a century and a half ago, Henry David Thoreau mused in *Walden* (1854) about a world in which ice cut from Walden Pond was exported to chill the glasses of the "sweltering inhabitants" of "Bombay and Calcutta"—a global world, in other words, in which "pure Walden water is mingled with the sacred water of the

Ganges" and New Englanders could "bathe [their] intellect in the stupendous and cosmogonal philosophy of the Bhagvat-Geeta." Today globalization has gone much further. Customer service personnel in Bangalore, India, field questions from Bostonians about their cell phones and Internet service providers. Hindus, Sikhs, and Buddhists attend American public schools from Cape Cod to San Francisco. American products and values permeate popular culture in Japan and China. And pop sensation Britney Spears has a baby blessed at a Hindu temple in Malibu, California.

Though the world is increasingly becoming one place, regional and religious differences abide. Sunnis battle Shiites in Iraq. Hindus rub up against Muslims in Kashmir and against Buddhists in Sri Lanka. Americans deserve to be equipped to make sense of these situations, and one simple way to equip them is to see to it that every public school student takes, in addition to a Bible course, at least one course on the world's religions.

This course should cover the seven great religious traditions of the world—Hinduism, Buddhism, Confucianism, Taoism, Judaism, Christianity, and Islam—but it should be tailored to local circumstances. Schools in New Mexico and Arizona might include units on Native American religions. Students in Stockton, California—home to the first Sikh *gurdwara* (temple) in the United States—might learn about Sikhism. Santeria could be discussed in Miami, a stronghold of that Afro-Caribbean faith.

In these world religions courses, students should learn about the origins of these religious traditions. They should study founders such as the Buddha, Confucius, Lao Tzu, Jesus, and Muhammad. They should also learn that some religions—Hinduism and Judaism, for example—have no founders. They should read portions of the scriptures of these traditions and discuss how different religions use scriptures in different ways. But these courses should not be stuck in the past, as if the world's scriptures were dead letters and these religions ancient relics. Students should learn about how today's Christians and Jews are adapting their religious traditions to modern life. American Hindus and Buddhists might be invited into these classes to talk about their holidays.

Teachers of both Bible and world religions courses must take pains not to argue for or against religion in general or any particular religion. They also need to be careful not to insist that all religions are essentially the same. If it is unconstitutional to preach the Christian gospel in public school classrooms, it is also unlawful to preach the gospel of religious relativism. Teachers should stick to describing and analyzing these religious traditions as objectively as possible, leaving it up to students to make judgments about the virtues and vices of any one religion, or of religion in general. In order to do all this, teachers need to be trained. We need more certification programs for public school religious studies teachers. We need more in-service training too. Much can be accomplished in weekend workshops sponsored by religious studies professors with expertise in the Bible or Islam. And there is tremendous value to bringing in an expert on the First Amendment to address teachers' fears about discussing religion in their classrooms.

The ground rules for public school courses on religion are fairly simple. They should be taught only if there are trained teachers ready and willing to teach them. Parents should be offered an opt-out provision if they consider any course to be objectionable on grounds of religion or conscience. Finally, these courses should be academic offerings *about* religion rather than devotional courses *in* religion. Teachers cannot be preachers. They need to inculcate knowledge rather than belief—religious literacy rather than faith. Their courses must be neutral, neither encouraging nor discouraging any particular religious belief or practice (or, for that matter, religion in general). This is not an easy assignment. As Justice Robert Jackson put it in his *McCollum* opinion, "The task of separating the secular from the religious in education is one of magnitude, intricacy and delicacy."[242] Given proper training and certification, however, public school teachers are more than up to the task.

One success story is a ninth-grade world religions course that has been required since 2000 in the public schools of Modesto, California, a city with a large evangelical Christian population as well as substantial populations of Hindus, Muslims, Jews, and Sikhs. A 2006 study, based on surveys of roughly four hundred students and interviews with teachers, administrators, and local religious leaders, found that this course was not a source of controversy in the community. It did not turn students into religious relativists or prompt them to change their religious beliefs. Most important, the study found that students' scores on a basic quiz concerning the world's religions and the First Amendment nearly doubled—from 37 percent before the course to 66 percent afterward.[243]

Constitutionality, Controversy, Cost

There are three main objections to the sort of religious literacy instruction proposed here: that it is not constitutional, that it is too controversial, and that it is too costly. As has already been discussed, the constitutional objection is misinformed: Supreme Court justices are all but begging public schools to teach about religion. As for the second objection, these courses will no doubt be controversial, but it is easy to overstate just how controversial they will be. Hundreds of school districts across the country already teach Bible and world religion courses as electives. And the overwhelming majority of Americans (roughly three-quarters in most surveys) say they do not object to teaching about the world's religions or the Bible in public schools.[244] Occasionally, a teacher will seize upon one of these courses as an opportunity to channel his inner Sunday school teacher or her inner atheist. And parental objections will sometimes escalate into lawsuits. But after these lawsuits are decided, parents and teachers adjust and life goes on. Allowing parents to pull their children out of courses that they find objectionable should also minimize the contention. But there is no way out of controversy here; teaching about religion is bound to be controversial, but so is ignoring it. The way forward is not to try to avoid disagreements but to tackle them head on.

Another objection to Bible and world religion courses is that they are too costly, not so much in dollars as in losses to other subject areas. Given a fixed number of school hours in any given day, a course added on religion is a course subtracted in some other topic; curriculum juggling *is* a zero-sum game. Nonetheless, religion is sufficiently important to warrant two courses out of every public school student's career. Not so long ago science was absent from secondary education and vocational instruction was unavailable. But public schools changed with the times, trading Latin for biology and Greek for shop. Our times demand changes too.

Admittedly, this is a difficult climate for adding subjects in public schools. President George W. Bush's "No Child Left Behind" law and the current vogue for standardized testing have forced elementary and secondary instructors to teach to the tests. In some elementary schools hardly anything other than reading and arithmetic is being taught on any given day. But the changes proposed here apply to secondary schools, and there are slots in any given middle school and high school that can be made available for the study of religion. "How can anyone believe that a college-bound student should take twelve years of mathematics and no religion rather than eleven years of mathematics and one year of religion?" Warren Nord asks. "Why require the study of trigonometry or calculus, which the great majority of students will never use or need, and ignore religion, a matter of profound and universal significance?"[245] Where to find space for instruction about religion should be left to local school districts—math is only one possibility—but there is no getting around the fact that a student ignorant of the Bible and the world's religions cannot be said to be ready for either college or citizenship.

One final objection to teaching about religion in the public schools is so silly that it hardly bears mentioning. It goes like this: Because American political life should be utterly secular and religious reasons should be out of bounds in political discourse, citizens don't need to know anything about religion. I hope the foolishness of this argument is evident. Assume for a moment that liberal philosophers such as John Rawls and Richard Rorty are right—that religious reasons ought to be banned from the public square because they are by definition irrational and therefore not susceptible to civil debate. Assume that religious people should be forced either to translate the religious reasons for their public policy stances into secular speech or to remain mum. Assume that the *polis* is not and will never be sufficiently tolerant to allow for God talk of any sort, that anything less than a "naked public square" means a return to the religious warfare of early modern Europe. Finally, assume that the counterarguments here—that banning religion from politics is undemocratic and that religious people are just as capable as secular people of reasonable debate—are all specious. Even if all these assumptions are correct (and they are not), the fact is that American political life is, as a factual matter, awash in religious reasons, religious arguments, and religious motivations. What good can it possibly serve for citizens, religious or otherwise, to be ignorant of all this?

Religious Studies in Higher Education

At least one course in religious studies should also be required of all college graduates. Since the 1960s the academic study of religion has found a home at many private and public colleges and universities in the United States. Programs and departments in religious studies at roughly eight hundred schools offer a major, and courses on the Bible and world religions count toward general education requirements at most of those schools. Religious studies courses are required of all students in most Catholic and evangelical Protestant institutions. Yet the vast majority of public and nonsectarian private colleges do not require a single course in the subject. Every year colleges provide bachelor's degrees to students who cannot name the first book of the Bible, who think that Jesus parted the Red Sea and Moses agonized in the Garden of Gethsemane, who know nothing about what Islam teaches about war and peace, and who cannot name one salient difference between Hinduism and Buddhism. Think of the ripple effects if recipients of BA degrees in communications—our future journalists, newscasters, television producers, and film directors—knew something about Christianity and the world's religions. Or if college graduates going into politics or business were even mildly conversant with the Quran.[246]

George Marsden of the University of Notre Dame and Warren Nord of the University of North Carolina have both argued for the return of "normative religious teaching" to American colleges and universities. They want professors not only to describe religious traditions but also to weigh in on their vices and virtues. Each has also argued that it is essential for students to learn "religious perspectives" in disciplines other than religious studies—to study theological critiques of economic theory and "religious interpretations of history." "There should be room," writes Nord, for both objective analysis of religion and "*normative* reflection on religion."[247]

At the public school level, all this would be unconstitutional. At colleges, however, there is doubtless a place for some mixing of theology and religious studies. But courses required of all college graduates should stick close to the facts. Although both Marsden and Nord disavow any desire to resurrect the Protestant establishment of the nineteenth century, each seems to long to return to the glory days when theology was the queen of the sciences and then to make her queen of the social sciences and the humanities too. There is more nostalgia than wisdom in this approach, and more than a modicum of intellectual imperialism. The time when college presidents were preachers and schoolchildren learned to read by poring over the Bible is long past, and the clocks are not turning back. But even if we wanted to return to the era of the *New England Primer* and mandatory chapel at college, such a return is no more likely than reconstructing Eden itself. The Supreme Court has made it plain that it will not cotton to proselytizing in the public schools, and Euro-secularity has advanced in higher education to a point where it is not realistic to imagine that our colleges and universities will give their hearts over to Eliot-style nonsectarian Protestantism (much less the Calvinist fervor of the founders of Harvard and Yale).

What Marsden and Nord seem to want is to make colleges and universities (or pockets of them) into religious places once again—to resurrect the big questions of God and creation and sin and judgment not only in departments of religion but also in courses in philosophy and economics and history and political science. This book aims at something more basic and less controversial. There is nothing wrong with college professors raising theological arguments for or against monarchy, capitalism, or evolution. But the present proposal is more modest than that. Rather than protesting "the exclusion of all religious concerns" from our universities, we should be concerned about the exclusion of the most basic religious information from the average student's course of study.[248] Rather than insisting that professors get up sophisticated theological critiques of neoclassical economics, we need to convince our private and public colleges to stop trivializing religion. There is no reason not to expect from America's future leaders minimal religious literacy.

For this agenda to succeed, it is crucial that the distinction between religious studies and theology—between teaching and preaching—be maintained in required courses in higher and secondary education. School superintendents and university administrators already have a difficult time understanding the difference between studying religion and doing religion. So does the general public. Given this confusion, it is important to draw a sharp distinction, in colleges as in public schools, between studying religion as an academic enterprise and thinking about the divine on behalf of one's religious community.

Beyond Character Education

It is also important to distinguish between religious studies and character education. During the nineteenth century one of the main aims of public schooling was to transform unruly children into law-abiding adults. Today calls for teaching about religion in the public schools are often yoked to efforts by character education advocates to spread such common values and sensibilities as open-mindedness, multiculturalism, tolerance of diverse viewpoints, and empathy for alternative ways of life. Boston University law professor Jay Wexler's call for religious studies courses in the public schools is based in part on the argument that such courses will foster "tolerance, empathy, and mutual respect." Likewise, Diana Eck's Pluralism Project aims not only to teach Americans about the religious traditions of their neighbors but also to foster a "public commitment" to the ideals of multiculturalism and religious pluralism. A firm believer in interreligious dialogue, Eck is convinced that we will get along better if we understand one another, and she views the study of religion as a way to do just that.[249]

There is nothing wrong with either empathy or mutual respect—or with moral education that emphasizes such time-honored virtues and values as honesty and hard work, justice and compassion. Still, two problems arise with thinking of religious literacy as moral instruction. First, this approach tends, at best, to confuse the agenda of spreading religious knowledge with the agenda of inculcating particular virtues. At worst, it sacrifices the former at the altar of the latter. In either case the educational goal shifts from making religiously literate citizens to making ethical citizens. In the process religion is reduced once again to "values," as if the world's religions cared not a bit about God, truth, or the afterlife.

The second problem with teaching religion as morality is that not all of the ostensibly common values character education aims to inculcate are truly shared. For every person clamoring on the left to use religious studies to teach multiculturalism, there is someone on the right intent on using religious studies to re-Christianize public education. School districts should teach religious tolerance and the First Amendment. That is not negotiable. But teaching the ideal of religious pluralism is another matter since Americans disagree strongly about its virtues and vices. It is quite possible that learning about Buddhism will make Christian students more respectful of Buddhist ways of being. It is also possible that learning about Buddhism will make these students more committed to showing Buddhists the errors of their ways—perhaps by becoming missionaries to Thailand or Korea. These contentious theological matters should not be mixed up with the crucial civic agenda of uprooting our collective ignorance of religion. Teaching about religion is controversial enough without mucking it up in moral or political agendas. Courses in religious studies should allow students to decide such normative questions for themselves. They should not be turned into exercises in political correctness or religious relativism.

For some reason some people who rightly see how inappropriate it is to insist that all religions are false or that only one religion is true think it perfectly appropriate (morally necessary, even) to preach to their students the equality of all religions. Setting aside the logical problem of how religions that affirm only one god, those that affirm multiple gods, and those that deny any god can be equally true, the fact is that the world's religions disagree fundamentally on the most basic matters. They do not agree on the problems they are trying to solve, on the goals they are trying to reach, on the paths to get to those goals, or on what sort of people (saints, bodhisattvas, renunciants, and so on) best chart these paths. In *The Great Transformation* (2006), a book about the emergence of many of the world's religions some two and a half millennia ago, writer Karen Armstrong tries to harmonize the cacophony of discordant beliefs and practices of these religions into one simple message. To the Buddha, Confucius, and other founders of these faiths, Armstrong writes, "what mattered was not what you believed but how you behaved." Most of these sages "had no interest whatever in doctrine or metaphysics." "For them, religion *was* the Golden Rule."[250]

What we have here is yet another effort to turn religion into a water boy for morality. In this regard Armstrong the liberal is nearly indistinguishable from William Bennett, the conservative Secretary of Education under President Reagan and author of *The Book of Virtues* (1993), who, more than anyone else in contemporary American public life, is to blame for popularizing the collapse of religion into "values." But in *The Great Transformation*—and here Armstrong differentiates herself from Bennett—we also have an effort to effect a Great Erasure, to wish away the many differences between the world's religions, to conflate Judaism's God, Buddhism's nirvana, Hinduism's Brahman, and Taoism's Way, as if these concepts were nothing more than different names for one ultimate reality. Armstrong has good ethical reasons for attempting this sleight of hand, not least a desire to "save our planet" from the terrors of "militant piety."[251] But her good will gets in the way of her understanding. Buddhism's goal of nirvana, or the elimination of suffering, is a far cry from the Christian goal of salvation, or the absence of sin, and still farther afield from the Jewish conception of God as a personal Creator, Lawgiver, and Judge. In fact, in Buddhism there is no judgment; ethics operates impersonally, by the law of karma.

Tolerance is doubtless a necessity for civil society. It is enshrined in the First Amendment and should be taught (and celebrated) in public school social studies courses. But a commitment to tolerance by no means entails indifference to either religious doctrines or religious differences. In fact, tolerance is an empty virtue in the absence of firmly held and mutually contradictory beliefs.

A Modest Proposal

Thinkers who argue for greater attention to religion in public life are often assumed to have a theological agenda. These assumptions are often correct. My goal, however, is civic rather than theological. Making American schools and colleges more religious is not my purpose. My brief for religious literacy proceeds on secular grounds, on the theory that Americans are not equipped for citizenship (or, for that matter, cocktail party conversation) without a basic understanding of Christianity and the world's religions.

Cynics might reply that this is too little, too late—that our collective amnesia is far too advanced. Perhaps so. Perhaps anti-intellectualism is endemic to democracy; perhaps religious believers will continue to undermine education about religion. But the time seems ripe for change. In America's past, ignorance of religion was fueled by a series of commitments to religious tolerance that insisted, typically for moral reasons, on obscuring the differences between religious traditions. In the aftermath of the Second Great Awakening Americans obscured the differences between Protestant denominations. During the religious revival that followed World War II they obscured the differences between Christianity and Judaism. More recently they have been trying to transform Muslims, Christians, and Jews into followers of the same God, even as Armstrong and others in the "spiritual but not religious" camp have been obscuring—in the name of compassion—crucial differences between Buddhism and Christianity, Hinduism and Judaism.

But a countervailing impulse now seems to be at play—a recovery of particularity in both academia and American culture writ large. The melting pot is now widely seen as a myth. We are, as Catholic writer Michael Novak put it, "unmeltable ethnics."[252] But we are proud not just of our Irishness or our Africanness, of being black or brown or red. We are proud as well of our Coptic Orthodoxy and our Tibetan Buddhism, our Ultra-Orthodox Judaism and our Sunni Islam, our Roman Catholicism and our evangelical Protestantism. Recent immigrants from India to the United States report few pressures to give up Hinduism. In fact, Hindus typically become more religious, not less, upon moving here. Today even conservative Christian critiques of the "naked public square" are often framed in terms of this sort of particularity. If it is acceptable to be a follower of Vishnu, why isn't it acceptable to be a born-again Christian—to come out of the closet (or a university professorship) as someone who has accepted Jesus as Savior and Lord? Why can't the diversity ethos that has made room in the academy for women and blacks, Catholics and Buddhists make room for evangelicals too?

There is a widening gap in the United States between what we actually know about religion and what we ought to know. But there is also a determination to narrow that gap—a sense of shame, or guilt at least, about our forgetfulness, about breaking the chains of memory that once bound our ancestors to one another and to the particular religious traditions they held dear.

When it comes to religion, we have had good reasons for our collective amnesia. More often than not it was tolerance—first for other Protestants, then for Catholics, then for Jews, and more recently for Muslims, Buddhists, and Hindus—that drove us to jettison theology for morality, to trade in the doctrines and stories of our religious traditions for the promise of social order. There are doubtless many today who are delighted to have the not-so-golden age of bitter sectarian disputes about infant baptism behind us, who are convinced that nothing good can come of learning about how theologians calculate the number of angels dancing on the head of a pin. But the costs of perpetuating religious ignorance are too high in a world in which faith moves, if not mountains, then at least elections and armies. It does nothing for the Secular Left to remain ignorant of the Religious Right (or vice versa). And it puts America at risk to remain ignorant as a society of the beliefs and practices of Buddhists in Sri Lanka, Hindus in Kashmir, and Muslims in Iran.

In debates about life and death and war and peace, the stakes are too high to defer to politicians and pundits. Given the ubiquity of religious discourse in American public life and the public power of religion at home and abroad, we Americans—liberals and conservatives, believers and unbelievers—need to learn about evangelicalism and Islam for ourselves, to see for ourselves what the Bible says about family values, homosexuality, war, and capital punishment, and what Islam says about many of these same things.

The Mother of Devotion

Given the paradox of religion's vitality in a nation in which so many know so little even about their own religious traditions, one might rightly wonder whether fervent faith depends on religious illiteracy, whether the health of American religion depends not on religious knowledge but on religious ignorance. This was the troubling question I took away from my around-the-photocopier-conversation with my Austrian colleague a few years ago, when he told me about the differences between his educated-but-irreligious students in Europe and his uneducated-but-pious students in the United States. Might religious education have doomed European religion? Might American religion be thriving precisely because of Americans' religious illiteracy? This was the suspicion of historian Richard Hofstadter, who wondered throughout *Anti-Intellectualism in American Life* whether "ignorance is the mother of devotion." And it was the conviction of the infamous nineteenth-century agnostic Robert G. Ingersoll, who once contended that the reason everybody in the United States believes in the Bible is that no one actually reads it.[253]

It could well be that faith without religious knowledge stands on exceedingly sandy soil. The Bible says—in a passage repeatedly quoted by Senator John Kerry in his 2004 presidential bid—that "faith without works is dead" (James 2:26). Faith without knowledge is likely no more vital. But the more germane point is that faith without knowledge is dangerous. Each of the world's great religions has wrestled for centuries with the foundational questions of life and death and whatever (if anything) lies beyond. Each has developed sophisticated theologies for making sense of other religions, for regulating war, and for fighting injustice. But we as a nation are forgetting these hard-won theologies, replacing them in many cases with bromides only an advertising hack could be proud of— bromides, it should be noted, that are themselves ripe for replacement whenever a sexier advertising pitch comes along. Moreover, the politicians and pundits eager to exploit these bromides for partisan purposes— to turn God, Jesus, and Muhammad into pawns in their political and military games—are legion. Faith without knowledge may or may not be dead, but our current mix of fervent religious belief and widespread religious ignorance is surely a dangerous combination.

Just before Christmas in 1949 one of the founding members of the National Association of Bible Instructors observed that the "younger generation" was "pitifully bewildered" about the Bible. "Protestantism," he concluded, "stands doomed." It is tempting to conclude this book with some similar lamentation—to insist that the nation "stands doomed" unless we become religiously literate. That is too dramatic. But Americans are doomed to repeat their recent mistakes if they do not start to reconstruct the chain of memory that bound their ancestors to Protestantism, Catholicism, Judaism, Islam, and other religions. And those who are not religiously literate are doomed to marginalize themselves from debates on matters of no less importance than the fate of the Middle East, the religious freedoms of the First Amendment, the politics of Islam, and the propriety of gay marriage.

From this nation's beginnings it has been widely understood that the success of the American experiment rested on an educated citizenry. In today's world it is irresponsible to use the word *educated* to describe high school or college graduates who are ignorant of the ancient stories that continue to motivate the beliefs and behaviors of the overwhelming majority of the world's population. In a world as robustly religious as ours it is foolish to imagine that such graduates are equipped to participate fully in the politics of the nation or the affairs of the world.

But becoming religiously literate is not just a civic duty; it can also be a personal desire. Who hasn't felt edged out of an important conversation by a lack of understanding of this religion or that? Wouldn't we all feel more empowered to question media misrepresentations of our own traditions if we knew more about them, or to defuse tensions in our hometown about the construction of a mosque or a Hindu temple if we were more conversant with Islam or Hinduism?

It is now commonplace to outsource computer programming and customer service work to developing nations. But democracy cannot be outsourced. To continue to defer to demagogues on matters as important as the political theology of Islam, the biblical view of marriage, or what Jesus would do about the environment is to recuse ourselves from democracy itself. The alternative is to "get" religion—to cultivate in ourselves and our children basic literacy about the Bible and the world's religions.

Moving forward on the problem of religious illiteracy will require compromise on both the Secular Left and the Religious Right. In *Divided by God* (2005) Noah Feldman charts a creative middle path between "values evangelicals" and "legal secularists." On the broader question of religion in the public square Feldman proposes a compromise that allows for "greater latitude" on "public religious discourse and religious symbolism" yet "a stricter ban on state funding of religious institutions and activities." Setting aside the merits of this particular effort to reunite a nation "divided by God" into blues and reds, Feldman is right to sense a desire for reconciliation here. Most Americans are weary of the culture wars, which owe their continued existence almost entirely to partisan politicians and media talking heads—in other words, to that minuscule portion of the population that owes its livelihood and celebrity to biased bickering. No one wants to revive the "Bible wars" in public schools, yet the vast majority want their children to learn more about religion. Progress on this score will take compromise too. The Secular Left will need to yield on the dogma that religion has no place in the public square. The Religious Right will need to give up its desire to use the public schools for proselytizing purposes. The middle path here—in both secondary and higher education—is teaching about religion that takes believers seriously yet refuses to plump either for or against what they believe. This path leaves responsibility for inculcating faith where it rightly belongs: in homes and religious congregations. But it is not complicit in the conspiracy of silence that continues to keep Americans religiously illiterate.[254]

For those of us beyond our high school and college years, the solution is to educate ourselves—to follow the ancient admonitions of the Hebrew Bible to "remember," to resolve to read Genesis or Matthew or the

Quran, and to reconstruct the chain of memory that binds us not only to our ancestors' religious traditions but also to America's first citizens, who understood attaining religious knowledge as both a personal challenge and a civic duty of the highest order.

Six

A Dictionary of Religious Literacy

In *Cultural Literacy* E. D. Hirsch provided a sixty-four-page appendix of terms literate Americans supposedly already knew. Hirsch did not define those terms. He said that you should know who the Abominable Snowman is, but he didn't tell you that you could find him in *Rudolph the Red-Nosed Reindeer* (or for that matter in Himalayan mythology). The following dictionary, instead of providing a similarly exhaustive accounting of what religiously literate Americans ought to know, offers a more modest list. Learning five thousand terms is not necessary; a hundred or so is a good start. But knowing what these terms mean is essential. So unlike Hirsch's appendix, this chapter provides definitions of its terms.

This dictionary does not try to duplicate the information you might learn in a Religion 101 course. It focuses instead on information US citizens need to make sense of their country and the world—the key stories, doctrines, practices, symbols, scriptures, people, places, phrases, groups, and holidays of the world's major religions. When it came to preparing this list, the key question was: What does one need to know to understand and participate in religiously inflected public debates? Consider Sufism: a primer on Islam would doubtless deal with Sufi mysticism, but this dictionary ignores Sufism in order to focus on sectarian divisions inside Islam that are more salient in the contemporary United States (including Wahhabism, which has ridden a wave of Saudi money into American mosques). Or consider Hanukkah. As any rabbi can tell you, this is a minor Jewish holiday. So why is it included here while more important festivals—Yom Kippur (Day of Atonement) and Rosh Hashanah (Jewish New Year)—are not? Because Hanukkah comes up repeatedly in public disputes about Christmas, including lawsuits about the constitutionality of nativity displays (some of which include menorahs and other Hanukkah symbols) on public property. Another of this dictionary's principles of inclusion is public confusion. Terms that are widely misunderstood or misused—*evangelicalism* and *fundamentalism,* for example—are stressed here.

In addition to defining these terms, this dictionary tries to make them relevant by noting how they are used (or abused) in public policy discussions—how the Genesis story of Adam and Eve is cited in debates about gay marriage or the Good Samaritan is drafted into fights over immigration law. In discussing American Christianity, it notes that Catholics are underrepresented in the US Congress relative to their overall population while Episcopalians and Presbyterians are overrepresented.

This chapter begins with a short section called "Religion by the Numbers." This section includes such basics as the 4 Noble Truths of Buddhism, the 5 Pillars of Islam, and the 10 Commandments. The rest of this chapter proceeds alphabetically with "What Americans Need to Know." Those who master this dictionary will be prepared to engage the controversial social and political issues of our time. Closer to home, they will also be able to understand what is being said (and implied) in town meetings and school committees. And they will have the confidence to participate in conversations about religion among coworkers and friends.

One final note: Much of the information included here derives from sources that are not without a point of view—from Lutherans or Shiites, the Bhagavad Gita or the Quran. Accuracy might dictate the repeated inclusion of caveats such as "according to the Bible" or "from the Buddhist perspective." But felicity of expression dictates otherwise. The reader should know that if I write that Joseph Smith Jr. found gold plates in the hills of New York in the 1820s I am not reporting the facts or even the facts as I understand them but rather the facts as Mormons believe them to be.

Religion by the Numbers

4 Gospels. The four narratives of the life of Jesus included in the New Testament of the Christian churches. They are: Matthew, Mark, Luke, and John. In Greek, the language in which these books were written, the term *gospel* refers to "good news." So these Gospels are the "good news" of the birth, teachings, miracles, death, and resurrection of Jesus. Although these books all narrate Jesus' life, they have different emphases. Matthew shows how Jesus fulfills Old Testament prophecies. Mark structures his story around the "messianic secret" that Jesus is the long-awaited messiah of the Jews. Luke accents Jesus' concern for women and the poor. John contains a variety of "I am" sayings, which underscore Jesus' divinity. Mark (circa 70 CE) is likely the earliest of the Gospels, which were written in the late first century. Matthew and Luke are probably based in part on Mark. Because of their similarities in structure and content these three books are called the synoptic Gospels. Of the Gospels, Americans' favorite is Matthew, followed by John, then Luke, then Mark. In recent decades noncanonical gospels such as the Gospel of Thomas have piqued considerable interest. The best-selling novel *The Da Vinci Code* (2003) spurred interest in the Gospel of Mary, and the publication in 2006 of the long-lost Gospel of Judas, which depicts Judas not as Jesus' betrayer but as his closest confidante, caused a stir.

4 Noble Truths. Buddhism's core teachings, delivered by the Buddha in his first sermon at Sarnath, outside Varanasi in what is now northern India. The first truth (the Existence of Suffering) states that human life is characterized by *dukkha,* which is usually translated as suffering but also means unsatisfactoriness. The second truth (the Origin of Suffering) says that suffering is caused by clinging, which is caused in turn by ignorance, particularly ignorance of the impermanence of things. The third truth (the Cessation of Suffering) says that the chain of cause and effect that produces suffering can be reversed, resulting in liberation from suffering or nirvana. The fourth truth (the Path to the Cessation of Suffering) outlines the way to nirvana via the Eightfold Path of Buddhist practice.

5 Ks. Symbols that identify male members of a Sikh order called the Khalsa, so called because each begins in Punjabi with the letter *k.* They are: *kes,* uncut hair; *kangha,* comb; *kirpan,* ceremonial sword; *kara,* steel wrist bangle; *kachh,* short pants. The 5 Ks were instituted in 1699 by Guru Gobind Singh, Sikhism's tenth guru, as a way to distinguish Sikhs from surrounding Hindus and Muslims. The kirpan has prompted many controversies in the United States. Public schools have wrestled with whether, as a matter of religious freedom, Sikhs should be allowed to wear kirpans at schools while Sikhs have struggled with whether it is permissible, in order to comply with school weapons bans, to dull their kirpans' blades or confine them permanently in their sheaths. After 9/11 one of the people arrested was a turbaned Sikh man innocently carrying a kirpan on a train in Providence, Rhode Island.

5 Pillars of Islam. The key practices of Islam, obligatory for all Muslims. They are: *Shahadah,* or witnessing that "There is no god but God, and Muhammad is the messenger of God"; *salat,* or prayer in the direction of Mecca five times a day (dawn, noon, afternoon, sunset, and evening); *sawm,* or fasting (from sunrise to sunset) during the lunar month of Ramadan; *zakat,* or almsgiving to the poor (via an asset tax); *hajj,* or pilgrimage to Mecca, once in a lifetime for all who are physically and financially able. Some critics of Islam wrongly claim that jihad is one of the Five Pillars. It is not. Muslims' emphasis on these Five Pillars underscores the fact that Islam is more focused on right practice (orthopraxy) than on right belief (orthodoxy).

7 sacraments. A sacrament is a religious rite that involves the manipulation of some tangible object (water, oil, bread, wine) and conveys God's grace to participants. Catholics (and most Orthodox Christians) acknowledge seven sacraments: baptism, confirmation, reconciliation (also known as penance or confession), Holy Communion, marriage, ordination of priests, and anointing of the sick (once referred to as last rites). Protestants classically acknowledge only two—baptism and Holy Communion—while some Protestant sects, notably the Quakers, reject sacramentalism altogether. Early twenty-first century debates about gay marriage highlighted the question of the sacramentalism of matrimony. If marriage is purely contractual, perhaps it can change with the times. But if marriage is ordained by God—"the visible form of invisible grace," in Saint Augustine's terms—the barriers to gay marriage are much higher.

7 deadly sins. In Roman Catholicism the most weighty human failings, sometimes referred to as the Seven Capital Sins. The standard list, which the thirteenth-century Catholic theologian Thomas Aquinas dated to Pope Gregory the Great (540–604), includes: pride, envy, greed, anger, sloth, lust, and gluttony. In the 1995 film *Se7en* detectives try to track down a murderer who kills in keeping with the Seven Deadly Sins.

8-Fold Path of Buddhism. Buddhism's Eightfold Path, the culmination of the Four Noble Truths, charts the course from suffering to nirvana. This practical path is classically divided into three parts: wisdom (right view and right intention); morality (right speech, right conduct, right livelihood); and concentration (right effort, right mindfulness, and right concentration). It is often described as a "middle way" between asceticism and hedonism.

10 Commandments. Religious and moral laws given by God to Moses on Mount Sinai and inscribed on two stone tablets. Also known as the Decalogue or the Ten Words, these laws begin with human beings' duties to God and conclude with their obligations to one another. The Bible contains two versions of the Ten Commandments, in Exodus 20:1–17 and Deuteronomy 5:6–21, which are also scattered throughout the Quran. The Bible does not number these commandments, however, so Jews, Catholics, and Protestants have different iterations of them. There is no single Jewish version, but one widely used version begins with "I the Lord am your God who brought you out of the land of Egypt, the house of bondage." Then follows, "You shall have no other gods besides me." The Protestant version and the Catholic version (also accepted by most Lutherans) collapse these two injunctions into one. The Protestant Decalogue includes a prohibition against "graven images" not found in the Jewish or Catholic lists. The most important difference is between the Jewish commandment not to "murder" and the Catholic and Protestant commandment not to "kill." Capital punishment and war would seem to be permissible in the former case, since arguably neither is murder, but not in the latter, since both involve killing. These three versions also differ at the end—to enable each to add up to ten. While Catholics conclude with separate injunctions against coveting your neighbor's wife and coveting your neighbor's goods, Jews and Protestants compress covetousness into a single commandment.

The Decalogue has a long history in American public life. Cecil B. DeMille directed a popular silent version of *The Ten Commandments* in 1923, and his 1956 remake of the same name was a blockbuster. Inspired by the remake, which starred Charlton Heston as Moses, a Catholic group called the Fraternal Order of Eagles began constructing Ten Commandments monuments on public lands across the country. These displays occasioned a flurry of litigation in the 1990s and beyond. In 2005 the Supreme Court, whose courtroom is itself adorned with a carving of Moses and other lawgivers, banned two such monuments (both Protestant versions in Kentucky courthouses) and approved another (a Judeo-Christian version in the Texas capitol). The most famous recent spat on this subject featured the "Ten Commandments Judge," Roy Moore, who, after refusing a court order to remove a Ten Commandments monument he had installed at Alabama's state judiciary building, was removed from his post as Alabama's chief justice in 2003. Most Ten Commandments controversies have concerned displays on public property. A nonprofit group called Project Moses erects similar displays on private land. This organization is also lobbying for a Ten Commandments monument on the National Mall in Washington DC.[255]

Jewish Version

1. I the Lord am your God who brought you out of the land of Egypt, the house of bondage.
2. You shall have no other gods besides Me.
3. You shall not swear falsely by the name of the Lord your God.
4. Remember the Sabbath day and keep it holy.
5. Honor your father and your mother.
6. You shall not murder.
7. You shall not commit adultery.
8. You shall not steal.
9. You shall not bear false witness against your neighbor.
10. You shall not covet your neighbor's house; you shall not covet your neighbor's wife, or ... anything that is your neighbor's.

Catholic Version

1. I am the Lord your God: You shall not have strange Gods before me.
2. You shall not take the name of the Lord your God in vain.
3. Remember to keep holy the Lord's Day.
4. Honor your father and your mother.
5. You shall not kill.
6. You shall not commit adultery.
7. You shall not steal.
8. You shall not bear false witness against your neighbor.
9. You shall not covet your neighbor's wife.
10. You shall not covet your neighbor's goods.

Protestant Version

1. I am the Lord your God, who brought you out of the land of Egypt, out of the house of bondage. You shall have no other gods before Me.
2. You shall not make yourself a graven image.
3. You shall not take the name of the Lord your God in vain.
4. Remember the Sabbath day, to keep it holy. Six days you shall labor, and do all your work.
5. Honor your father and your mother.
6. You shall not kill.

7. You shall not commit adultery.
8. You shall not steal.
9. You shall not bear false witness against your neighbor.
10. You shall not covet your neighbor's house; you shall not covet your neighbor's wife, or ... anything that is your neighbor's.

12 apostles. The original followers, or disciples, of Jesus, dispatched by him to spread the Christian message, are referred to as the twelve apostles (from the Greek for "those who are sent forth"). They are: Peter, Andrew, James (the greater), John, Philip, Bartholomew (aka Nathaniel), Matthew, Thomas, James (the lesser), Jude, Simon, Judas. After Judas betrayed Jesus and committed suicide, he was replaced by Matthias.

What Americans Need to Know

Abraham. The Hebrew Bible patriarch and father of the "Abrahamic" religions of Judaism, Christianity, and Islam. According to Genesis, Abraham and God enter into a covenant. Although Abraham is old and his wife, Sarah, is barren, God promises to make him the father of a great nation residing in a Promised Land, and Abraham agrees in turn to circumcise his male children. Abraham is best known for obeying God's command to sacrifice his son Isaac. After Abraham bound Isaac on an altar and raised a knife to slay him, an angel stayed his hand and a nearby ram was sacrificed instead. Abraham is also revered among Christians, who see him as a person of great faith, and by Muslims, who call him Ibrahim and cite the story of the binding of his son (not Isaac but Ishmael— Ismail in Arabic—according to Muslims) to support their view of him as the first Muslim, and their understanding of themselves as heirs of his promises (including the Land of Canaan). Toward the end of the twentieth century, and particularly after the events of September 11, 2001, Americans began to speak of Judaism, Christianity, and Islam as "Abrahamic religions." In September 2002 Abraham appeared on the cover of *Time* magazine as the father of these faiths.

Abrahamic tradition. See Judeo-Christian-Islamic.

Adam and Eve. The Bible begins in the book of Genesis with two creation accounts. In the latter God creates Adam as the first human. God then creates Eve, the first woman, out of one of Adam's ribs and instructs the two not to eat from the Tree of the Knowledge of Good and Evil. Tricked by a serpent, however, they eat this "forbidden fruit," prompting God to banish them from Eden. According to many Christians, who describe this catastrophe as the Fall, all subsequent humans were born with a rebellious nature called original sin. At least since the publication of *The Woman's Bible* (1895), Jewish and Christian feminists have wrestled with the gender implications in this story, which according to some interpreters makes women both secondary and subordinate to men—Eve is described as Adam's "handmaid" or "helper"—and blames a woman for the Fall. Feminists have responded by emphasizing the first creation account, which refers to God creating male and female at the same time and both in the divine image. Muslims wrestle with similar questions. The story of the first woman's creation from Adam's rib appears in the hadith, but in the Quran most references to creation speak of God fashioning male and female from the same substance.

In the contemporary gay marriage debate, opponents have invoked the Garden of Eden story, arguing that in Genesis God ordains marriage as a contract between one man and one woman. In the beginning, they argue, it was "Adam and Eve," not "Adam and Steve." There is no mention in Genesis, however, of Adam and Eve getting married.

Adventism. See Seventh-Day Adventism.

African Methodist Episcopal Church. One of the largest black church denominations in the United States, the AME (as it is popularly called) was founded in Philadelphia in 1816 by Richard Allen, who went on to become this denomination's first bishop. The AME boasts over a dozen colleges and seminaries in the United States and roughly 3.5 million American members.

ahimsa. Term in Hinduism, Buddhism, and especially Jainism, often translated as nonviolence, referring to not harming or wishing to harm. Described by Jains as the highest moral duty, this ideal informs such diverse practices in India as vegetarianism and the veneration of cows. It also motivates Jain ascetics to wear face masks and sweep the ground before them in order to avoid injuring even tiny insects. *Ahimsa* profoundly influenced Mohandas Gandhi (1869–1948) and his nonviolent campaign for Indian independence, though Gandhi creatively reinterpreted this ideal in more positive terms—as universal compassion. Through Gandhi, *ahimsa* also informed the nonviolent struggles of the

Reverend Martin Luther King Jr. and the civil rights movement. Today this ideal plays a major part in the Dalai Lama's nonviolent struggle for Tibetan cultural autonomy.

Allah. Term for God in Arabic and Islam. In the Quran Allah is described as merciful, gracious, and compassionate and is said to be the creator, sustainer, ruler, judge, and redeemer of the universe. Muslims traditionally ascribe to God ninety-nine "beautiful names," including "The Just," "The Mighty," and "The Perfectly Wise." The most important teaching about Allah, however, is *tawhid,* or divine oneness, a view inscribed in the *Shahadah,* or Muslim creed, as "There is no God but God." Rival understandings of God, including polytheism and the Christian view that God is somehow three in one, Muslims reject as *shirk,* or ascribing partners to Allah (who alone is divine).

One of the most common Muslim sayings is *"Allahu Akbar,"* or "God is great." These words were the last sounds recorded on the cockpit voice recorder for United Flight 93, which terrorists crashed in rural Pennsylvania on September 11, 2001, and there is a Muslim tradition of reciting this saying when going into battle to defend Islam. But *Allahu Akbar* is more commonly heard in both the traditional call to daily prayers and in the prayer ritual itself. Since 9/11 Americans have debated whether, as Muslims have traditionally claimed, the Islamic God is the same as the Jewish and Christian God. After 9/11 President George W. Bush affirmed that Muslims and Christians "worship the same God," but many evangelicals disagreed. "We should always remember," Richard Land of the Southern Baptist Convention said of Bush, "that he is commander in chief, not theologian in chief."[256]

al-Qaeda. International terrorist organization founded in the late 1980s by the wealthy Saudi-born financier Osama bin Laden (b. 1957). Al-Qaeda is best known for hijacking three jets on September 11, 2001, and crashing them into the World Trade Center, the Pentagon, and a Pennsylvania field. Influenced by Wahhabism and other forms of Islamist thought, al-Qaeda ("the base" in Arabic) emerged in 1989 out of an organization bin Laden used to finance the struggle of the Mujahideen ("holy warriors") against Soviet occupation of Afghanistan—a struggle funded in part by the United States. After the Soviets withdrew that same year, al-Qaeda enjoyed safe haven in Afghanistan under the Taliban, a theocratic Sunni state that punished theft by amputation, banned television, and mandated that women wear the full *burqa* (veil covering the entire body) in public. From that base al-Qaeda launched a "holy war" against Western occupation of Muslim lands, especially the presence of American troops in Saudi Arabia. That jihad, as members called it, proceeds on two fronts: against the "near enemy," Muslim-majority states—Saudi Arabia chief among them—that it regards as apostate; and against the "far enemy" of the United States and other Western powers that support those apostate regimes.

What al-Qaeda opposes is plainer than what it desires, but the organization seems to seek a transnational Islamic empire that adheres to a strict interpretation of Islamic law. In the nearer term al-Qaeda seems intent on instigating a "clash of civilizations" between Muslims and "the Zionist-crusaders alliance"—a clash that goes back to medieval crusades and the life of Muhammad himself. Their hope is that such a struggle will, as another al-Qaeda leader, Ayman al-Zawahiri (b. 1951), put it, "purge our land from the aggressors."[257]

Responding to suicide bombings against US embassies in Kenya and Tanzania in 1998, the US military bombed al-Qaeda training camps in Afghanistan and a pharmaceutical plant in the Sudan that was reportedly making nerve gas for bin Laden. After 9/11 the United States invaded Afghanistan and ousted the Taliban, sending bin Laden and his organization scattering. Although bin Laden eluded capture, roughly one thousand al-Qaeda members were arrested in dozens of countries, but al-Qaeda continued to operate.

Anglicanism. See Episcopalianism.

Apocalypse. Catastrophic end times battle in which the forces of good triumph over the forces of evil and usher in of a new age of justice and peace. In Greek, the term *apocalypse* refers to the unveiling of hidden things; what is being disclosed here is the messiah or the Christ and the horrors and glories that attend his coming. The most famous apocalyptic literature in the West is the New Testament book of Revelation, which is sometimes referred to as the Apocalypse. However, Christians borrowed the genre, which classically attends to such matters as the bodily resurrection and the last judgment, from Jews. This genre lives on in secular films such as *Apocalypse Now* (1979) and the pious *Left Behind* novels (1995–) of Tim LaHaye and Jerry Jenkins. Many of America's new religious movements have anticipated an impending apocalypse. Seventh-Day Adventism emerged out of the prophecies of the Baptist farmer William Miller that the world would end on October 22, 1844. And the Branch Davidians of Waco, Texas, believed that their leader, David Koresh, was close to decoding the Seven Seals of Revelation when their compound went up in flames in 1993. Apocalypticism also plays a role in contemporary American politics, motivating many evangelicals and fundamentalists to support the state of Israel on the theory that the Jews must return to the Holy Land promised by God before Jesus will return to establish his kingdom. In a secular guise apocalypticism fueled the Y2K frenzy, which led many to fear that a minor computer bug would lead to a global economic meltdown on January 1, 2000.

Apostles' Creed. Short statement of Christian beliefs, traditionally attributed to Jesus' apostles but actually composed long after their deaths. The most popular creed in Christian worship services in the West, it reads (in one traditional English version):

I believe in God the Father Almighty, Maker of heaven and earth.
And in Jesus Christ his only Son our Lord; who was conceived by the
    Holy Ghost, born of the Virgin Mary, suffered under Pontius
    Pilate, was crucified, dead, and buried; he descended into hell; the
    third day he rose again from the dead; he ascended into heaven,
    and sitteth on the right hand of God the Father Almighty; from
    thence he shall come to judge the quick and the dead.
I believe in the Holy Ghost; the holy catholic Church; the
    communion of saints; the forgiveness of sins; the resurrection of the
    body; and the life everlasting. Amen.

Armageddon. This Christian term, which appears only once in the Bible—Revelation 16:16: "the place that in Hebrew is called Armageddon"—refers most narrowly to the place where the fiery battle between good and evil will take place in the last days. More broadly, it refers to this battle itself. Armageddon has captured the imaginations of many Christians and inspired a variety of best-selling novels, including Hal Lindsey's *The Late Great Planet Earth* (1970) and the *Left Behind* series (1995–) of Tim LaHaye and Jerry Jenkins. This term, which is employed regularly in US House and Senate debates, has also been used to describe many historical conflicts, including the Civil War, World War I, and World War II. It is a transliteration of the Hebrew for "Mount Megiddo" in northern Israel.

atheism. Denial of the existence of any and all gods. Although many commonly believe that affirming God is a prerequisite for any religion, some religions are atheistic; neither Buddhists nor Taoists typically worship any divinity. Atheism has made some inroads in Europe but few in the United States. According to recent polls, most Americans say that they would not vote for an atheist for president. Some local and state governments still have laws on the books forbidding atheists from testifying in court or running for office.

atonement. For Christians, the death of Jesus on the cross, which somehow gets sinners right with God and wins them salvation. The "somehow" here is significant since Christians disagree on how the atonement operates, whom it affects, and what metaphors—sacrifice? ransom? payment?—best describe it. Substitutionary views, held by many conservative Christians, claim that on the cross Jesus either took upon himself the punishment brought on by human sins or paid a ransom to the devil to free humans from everlasting torment. Exemplary views, typically held by liberal Christians, see Jesus' death as an example of divine love. Theologians have also differed over whether Jesus died for everyone (unlimited atonement) or just for the elect (limited atonement) and over whether the benefits of the atonement are available, as Protestants believe, to anyone who has faith or, as Catholics have traditionally affirmed, only to those who partake of the Catholic sacraments.

Atonement is also a feature of Judaism. On Yom Kippur (Day of Atonement), which falls in the Jewish calendar just after Rosh Hashanah (Jewish New Year), Jews fast and pray, asking God to forgive them for sins committed in the prior year. Christian atonement theories were widely discussed after the release of the film *The Passion of the Christ* (2004) reinvigorated an ancient debate about whether Jews are responsible for Jesus' crucifixion, but for the most part concerns about the atonement are muted in the contemporary United States, probably because hell is no longer a real and present danger for most Americans.

baptism. Rite of initiation into the Christian community in which candidates are immersed in water or water is sprinkled or poured over them. Christians describe this practice, which they trace to Jesus' baptism by John the Baptist, as dying and rising to new life, a cleansing of sins, and an infusion of the Holy Spirit. Baptism has provoked some of the most bitter disputes in Christian history. Is baptism a sacrament? Catholics and most Protestants say yes, but Quakers say no. Should it be administered to infants? Most Christians say yes, but Baptists insist on believers' baptism. The Salvation Army does not baptize at all; and "Jesus Only" Pentecostals baptize in Jesus' name alone rather than in the name of the Father, the Son, and the Holy Spirit. A related practice is the baptism of the Holy Spirit (or spirit baptism), which Holiness, Pentecostal, and charismatic groups see as separate from water baptism and believe conveys such gifts of the Holy Spirit as speaking in tongues.

Baptists. The largest Protestant group in the United States. Baptists distinguish themselves from other Christians chiefly by their rejection of infant baptism in favor of believers' baptism. Baptism, they argue, is not a means of grace but a sign of grace already received. Throughout American history Baptists have been staunch advocates of the separation of church and state. Thomas Jefferson's famous 1802 letter to Baptists in Danbury, Connecticut, commending a "wall of separation between church and state" was preaching to the choir; and one of the most powerful voices for strict church/state separation was Baptist Supreme Court justice Hugo Black, who grafted the "wall" metaphor onto the Constitution in *Everson v. Board of Education* (1947). Since the 1980s, however, Baptists—Jerry Falwell and the "Ten Commandments Judge" Ray Moore among them—have been some of the most vocal opponents of strict separationism. Like most US Protestant denominations, Baptists split regionally (into North and South) and racially (into black and white) in the nineteenth century. Their largest denomination today is the Southern Baptist Convention, which claims about twenty million members. The other major white Baptist group, American Baptist Churches in the USA, reports just under two million members and is more liberal both theologically and politically. Black Baptists cluster in four denominations: National Baptist Convention, USA; National Baptist Convention of America; Progressive National Baptist Convention; and National Missionary Baptist Convention of America.

Although Baptists came to prominence during the Second Great Awakening of the early nineteenth century, they did not place a member in the White House until Warren Harding in 1921. Three more Baptist presidents—Harry Truman, Jimmy Carter, and Bill Clinton—followed. Carter was a Southern Baptist, but he cut ties with that denomination in 2000 after it lurched to the right in the Reagan era. Despite a widespread perception among secularists that Christian conservatives are overrunning American politics, Baptists are actually underrepresented in the Capitol. On surveys that ask Americans to name their religious preference, roughly

16 percent call themselves Baptists, but Baptists constituted only 14 percent of US Senators and House members in the 109th Congress.

Bhagavad Gita. The most popular scripture in contemporary Hinduism, part of a Hindu epic called the Mahabharata, written in Sanskrit between 200 BCE and 200 CE. Central to the Gita is a battlefield discussion of Hindu ethics between an Indian warrior named Arjuna and the Hindu god Krishna (disguised as Arjuna's charioteer). A classic example of *bhakti* (or devotional) Hinduism, the book popularizes the teachings of the earlier and more philosophical Upanishads by describing three different paths to God: the disciplines of devotion (*bhakti* yoga), action (*karma* yoga), and knowledge (*jnana* yoga). First translated into English in 1785, the Gita became a favorite of the Transcendentalists, and Ralph Waldo Emerson once mistakenly referred to it as "the much renowned book of Buddhism."[258] Among American Hindus today it is the Hindu holy book par excellence, read and discussed in Gita study groups that mimic Christian Bible study groups. Robert Oppenheimer, who as a member of the Manhattan Project helped to design the first atomic bomb, reports that a quotation from the Gita came to mind when he witnessed the first nuclear explosion in New Mexico in 1945: "I am become death, the destroyer of worlds."

Bible. The Jewish and Christian scriptures are both referred to as the Bible. The Hebrew Bible consists of twenty-four books divided into three sections: the Law, consisting of the Pentateuch, or the five books attributed to Moses (Genesis, Exodus, Leviticus, Numbers, Deuteronomy); the Prophets (Jeremiah, Isaiah, and so on); and the Writings (various additional books, including Psalms, Proverbs, and Job). The Hebrew Bible is also called the Tanakh, which is an acrostic for the Hebrew words for each of these three parts (*Torah* for Law; *Neviim* for Prophets; and *Ketuvim* for Writings). The Christian Bible consists of the Old and New Testaments. Most Christian groups restrict the New Testament to twenty-seven books: four Gospels (Matthew, Mark, Luke, and John); the Acts of the Apostles; twenty-one letters, or Epistles, many attributed to Paul; and the apocalyptic book of Revelation. The Protestants' Old Testament mirrors the content of the twenty-four books of the Hebrew Bible but divides them into thirty-nine books, for a total of sixty-six biblical books. Roman Catholic Bibles include seven additional Old Testament books, known to Protestants as the Apocrypha, for a total of seventy-three (or, if Prophecy of Jeremias and Lamentations of Jeremias are published as one book, seventy-two). Of the many English translations of the Bible, which was originally written in Hebrew and Greek, the most popular is the King James Version (1611). Today Americans can select from dozens of different translations, including New Testaments published as glossy magazines for youth and inclusive-language Bibles sensitive to feminist sensibilities.

The Bible has enjoyed a long and winding afterlife in American culture, inspiring thousands of novels, poems, films, plays, paintings, sculptures, songs, and other works of the imagination. It is the best-selling book in American history and an oft-invoked text in American public life. ("Both read the same Bible and pray to the same God, and each invokes His aid against the other," President Lincoln said of the North and the South in 1865 in his Second Inaugural Address.) Many Americans regard the Bible as the Word of God, yet it is not universally beloved. Thomas Paine, whom Theodore Roosevelt once blasted as a "filthy little atheist," called the Bible "a book of lies and contradictions and a history of bad times and bad men." This is a minority view.

bin Laden, Osama (b. 1957). Saudi-born head of the international terrorist organization al-Qaeda, one of the CIA's most wanted men, and a Che Guevara–style hero to many Muslim youth. Bin Laden inherited considerable wealth when his father, a Yemeni construction magnate, died in 1968. In 1979 bin Laden went to Afghanistan to fight with the Mujahideen ("holy warriors") against Soviet occupation of that Muslim-majority nation. He later founded and financed a Sunni organization devoted to this cause, which would evolve into al-Qaeda ("the base"). Returning to Saudi Arabia after the Soviets withdrew from Afghanistan, bin Laden became incensed when, following the 1990 Iraqi invasion of Kuwait, the Saudis allowed US troops to be stationed in that country, which is home to Islam's two most sacred cities. Expelled from Saudi Arabia for his public assertion that his country had abandoned Islamic law, he moved to Sudan in 1991. Expelled by the Sudanese in 1996, he found safe haven in Afghanistan under the Taliban, a theocratic Sunni state. That same year he declared a holy war against US forces. Two years later he issued a so-called fatwa—"Jihad Against Jews and Crusaders"—referring to American soldiers as "crusader armies spreading in [the Arabian Peninsula] like locusts, eating its riches" and urging all Muslims "to kill the Americans and their allies—civilian and military."[259] Bin Laden has been linked to terrorist attacks in many different countries, but none as spectacular as the September 11, 2001, attacks that killed thousands of people in New York City, Washington DC, and rural Pennsylvania. Following these attacks the United States military invaded Afghanistan, uprooting the Taliban and forcing bin Laden into hiding. Since 9/11 he has appeared on a series of video and audio tapes.

Bin Laden, whom scholars describe as a brilliant writer and popular polemicist, is said to have been influenced by Wahhabism, the dominant school of Islamic thought in Saudi Arabia, but the stronger influence is "the father of Islamist fundamentalism," the Egyptian scholar Sayyid Qutb (1906–1966). Many themes in Qutb's thought—an emphasis on holy war, demonization of Christians and Jews, hostility to secularism and democracy, and denunciation of Muslim-majority societies that do not scrupulously follow Islamic law—are also themes of bin Laden.

Black Muslims. Members of the black nationalist sect the Nation of Islam (NOI) founded in Detroit in the 1930s by W. D. Fard (?–1934?) and led today by Louis Farrakhan (b. 1933). Under the leadership of Elijah Muhammad (1897–1975), who spearheaded this group after Fard's disappearance in 1934, the NOI preached a heterodox combination of black nationalism and Islam that denounced whites as "blue-eyed devils" and hoped for a separate black nation. More traditional Muslims looked askance at the Black Muslims' doctrines (the view that Fard was divine) and practices (fasting in December instead of Ramadan), but the movement grew throughout the sixties, particularly among black males in prisons, who gravitated to its strict discipline and its emphasis on self-help and self-respect. One prison convert was Malcolm X (1925–1965), who before his assassination in 1965 was the most powerful alternative to the more moderate civil rights message of the Reverend Martin Luther King Jr. The most famous convert was the heavyweight boxing champion Cassius Clay, who proclaimed his conversion to Islam and changed his name to Muhammad Ali in 1964.

After Elijah Muhammad died in 1975, his son and successor, Warith Deen Muhammad (b. 1933), took the Nation of Islam in the direction of orthodox Sunni Islam, admitting whites and renaming it the American Society of Muslims. In 1977 Farrakhan led a group that disagreed with Warith Deen Muhammad's mainstreaming strategy into a reconstituted Nation of Islam. Although his explosive rhetoric led many to denounce him as racist and anti-Semitic, Farrakhan retained sufficient clout among African Americans to organize the Million Man March on Washington DC in 1995. Not all African American Muslims are Black Muslims. In fact, the overwhelming majority of African American Muslims are members of far more traditional Sunni Muslim groups.

born-again Christian. Someone who has accepted Jesus as his or her Savior and Lord, typically in a sudden conversion experience or "new birth." This rather imprecise term comes from John 3:7, where Jesus says, "Ye must be born again." Pollster George Barna draws a sharp distinction between born-again Christians and evangelicals, defining the former as people (roughly 40 percent of Americans) who say they have had a "new birth" experience and the latter as a much smaller subset of born-again Christians (about 7 percent of Americans) who exhibit additional criteria, including belief in Satan and the conviction that salvation comes through grace alone. This distinction has not caught on. For the most part the terms *born-again Christian* and *evangelical* are synonymous.

Buddhism. Religion founded in northern India by Siddhartha Gautama, who became known as the Buddha ("Awakened One") after experiencing enlightenment. Many Buddhists trace the life of the Buddha (and thus the origins of Buddhism) to the sixth and fifth centuries BCE, but the scholarly consensus is that he lived and died during the fourth century BCE. Converts to Buddhism vow to "take refuge" in the "Three Jewels": the Buddha; the Dharma (teaching); and the Sangha (Buddhist community). They see *dukkha* (suffering or unsatisfactoriness) as the core human problem and trace the origin of suffering to ignorance. They refer to the uprooting of ignorance and suffering as enlightenment, or nirvana. One of their most difficult and distinctive teachings is that the person we refer to as "I" is actually a composite of other things (or, in some interpretations, a figment of our imagination). In Buddhism practitioners seek to bring an end to suffering by eliminating desire and ignorance. They do so via a variety of techniques, including chanting and meditation. And they do not traditionally see the Buddha as a god.

The Buddhist tradition is divided into three major "vehicles": Theravada, Mahayana, and Vajrayana. Theravada ("Way of the Elders") is the oldest of the three. Popular in South and Southeast Asia, it is a difficult path oriented around the efforts of monks and nuns to achieve wisdom for themselves. According to this tradition karmic merit can be transferred only with great difficulty. So you have to earn nirvana by self-help. Mahayana ("Great Vehicle") is popular in China, Japan, Korea, and elsewhere in East Asia. According to this easier path, karmic merit can be transferred fairly simply, so it is possible to win nirvana—and even become a Buddha yourself—with the help of others. Here the key virtue is not wisdom but compassion, which is embodied in the *bodhisattva,* who takes a vow to help all beings achieve nirvana. The third major Buddhist vehicle, Vajrayana, combines elements of the Theravada and Mahayana traditions and is most popular in Tibet and Mongolia. Vajrayana Buddhists use a variety of techniques, including esoteric texts called *Tantras,* cosmic maps called mandalas, and sacred sounds called mantras, to achieve nirvana. They are represented by the Dalai Lama, who serves both as the political leader of the Tibetan people in exile and the spiritual leader of Vajrayana's "Yellow Hat" (Gelugpa) sect.

Buddhism first came to America through Chinese immigration in the 1840s. Since that time the United States has experienced a series of Buddhists awakenings, including a Japanese Buddhist vogue in the late nineteenth century and a Zen vogue in the 1950s. The most recent Buddhist boom came during the 1990s, which saw three different feature films about Buddhism—*The Little Buddha* (1993), *Kundun* (1997), and *Seven Years in Tibet* (1997)—plus a *Time* magazine cover on "America's Fascination with Buddhism" (1997). Although many college students embraced the Free Tibet cause during the 1990s and Vice President Al Gore was embroiled in a fund-raising scandal at a Buddhist temple during that same decade, Buddhists have not been particularly active in American politics. However, the Buddhist Churches of America, which dates to the 1890s and is the closest the United States gets to a Buddhist mainline, has spoken out against school prayer and for same-sex marriage. Buddhism also has a presence in American higher education—in Naropa University, founded in 1974 in Boulder, Colorado, by the Tibetan Buddhist teacher Chogyam Trungpa; and in Soka University of America, which opened in 2001 in Aliso Viejo, California, under the auspices of the Japan-based Soka Gakkai International.

Calvinism. Protestant theological tradition based on the teachings of the Swiss theologian John Calvin (1509–1564), established in the North American colonies through the Puritans, and spread nationwide through Congregational and Presbyterian churches. Also known as Reformed theology, Calvinism draws its dynamism from two foundational tenets: the absolute sovereignty of God and the total depravity of human beings. One controversial doctrine that flows from these tenets is double predestination: the belief that God fated every human being, before birth, to either heaven or hell. Calvinism is most carefully encapsulated in the Westminster Confession of Faith (1647). It is most succinctly summarized in the Five Points of Calvinism of the Synod of Dort (1618–1619), which can be remembered via the acronym *TULIP:* total depravity, unconditional election, limited atonement, irresistible grace, and the perseverance of the saints. Calvinism dominated American theology until the late eighteenth and early nineteenth centuries, when Arminianism—the view, popular among evangelicals, that humans are free to accept or reject the saving grace of Jesus—took hold. German sociologist Max Weber argued that Calvinism gave birth to capitalism by producing powerful theological motivations for both working hard and saving money.

Catholicism, Roman. One of Christianity's three main branches, along with Eastern Orthodoxy and Protestantism, and the largest of the three. The term *catholic* means universal, and Catholics have always tried to be the church for the whole world. But as the adjective *Roman* implies, this church is centered in Rome and is led by a pope who doubles as that city's bishop. Roman Catholicism is administered by a hierarchy of bishops and priests, and since 1870 the pope has been empowered to speak infallibly on matters of faith and morals. While Protestants recognize only two sacraments, Catholics recognize seven: baptism, confirmation, reconciliation (also known as penance or confession), Holy Communion, marriage, ordination of priests, and anointing of the sick (once referred to as last rites). Catholics also differ from Protestants in their veneration of the Blessed Virgin Mary and other saints, their insistence that the Bible be read in light of church traditions, and their restriction of the priesthood to males who take a vow of celibacy.

Roman Catholics preceded Protestants to the New World, planting their faith in both New Spain and New France, and were welcomed in the colony of Maryland, which was founded as a safe haven for Catholics in a sea of antipathetic Puritans and Anglicans. Catholics did not come in large numbers to the United States until the 1830s, but by 1860 they were the nation's largest single Christian denomination. Still, anti-Catholicism remained a major theme in American history well into the twentieth century; the country did not have a Catholic president until John Kennedy in 1960. American Catholics have a long history of speaking out on issues of war and peace, poverty and inequality. But the capacity of Catholic leaders to speak authoritatively on such matters was crippled in the early twenty-first century by a series of scandals involving sex between priests and young male parishioners.

Today American Catholics cluster in New England, the upper Midwest, and the Southwest, including southern California. Catholics are underrepresented in the US Congress but overrepresented in the Supreme Court. Five of its nine justices, including Chief Justice John Roberts, are

Catholics, making the current Supreme Court the first in US history with a Catholic majority.

Christ. Although sometimes mistaken for Jesus' last name, *Christ* is actually a title derived from *christos,* the Greek term for messiah, or "anointed one." To call Jesus the Christ, therefore, is to make a theological claim—that he is the messiah long expected by the Jews. It is from this term that the word *Christian* arises.

Christian Coalition. A successor of sorts to the Moral Majority, this conservative political pressure group, supported largely by white evangelicals and Catholics, was established in 1989 by Pat Robertson (b. 1930) after his failed bid for the Republican presidential nomination. Under the direction of Ralph Reed (b. 1961), who led it during its heyday in the mid-1990s, the Christian Coalition claimed more than 1.6 million members. It fell on hard times, however, in the early twenty-first century, in part because the Republican Party's ascent to power complicated its identity as a group of outside agitators. Today the Christian Coalition of America, as it is formally known, bills itself as a promoter of "family values" and "America's leading grassroots organization defending our godly heritage." One testament to this group's success is a competing organization, called the Secular Coalition of America (established 2002), which represents the political interests of the American Humanist Association, Atheist Alliance International, and other skeptics.

Christianity. The largest of the world's religions, with perhaps one-third of the world's population. Christians see sin as the core human problem and describe liberation from sin as salvation. The key to salvation, which brings with it eternal life in heaven, lies in the incarnation, crucifixion, and resurrection of Jesus. The Jesus story is recorded in the New Testament, which along with the Old Testament constitutes the Christian Bible and is interpreted through church documents such as the Nicene Creed of the fourth century. In the New Testament Jesus is variously described as Son of God, Son of Man, and Christ (from the Greek word for messiah), and over the centuries Christians have debated precisely who he was (and is). The dominant view, expressed in the Nicene Creed, has been that Jesus is "very God of very God"—one of the three persons (with the Father and the Holy Spirit) of the Trinity—and that his death on the cross somehow makes salvation possible. Christianity's key practices include baptism, a rite of initiation by water, and Holy Communion, a reenactment of the Last Supper, which Jesus shared with his followers right before his arrest, trial, and execution.

Eastern Orthodoxy, Roman Catholicism, and Protestantism are Christianity's three main branches. Christianity split into Roman Catholicism and Orthodoxy in 1054, and Protestantism splintered off of Roman Catholicism during the Reformation of the sixteenth century. Of these three branches, Roman Catholicism is the largest, followed by Protestantism and then Eastern Orthodoxy. In the United States, however, Protestantism accounts for well over half of the total population, and Roman Catholicism for roughly one-quarter. Americans have long debated whether the United States is a "Christian nation." The country is secular by law, but Christmas is a national holiday here, the Bible is the unofficial scripture of political rhetoric, and every US president has pledged his allegiance to Jesus.

Christmas. Typically celebrated on December 25, Christmas is both a Christian holy day commemorating the birth of Jesus Christ in a manger in Bethlehem and an official US holiday marked by Santa Claus, trees, and gift exchanges. The Supreme Court has repeatedly been asked to rule on how secular and how sacred Christmas is. Many of its Christmas cases concerned the constitutionality of nativity scenes (displays of Mary and Joseph with Jesus in the manger) placed on municipal properties. During the early twenty-first century, Fox News personality Bill O'Reilly and other cultural conservatives decried a "war on Christmas" by the Secular Left. The first American opponents of Christmas, however, were New England's Puritans, who considered the observation of Christmas a Roman Catholic abomination and passed legislation outlawing its celebration in 1659. The climate is quite different today. According to a 2000 poll, 96 percent of Americans—including many non-Christians—say that they celebrate Christmas.

Church of Jesus Christ of Latter-day Saints. See Mormons.

city upon a hill. This biblical image became part of the American public lexicon through a sermon delivered in 1630 on board the *Arabella* off the New England coast by the Massachusetts Bay Colony governor John Winthrop. "We shall be as a city upon a hill," Winthrop said. "The eyes of all people are upon us." President Ronald Reagan later popularized and reinterpreted the phrase, which in his usage typically became "shining city on a hill." The core concept here is that Americans will lead by example. For Winthrop, however, the idea was conditional. Only if God's people acted well would God bless them. For Reagan, however, there was little conditional about this covenant between God and his chosen people. Winthrop's image derives from Matthew 5:14: "Ye are the light of the world. A city that is set on a hill cannot be hid."

Confucius. See Confucianism.

Confucianism. Religion (or, according to some, simply a philosophy) founded by Confucius (551–479 BCE) during the Warring States period of Chinese history. Preserved in the Analects, Confucius's teachings focus on this world rather than the next and show scant interest in theological speculation. Confucius's goal was social harmony, which resulted in his view from a combination of individual self-cultivation and social rites. He emphasized virtues such as humaneness (*jen*) and filial piety (*hsiao*) and described the noble person who embodied them as a sage (*chun-tzu*). But Confucius also stressed the importance of ritual propriety (*li*), especially when it came to what he called the Five Great Relationships: between parent and child; between elder and younger siblings; between husband and wife; between friend and friend; and between ruler and subject. Confucius also taught the Negative Golden Rule: "Do not do to others what you do not want them to do to you."

Confucianism, which along with Taoism and Buddhism constitutes one of China's "Three Teachings," had a profound impact on China after it became the official state religion of the Han dynasty during the second century BCE. It subsequently spread across East Asia, where its emphasis on ancestor veneration and respect for elders resonate today. Confucianism came to the United States with Chinese immigrants as early as the 1840s. Today a group of Boston-area philosophers refer to themselves as Boston Confucians.

Congregationalism. One of the mainline Protestant denominations, most visible in contemporary America in the United Church of Christ. Congregationalism arrived in the United States when the Pilgrims landed in Plymouth and the Puritans established the Massachusetts Bay Colony. During the Great Awakening of the early eighteenth century Congregationalism split into prorevival (New Light) and antirevival (Old Light) factions. It later split along Trinitarian/Unitarian lines. In 1957 various Congregational groups merged into the United Church of Christ, whose 1.7 million members make it America's largest Congregationalist group.

Congregationalists get their name from their insistence on the autonomy of the local congregation—a form of church governance that characterizes some other denominations, including the Baptists, and many non-Christian groups.

Conservative Judaism. Middle path between Orthodox and Reform Judaism originally known as "Historical Judaism." Conservative Judaism, which arose in nineteenth-century Europe in response to perceived excesses of Reform Judaism, is closer to Orthodox Judaism when it comes to observing the Sabbath and kosher dietary laws. Like Reform Jews, however, Conservative Jews accept the ordination of women, mixed-gender seating in synagogues, and biblical criticism. In the United States Conservative Judaism traces its roots to the opening in 1887 of the Jewish Theological Seminary (JTS), which was established in opposition to the Reform Jews' Pittsburgh Platform of 1885 (and a notorious banquet at Hebrew Union College in Cincinnati where guests were served shrimp, a food forbidden by Jewish dietary laws). Thanks to the leadership of JTS president Solomon Schechter (1847–1915), Conservative Judaism took organizational shape with the founding in 1913 of the United Synagogue of America (now United Synagogue of Conservative Judaism), a group that currently accounts for roughly one-third of all religiously observant American Jews. Outside the United States Conservative Judaism is known as *Masorti* ("Traditional") Judaism. Reconstructionist Judaism, which views Judaism as a civilization and not just a religion, is an offshoot of the Conservative movement.

creationism. The belief that the creation account in Genesis is historically and scientifically correct. The key claim here is not so much that God created the world in precisely seven days—creationists differ on this point—but that God created all species in a short time span and that human beings are not the result, as Charles Darwin argued, of the random process of natural selection. This creationist view, which has its roots in *What Is Darwinism?* (1874) by Princeton Theological Seminary theologian Charles Hodge, is often associated with the fundamentalist fringe. But surveys show that most Americans side in this debate with Hodge and only a small minority with Darwin.[260] The battle between creation and evolution stood at the center of the Scopes "Monkey Trial" of 1925, which featured a Dayton, Tennessee, science teacher accused of violating a state law forbidding teachers from mentioning "any theory that denies the Story of Divine Creation of man as taught in the Bible." In 1987 the

Supreme Court struck down a Louisiana law requiring public school districts that teach evolutionary theory to give equal treatment to "creation science."

Since then Darwin's critics have increasingly spoken of "intelligent design" (ID) rather than creationism. According to intelligent design theory, both the universe and individual organisms in it are too complex to be the result of either chance or natural selection and must instead have been caused by an intelligent designer. Almost all scientists view this theory as pseudoscientific. In a lawsuit challenging the constitutionality of an ID curriculum in public school biology classes in Dover, Pennsylvania, a US district judge agreed. Intelligent design may or may not be true, he ruled in 2005, but there is "overwhelming evidence" that it is "a religious view, a mere re-labeling of creationism, and not a scientific theory." Still, ID has its supporters, particularly on the Religious Right. President George W. Bush said in 2005 that public schools should teach both evolutionary theory and intelligent design.

crusades. Medieval military campaigns of the eleventh through the fifteenth centuries waged by Christians to recapture the Holy Lands from Muslims. The church offered indulgences for the remission of sins to crusaders, as Christian participants were called, and lauded those who died in these "holy wars" as martyrs. Although successful militarily, the crusades badly damaged Christian-Muslim relations, bringing on an era of mistrust and hostility that continues to characterize these relations today. In September 2001 President George W. Bush referred to the war on terrorism as a "crusade," sparking anger among Muslims aware of the history of medieval crusades and the religious meaning of the term as "taking the cross." Meanwhile, Osama bin Laden referred to the war on terrorism as "a crusade against Islam," and his followers lauded him as "the Second Saladin"—a reference to the Muslim hero who took Jerusalem by force in 1187.

Dalai Lama (b. 1935). The spiritual leader of the Gelugpa lineage of Tibetan Buddhism and the political leader of the Tibetan people, understood by his followers to be the reincarnation of the bodhisattva Avalokiteshvara and, as such, a person of extraordinary wisdom and compassion. Like the terms *Christ* and *Buddha, Dalai Lama* ("Ocean of Wisdom") is a title rather than a proper name. Today's Dalai Lama, born Lhamo Dhondrub in 1935, is the fourteenth in a lineage that began in the fifteenth century. While still an infant, he was recognized as a reincarnation of the thirteenth Dalai Lama and given the name Tenzin Gyatso.

(Each Dalai Lama is said to be a reincarnation of his predecessor.) He fled to India in 1959 after the Chinese government occupied Tibet and now operates the Tibetan government in exile in Dharamsala, India. The Dalai Lama was awarded the Nobel Peace Prize in 1989. In the United States he has become something of an icon, personifying both Buddhism itself and the ongoing struggle for a free Tibet. He has met with a series of US presidents, beginning with George H.W. Bush in 1991, and was featured in the "Think Different" advertising campaign of Apple Computer.

Daoism. See Taoism.

David and Goliath. Antagonists in a classic underdog story that appears in the Hebrew Bible in 1 Samuel 17. David was a small Israelite shepherd boy who would later become the second king of Israel and the author of the Psalms. Goliath was a Philistine giant. While the Israelites and the Philistines were engaged in battle, David felled Goliath with a single stone rocketed from his slingshot. This act of bravery scattered the Philistines and propelled the Israelites to victory. This story provides the template for hundreds of Hollywood sports movies—a template made explicit in the film *Hoosiers* (1986) when a prayer before the Indiana high school state championship basketball game specifically likens the small-town heroes to David and their big-city antagonists to Goliath.

Decalogue. See 10 Commandments.

Deism. Rationalistic religion based on reason and nature rather than revelation. Rejecting both miracles and prayer, Deists classically describe the Almighty as a Watchmaker, who, after creating the world, sits back and observes history without intervening in it. They are critical of "priestcraft" and institutional religion. They believe in one God and in afterlife rewards and punishments. And they see morality as the essence of religion. ("My religion," wrote Thomas Paine, "is to do good.") Deism, which emerged in seventeenth-century Europe and spread under the influence of the Enlightenment, was popular in the colonies at the time of the American Revolution and was the faith of many of the nation's founders. It was quickly overrun, however, by forms of faith that were more heartfelt and more recognizably Christian.

Disciples of Christ. One of American Protestantism's mainline denominations, the Christian Church (Disciples of Christ) emerged in 1831 out of the efforts of Alexander Campbell's "Disciples," Barton W. Stone's "Christians," and other "restorationists" to reconstruct modern Christianity in the image of the early church. Along with Methodists and Baptists, Disciples of Christ were one of the fastest growing denominations in nineteenth-century America. They accepted no creeds or catechisms, putting their faith in the New Testament instead. "Where the Scriptures speak, we speak," said restorationist leader Thomas Campbell. "Where the Scriptures are silent, we are silent." Citing the example of the early church, Disciples of Christ today perform baptism by immersion and celebrate Holy Communion every Sunday. Three American presidents—James Garfield, Lyndon Johnson, and Ronald Reagan—were raised in this denomination, and Garfield was an ordained Disciples of Christ minister.

Today the Disciples of Christ claim just over one million American members. The Churches of Christ, which split from the Disciples of Christ in the early twentieth century (in part over opposition to instrumental music in worship services), has a slightly larger membership than the Disciples of Christ.

dispensational premillennialism. Dispensationalism is a school of Bible interpretation that divides sacred history into distinct periods, called dispensations, in which different plans for salvation apply. Premillennialism is the view that Jesus will return before the thousand-year reign (millennium) prophesied in the New Testament book of Revelation. When put together, these two terms create a core teaching of Protestant fundamentalism: dispensational premillennialism. According to this teaching, the end of the current dispensation is imminent. It will conclude with the Rapture of believers into heaven, followed for those who are left behind by a Great Tribulation of seven years, which will include the appearance of the Antichrist and the battle of Armageddon. But Jesus will come down from the clouds, defeat the Antichrist, and establish a thousand-year reign of peace and justice. This eschatology (or theology of the last days) was developed by the British theologian John Nelson Darby (1800–1882), and it spread across the United States after the Civil War. Its greatest expression is the *Scofield Reference Bible* (1909) of Cyrus Ingerson Scofield (1843–1921). More popular manifestations include Hal Lindsey's best seller, *The Late Great Planet Earth,* and the *Left Behind* novels (1995–) of Tim LaHaye and Jerry Jenkins. Today dispensational premillennialism is the most popular form of prophecy belief in the United States, informing (among other things) conservative Christian support for the state of Israel.

Easter. The most important Christian holy day, commemorating the resurrection of Jesus three days after his crucifixion on Good Friday. In a
more secular guise, Easter is a popular spring celebration of fertility and
new life, replete with marshmallow bunnies, chocolate eggs, flowers,
and fancy new clothes.

Edwards, Jonathan (1703–1758). American philosopher, theologian, and
Congregationalist preacher whose church in Northampton, Massachusetts, stood at the center of the Great Awakening of the 1730s and
1740s. Edwards's writings on revivalism in particular and religious experience in general attempted to synthesize "head religion" and "heart religion," the intellect and the emotions. His broader theology combined
Calvinist orthodoxy, the philosophy of John Locke, and the physics of
Isaac Newton. After being dismissed by his Northampton congregation
in 1750, Edwards served as a missionary to Housatonic Indians in Stock-
bridge, Massachusetts. Shortly before his death in 1758 he was appointed
president of the College of New Jersey (now Princeton University).
Edwards's "Sinners in the Hands of an Angry God" (1741) may be the
most famous sermon in American history, but its fire-and-brimstone rhetoric is not at all characteristic of Edwards's preaching style.

Eid. This term, Arabic for "feast," refers to two festivals in the Muslim
calendar: Eid al-Fitr, the feast of the breaking of the fast at the end of the
month of Ramadan; and Eid al-Adha, the feast of sacrifice that concludes
the pilgrimage to Mecca. On Eid al-Fitr, the lesser of these two festivals,
Muslims pray, visit friends and family, and exchange gifts. On Eid al-
Adha, they sacrifice a lamb or some other animal to commemorate both
Abraham's willingness to offer his son Ishmael to Allah and Allah's mercy
in accepting a lamb instead. In February 1996 President Bill Clinton welcomed Muslim families into the White House to celebrate Eid al-Fitr,
prompting First Lady Hillary Clinton to call that holiday "an American
event."[261] In September 2001 the US Postal Service issued a postage
stamp (its first on a Muslim theme) celebrating both Eids. The calligra-
phy on the stamp read *"Eid mubarak"*—a traditional holiday greeting
meaning, "May your festival be blessed."

Eightfold Path of Buddhism. See 8-fold Path of Buddhism.

encyclicals. Official letters circulated by the Roman Catholic Church on
matters of faith, practice, and morals. Found in these influential

pronouncements are Catholic teachings on many controversial social issues—on labor-capital relations (*Rerum Novarum,* 1891), human rights (*Pacem in Terris,* 1963), contraception (*Humanae Vitae,* 1968), and abortion, birth control, euthanasia, and capital punishment (*Evangelium Vitae,* 1995).

Episcopalianism. The Episcopal Church in the United States of America is part of the international Anglican Communion, which claims some 70 million members in a worldwide fellowship of self-governing churches that trace their roots to the Church of England. This church was founded in 1534 when King Henry VIII (1491–1547) rejected papal authority and declared himself the head of the Church of England. Episcopalians take their name from the Anglican form of church governance, which is episcopal, meaning it includes bishops. Of all the major Protestant denominations, Episcopalianism is closest to the Roman Catholic tradition. Like Catholicism, it is liturgical, and its churches generally practice Holy Communion weekly. Also like Catholicism, Episcopalianism vests authority not only in scripture but also in tradition, though, unlike Catholics, Episcopalians add reason to this list of theological authorities.

The Church of England was established in colonial Virginia, South Carolina, Georgia, and Maryland, but it suffered mightily during and after the American Revolution since many of its clergy, particularly in the north, sided with the British. Still, many of the nation's founders, including George Washington and Thomas Jefferson, were Anglicans, as were two-thirds of the signers of the Declaration of Independence. Today Episcopal churches are suffering through membership declines. In 2000 the Episcopal Church in the USA claimed only 2.5 million members (down from 3.4 million in 1960), and its unity was severely tested in 2003 when the Diocese of Vermont elected Gene Robinson as the first openly gay Episcopalian bishop. But Episcopalianism continues to have influence in corridors of power way out of proportion to its numbers. Roughly one-third of all Supreme Court justices and one-quarter of all US presidents have been Episcopalians, far more than any other denomination. And Episcopalians commanded forty-two seats in the 109th Congress—about thirty-three more than their current share of the US population would warrant.

establishment clause. See First Amendment.

Eucharist. See Holy Communion.

evangelicalism. The term *evangelical* (from a Greek word meaning "good news") is often confused with the word *evangelistic,* which means intent on proselytizing. Although evangelicals are typically also evangelistic, the term *evangelical* has a more specific meaning. It refers to theologically conservative Protestants who stress the experience of conversion (being "born again"), view the Bible as the inspired and authoritative Word of God, emphasize evangelism, and believe that salvation comes by faith in the atoning death of Jesus Christ. Or, as British historian David Bebbington has put it, they affirm conversionism, Biblicism, activism, and crucicentrism.

Since the early nineteenth century, when evangelicalism became the dominant religious impulse in the United States, evangelicals have played a major role in American political and social life (often on the left), spearheading such movements as abolitionism, temperance, and women's rights, and otherwise acting as an informal yet potent Protestant establishment. Evangelicals largely disappeared from public view after the embarrassment of the Scopes "Monkey Trial" of 1925, only to reemerge—this time on the right—in the late 1970s.

Evangelicals should not be confused with fundamentalists. Whereas fundamentalists describe the Bible as the infallible Word of God, evangelicals insist merely that the Bible is divinely inspired. Fundamentalists also tend to be more antimodern than evangelicals, whose success in American culture can be attributed in considerable measure to their ingenuity in applying all manner of modern conveniences (books, magazines, radio, television, the Internet) to Christian ends.

Evangelicals are exceedingly unpopular among those on the Secular Left. A 2002 poll concerning non-Christians' perceptions of such groups as military officers, lawyers, and lesbians found that evangelicals ranked tenth out of eleven groups, ahead only of prostitutes. There is reason to believe, however, that this antipathy is based in part on misunderstanding. Although many evangelicals today are conservative Republicans, significant minorities describe themselves either as "liberal" or "moderate." Moreover, most evangelicals favor increasing taxes to help the poor and stricter government regulations to protect the environment. In 2004 the National Association of Evangelicals (established 1943) issued "an evangelical call to civic responsibility" that interpreted Genesis as a call to "show our love for the Creator by caring for his creation." In 2005 an Evangelical Climate Initiative, supported by many leading American evangelicals, urged the US government to tackle the problem of global warming by substantially reducing carbon-dioxide emissions.

Exodus. Exodus ("departure" in Greek) refers both to the second book of the Hebrew Bible and to the epic story told in that book—of the flight of the Israelites and their leader Moses out of slavery in Egypt and (after forty years in the wilderness and Moses's death) into the Promised Land. Key events in this grand narrative include Moses's receipt of the Ten Commandments on Mount Sinai, the Ten Plagues of Egypt, the parting of the Red Sea, the appearance of manna from heaven, and God's guidance of his chosen people by a pillar of cloud by day and a pillar of fire by night. This story has inspired a variety of American groups, who have read into it analogies with their own experiences. African Americans interpreted their passage from slavery to freedom to civil rights as an Exodus tale. Mormons also understood their trek from Illinois to the Great Salt Lake basin in Utah as an exodus, complete with Brigham Young (1801–1877) as their "American Moses." The Puritans too saw themselves as a chosen people in covenant with God in the Promised Land of New England. Exodus imagery also captured the imaginations of the nation's founders. Thomas Jefferson once suggested that the national seal should depict "the children of Israel in the wilderness, led by a cloud by day and a pillar of fire by night"; Benjamin Franklin favored an image of Moses and the Israelites crossing the Red Sea.[262]

Fall. See Adam and Eve.

Falwell, Jerry. See Moral Majority.

family values. Although this term sounds ancient, it is actually of recent vintage, first used in its current sense in the late 1960s and injected into American cultural politics in the late 1970s. The Republican Party platforms of 1976 and 1980 endorsed "family values" as an antidote to what conservatives saw as the moral degradation of American society brought on by the sexual revolution, rock 'n' roll, and the counterculture. By the early 1980s this phrase—and related ones such as *traditional values* and *moral values*—had come to serve as code for opposition to "atheistic schools, rampaging crime, God-forsaken homes, drugs, abortion, pornography, permissiveness and a sense of cynicism and spiritual desolation absolutely unprecedented in our country's history." At the 1992 Republican Party Convention, secretary of education William Bennett (b. 1943) called family values "a great dividing line between the parties," and presidential candidate Pat Robertson accused President Clinton of hatching "a radical plan to destroy the traditional family." Groups such as Focus on the Family (established in 1977) later extended the family values agenda to include support for parochial school vouchers and public school prayer.[263]

The term *family values* often serves as a proxy for "religious" in American political rhetoric. To be a family values candidate is to be a person of faith (and to appeal to conservative Christians). Many question, however, whether either Jesus or Paul exhibited family values. Both opposed divorce, but Paul preferred celibacy to marriage, and—*The DaVinci Code* (2003) notwithstanding—Jesus never married or had children. Moreover, Jesus repeatedly told his followers that he had come not to strengthen families but to set family members against one another: "If any man come to me, and hate not his father, and mother, and wife, and children, and brethren, and sisters, yea, and his own life also," he said, "he cannot be my disciple" (Luke 14:26).

fatwa. Islamic legal opinion given by a legal scholar (*mufti*) in the context of a particular school of law and in response to a specific question posed by a court or individual. Although many non-Muslims believe that fatwas are infallible declarations, most Muslims understand them to be binding only on those who recognize the authority of the legal scholar who issues them. This term burst into public prominence in the West after Iran's Ayatollah Khomeini (d. 1989) issued a fatwa calling for the assassination of Salman Rushdie, whose novel *The Satanic Verses* (1988) he deemed blasphemous. More recently, Americans have had to grapple with the 1998 "fatwa" of Osama bin Laden, which stated, "The ruling to kill the Americans and their allies—civilians and military—is an individual duty for every Muslim." Less well known is the July 2005 fatwa issued by the eighteen-member Fiqh Council of North America, which declared, "All acts of terrorism targeting civilians are *haram* (forbidden) in Islam." Many Muslim leaders have observed that bin Laden, who is not a legal scholar, has no authority to issue a fatwa. Even Taliban leader Mullah Muhammad Omar admitted that any so-called fatwas issued by bin Laden are "illegal and null and void."[264]

First Amendment. The First Amendment to the US Constitution contains—in addition to protections of freedom of speech, press, assembly, and petition—two clauses concerning religion: the establishment clause, which states that "Congress shall make no law respecting the establishment of religion," and the free exercise clause, which adds, "or prohibiting the free exercise thereof." Rejecting the European model of one religion per state, the First Amendment transformed the American religious landscape into a thriving spiritual marketplace in which different religions, and different versions of each, competed for believers, donations, and public power.

Upon its ratification in 1791, the First Amendment applied only to the federal government—Massachusetts maintained a Congregational establishment until 1833—but after the passage of the Fourteenth Amendment in 1868, all state and local laws had to answer to the entire Bill of Rights. In recent years the Supreme Court has turned to the First Amendment to decide establishment clause cases concerning "under God" language in the Pledge of Allegiance, school prayer, and Ten Commandments displays on public property. Free exercise cases have taken up animal sacrifice by Santeria practitioners and the ritual use of the hallucinogen peyote by members of the Native American Church. In the last of these cases, *Oregon v. Smith* (1990), the Supreme Court ruled that laws can restrict religious freedom as long as they are universally applicable; in this case, drug laws can abridge the religious freedom of Native Americans as long as those laws apply to all citizens and all religions. Strong opposition to this controversial decision, which severely restricted the range of religious freedoms protected by the First Amendment, led to the passage of the Religious Freedom Restoration Act, which became law in 1994 but was ruled unconstitutional by the Supreme Court in 1997.

Five Ks. See 5 Ks.

Five Pillars of Islam. See 5 Pillars of Islam.

Four Noble Truths. See 4 Noble Truths.

free exercise clause. See First Amendment.

Friends, Religious Society of. See Quakers.

fundamentalism. Many Americans today cannot tell an evangelical from a fundamentalist, but the differences are significant. Both groups stress conversion. Both typically oppose premarital sex, abortion, and homosexuality. Both also emphasize the Bible, though evangelicals usually speak of its divine inspiration, especially in matters of the spirit, while fundamentalists affirm its inerrancy on all subjects, including history and science. The most salient distinction between the two groups, however, concerns their attitudes toward modernity. Historian George Marsden once defined a fundamentalist as "an evangelical who is angry about something."[265] And what fundamentalists are angry about is modernity. Evangelicals, by contrast, are unabashedly modern, having taken to new technologies—from the radio to television to the Internet—with glee.

The roots of fundamentalism run to the late nineteenth century, when conservative Protestants first distilled their faith down to such basics as biblical inerrancy, the virgin birth of Jesus, miracles, the substitutionary atonement, and Jesus' bodily resurrection. But fundamentalism proper first emerged with (and took its name from) the publication of *The Fundamentals* (1910–1915), a twelve-volume series that sought to distinguish true Christianity from liberal Protestantism, which fundamentalists refused to recognize as legitimately Christian. Fundamentalists had their coming-out party at the "Monkey Trial" in 1925 in Dayton, Tennessee, where a public school science teacher was tried for illegally teaching evolutionary theory. William Jennings Bryan, who represented the creationists and the state of Tennessee, won the trial, but Clarence Darrow, his courtroom antagonist, won the public relations war, sending fundamentalists into self-imposed exile for decades. Although fundamentalists have long been stereotyped as anti-intellectual rubes, they have always stressed the importance of doctrine. *The Fundamentals* is a broadside against theological modernism, but it also criticizes evangelicals for neglecting truth in the name of experience.

Some scholars have tried to apply this term to other modes of religiously inspired antimodernism: to the Wahhabi school of Islam, which insists on reading the Quran literally and strictly applying its teachings to contemporary life; to right-wing Hindu nationalists in the Bharatiya Janata Party in India; or to Ultra-Orthodox Jews. But fundamentalism proper is a Protestant impulse that bears only superficial similarities to such movements.

Garden of Eden. See Adam and Eve.

Genesis. The first book in the Bible and the most influential biblical book in American life, Genesis has given the world an extraordinary rich religious and cultural legacy: characters such as Adam, Eve, the Serpent, Noah, Abraham, Sarah, Joseph, and the Pharaoh; places such as the Garden of Eden and Sodom and Gomorrah; events such as creation, the flood, and the binding of Isaac; and perennial themes such as the covenant between God and humans, the conflict between good and evil, and the battle of the sexes. Genesis' account of creation in seven days occasioned a pitched battle over the new geology before the Civil War and over evolution after it. That battle continues today in lawsuits over the propriety of teaching intelligent design in the public schools. On the contentious question of global warming and the environment, Green Christians read Genesis as commanding human beings to act as stewards of the Earth while those who dismiss Christian environmentalists as tree-hugging pagans read that same text as commanding humans to exert dominion over it.

Gnosticism (from *gnosis,* Greek for wisdom). A religious impulse, found in ancient Judaism, ancient Christianity, and other religions, that promises salvation through secret wisdom. Such noncanonical texts as the Gospel of Thomas, discovered in Egypt in 1945, fall into this tradition, as does the Gospel of Judas, first published in 2006. Literary critic Harold Bloom has argued that Gnosticism is the real American religion, and he finds evidence for his claim in Ralph Waldo Emerson and Walt Whitman, Mormonism and Pentecostalism.

"God Bless America." Over the last quarter century, US presidents routinely asked God to bless the nation at the end of their speeches. Whereas President Carter often concluded his speeches with a simple thank-you, President Reagan typically signed off with "God bless America." President George H. W. Bush followed with "God bless you, and God bless the United States of America." Presidents Bill Clinton and George W. Bush have made God-blessings part and parcel of presidential rhetoric. The phrase is also the title of the Irving Berlin song made famous by Kate Smith in the 1930s and, since 9/11, sung during the seventh-inning stretch at major league baseball games.

Golden Rule. The most common moral maxim in the world's religions, expressed by Jesus as, "Do to others what you would have them do to you" (Matthew 7:12, NIV). The Golden Rule is often confused with the related admonition to "love your neighbor as yourself," which appears repeatedly in both the Hebrew Bible and the New Testament. In his October 2000 presidential debate with Al Gore, George W. Bush (in response to a question on gun control) conflated these two commandments when he said Americans needed to follow the "larger law" to "Love your neighbor like you would like to be loved yourself." President Kennedy got the Golden Rule right in June 1963 in a televised speech regarding a court order to desegregate the University of Alabama. "The heart of the question," he said, "is whether all Americans are to be afforded equal rights and equal opportunities, whether we are going to treat our fellow Americans as we want to be treated." The Golden Rule has also been attributed to other religious leaders, including Confucius, Muhammad, and the first-century rabbi Hillel.[266]

Good Samaritan. The best-known parable of Jesus is a story of the kindness of strangers. When asked, "Who is my neighbor?" Jesus spoke of a man who had been attacked and left for dead by the roadside. Various people passed by, but a person from Samaria stopped to help. Like many of Jesus' parables, this one comes as a surprise. Jewish listeners would have regarded Samaritans as undesirables, but in this case the hero is a Samaritan. Today the Good Samaritan is a popular character in American public life. Stories of looting were endemic after attacks on the World Trade Center on September 11, 2001, and after Hurricane Katrina submerged New Orleans in 2005. But so were stories of Good Samaritans. During the last decade the US Congress has debated the "Good Samaritan Food Donation Act," the "Good Samaritan Tax Act," and a "Good Samaritan Exemption" to the Marine Mammal Protection Act. In March 2006 New York Senator Hillary Clinton said that Republican efforts to outlaw giving assistance to illegal immigrants would "criminalize the Good Samaritan and probably even Jesus himself."[267]

gospel of wealth. Capitalism's answer to the Social Gospel, the gospel of wealth derives from a 1900 book of the same name by the steel magnate and philanthropist Andrew Carnegie (1835–1919). This theology was later popularized by "Acres of Diamonds," a sermon delivered over six thousand times by Baptist minister Russell Conwell (1843–1925). Part Calvinism, part social Darwinism, and part laissez-faire capitalism, the gospel of wealth teaches that prosperity is God's reward for morality and hard work. A frequently forgotten corollary is that the wealthy have a responsibility to give their wealth away. The gospel of wealth survives today—minus the philanthropy—in "prosperity theology," also known as the "Word of Faith" or "name it and claim it" theology, which promises that health and wealth are readily available to any Christian who asks God for either (or both) in faith.

Graham, Billy (1918–). The most visible religious leader to generations of twentieth-century Americans, Billy Graham served for decades as a globe-trotting evangelist, preaching to more people than anyone else in history. Raised a Southern Presbyterian in Charlotte, North Carolina, he was converted during a revival in his hometown in 1934 and began his career as an evangelist at Youth for Christ revivals in 1945. Although Graham got off on the wrong foot with President Harry Truman, who judged him a "counterfeit," he later served as an unofficial American Protestant pope, consulting and praying with Presidents Eisenhower, Kennedy, Nixon, Johnson, Reagan, Bush, and Clinton. President George W. Bush has credited Graham with helping to crack his drinking habit and to bring him to Jesus. Although often labeled a fundamentalist, Graham is actually an evangelical who has repeatedly drawn fire from fundamentalists for his policy of involving in his revivals (which he calls "crusades") all the Christian denominations in a given city, including liberal Protestant groups. Graham ceded many of the activities of his Billy Graham Evangelical Association to his son Franklin Graham in 2000.

Great Awakening. A series of revivals that shook the colonies between the 1720s and the 1760s. Led by such preachers as Dutch Calvinist Theodore Frelinghuysen, Presbyterian Gilbert Tennent, Congregationalist Jonathan Edwards, and Anglican George Whitefield, this movement broke out up and down the eastern seaboard, putting the experience of conversion front and center in American Protestant life and introducing a more extemporaneous and emotional style to both sermons and worship. In the process the Great Awakening split colonial Protestantism into two factions: prorevival "New Lights" and antirevival "Old Lights." It also helped to turn revivalism into a key component of American religion and to make evangelicalism the nation's dominant religious impulse. In the political realm the Great Awakening served to knit Americans of all colonies into one people—a perspective that contributed greatly to the coming American Revolution.

hadith. Islamic sacred tradition, second in importance only to the Quran, relating the words and deeds of Muhammad and his companions as transmitted by trusted confidantes. Muslims interpret the Quran in light of these hadith and use their teachings, which they believe to be divinely inspired, to conform their lives to the exemplary life of Muhammad. A given hadith contains two parts: a text and a chain of authority. The latter, which traces the transmitters of the text back to its source, is used to determine how much trust to place in a given hadith (which Muslim scholars classify as "sound," "good," or "weak"). Those who have compared the Quran in Islam to Jesus in Christianity—both are the revelations of God—see the hadith as analogous to the Christian New Testament. In any case, it stands alongside the Quran itself as one of two key sources of Islamic law. There are six major Sunni compilations, the most authoritative of which are the "authentic" compilations of *Bukhari* and *Muslim* (each named after its compiler). Shiites have their own collections of hadith, which include in addition to the sayings and deeds of Muhammad those of their imams.

"Hail Mary." See Mary.

hajj. See 5 Pillars of Islam.

Hanukkah. Jewish festival of lights, which lasts for eight days and roughly coincides with Christmas. This minor holiday commemorates a miracle first described in a compilation of rabbinic disputations called the Talmud. After foreign soldiers desecrated Jerusalem's Second Temple in the second century BCE, Judas Maccabee purified and rededicated it on the twenty-fifth day of the Jewish month of Kislev (when Hanukkah now starts). Although there was only a one-day supply of holy oil, that supply miraculously lasted for the eight days it took Maccabee to complete his work. Today Jews celebrate Hanukkah (lit. "dedication") by saying prayers and lighting candles each evening for eight days. The lamp that holds the eight candles is called a menorah.

In the United States Hanukkah has become something of a Jewish Christmas, with gift giving and (in some cases) tree trimming. The holiday has been widely discussed in US politics in the context of public displays of nativity scenes, which often include menorahs and other Hanukkah symbols to signal their interreligious nature (and therefore their constitutionality). In "The Hanukkah Song," comedian Adam Sandler pokes fun at fellow Jews who feel somewhat underserved by Hanukkah at Christmastime, offering them a long list of "people who are Jewish, just like you and me." "David Lee Roth lights the menorah," he croons. "So do James Caan, Kirk Douglas, and the late Dinah Shore-ah."

Hare Krishnas. Popular name for members of the International Society of Krishna Consciousness (ISKCON), a Hindu devotional movement based on the teachings of the Bengali mystic Caitanya (1486–1533) and brought to the United States in 1965 by A. C. Bhaktivedanta Swami Prabhupada (1896–1977). The devotional practices of this small group center on chanting a mantra to Krishna—"Hare Krishna, Hare Krishna; Krishna, Krishna, Hare, Hare; Hare Rama, Hare Rama; Rama, Rama, Hare, Hare"—whom devotees revere as the one true God. Hare Krishnas brought (and lost) a number of landmark lawsuits that helped to define First Amendment jurisprudence. In *Heffron v. ISKCON* (1981) the Supreme Court ruled that Hare Krishnas were subject to licensing regulations regarding distributing literature and soliciting donations at the Minnesota state fair. In *ISKCON v. Lee* (1992) the Supreme Court held that local regulations banning Hare Krishnas from asking for donations at airports were constitutional.

hijab. This Arabic term refers to any partition separating two things, but most commonly to a veil or head covering worn by some Muslim women. The Quran mandates modesty in female dress but does not say what form this modesty should take. So hijabs vary considerably from country to country and believer to believer, and many Muslim women wear no head coverings at all. Since the 1970s the veil has become a battleground between Muslims and Westerners. Many feminists see the veil as the symbol par excellence of the oppression of women in Islam. But many Muslim women, both in the United States and abroad, see head scarves as symbols of Muslim identity and of resistance to the sexual libertinism of Western societies. In the early twenty-first century American courts adjudicated many contests over whether the First Amendment's free exercise clause offers Muslim women the right to cover their hair when doing so would violate dress codes in public schools, jails, police units, or the armed forces.

Hinduism. Wildly diverse Indian religion manifested in beliefs such as reincarnation, practices such as yoga, and scriptures such as the Vedas, the Upanishads, and the Bhagavad Gita. Hinduism, which has no founder and no standard scripture or commentary, is often described as polytheistic, and it does feature hundreds of divinities—from the good-natured cowherd, Krishna, to the bloodthirsty goddess of cremation grounds, Kali. But many Hindus, especially in America, are monotheists who insist that underlying these diverse manifestations of divinity is one Absolute Reality.

Hinduism is the religion of roughly 80 percent of India's population of one billion. It first came to the United States in the person of Swami Vivekananda (1863–1902), a missionary who represented Hinduism at the World's Parliament of Religions in Chicago in 1893. Hinduism's most popular manifestation in America today is the contemporary yoga vogue, which began in the 1990s. Important American Hindu groups include the Vedanta Society, founded in New York in 1894 by Vivekananda, and the Self-Realization Fellowship, incorporated in 1935 by Swami Paramahansa Yogananda (1893–1952), the author of the countercultural hit *Autobiography of a Yogi* (1946). Hinduism burst onto the popular scene in the 1960s and 1970s through a series of gurus who came to the United States after the US Congress liberalized immigration from Asia in 1965. Thanks to the popularity of the Maharishi Mahesh Yoga (b. 1911) of Transcendental Meditation fame and A. C. Bhaktivedanta Swami Prabhupada of the Hare Krishnas, *Life* magazine declared 1968 the "Year of the Guru." In recent decades American Hinduism has become an immigrant phenomenon focused more on building temples than attracting Caucasians. Indian American Hindus have formed a few pressure groups, such as American Hindus Against Defamation, which combats negative stereotypes of Hinduism fostered by the media, but they have largely kept politics at arm's length. There are currently more than one million Hindus and a few hundred temples in the United States. In 2000, a Hindu priest opened a session of the US Congress with a prayer.

Holocaust. The mass murder of roughly six million Jews by the Nazis between 1933 and 1945, prompted in part by centuries of Christian theology that branded the Jews as Christ killers. Also known as the *Shoah* (Hebrew for "calamity"), this event, which included the murders of millions of homosexuals, Gypsies, Poles, Jehovah's Witnesses, the handicapped, and other non-Jewish minorities, has raised profound theological questions among believers about the existence and goodness of God in a world that is witness to such evil. It has also raised questions about the contributions of Christian theology to this act of genocide. Widespread revulsion at the efforts of the Nazi regime to exterminate the Jews helped to pave the way for creation of the state of Israel in 1948. The story of the Holocaust is told in the United States Holocaust Memorial Museum in Washington DC.

Holy Communion. A central act of Christian worship, also referred to as Eucharist, Lord's Supper, and Mass, this communal meal, typically celebrated with bread and wine (or grape juice), recalls the Last Supper of Jesus and his disciples on the night before his crucifixion—a rite that is popularly said to be based on the Passover Seder meal of the Jews. Christians differ over how important Holy Communion is, how often to celebrate it, how old you should be to participate, and to what extent Jesus' presence in the ritual is to be understood symbolically or literally. The Roman Catholic doctrine of transubstantiation teaches that the bread and the wine are somehow transformed during this liturgy into the body and blood of Jesus. Some liturgically minded Protestant groups, notably Episcopalians and Lutherans, deny transubstantiation yet insist on the "real presence" of Jesus. Less liturgically minded Protestants, such as the Methodists and the Baptists, see the rite simply as a memorial.

imam. To Sunni Muslims, an imam ("leader" in Arabic) is simply the man who leads a congregation in prayer. To Shiite Muslims, an imam is far more important: a descendant of Muhammad chosen by God to lead the community in all areas of belief and practice. Shiites disagree on whether there were five, seven, or twelve imams, but most believe that a "hidden imam" is coming at the last days to restore peace and justice on earth. During the Iranian Revolution of 1979 the Ayatollah Khomeini was referred to as an imam, in keeping with the Shiite practice of referring to jurists by that title. In the United States, *imam* has evolved into a title of respect, akin to *Reverend,* as in Imam Siraj Wahhaj of Brooklyn, who in 1991 became the first Muslim to offer a prayer before the US House of Representatives.

Immaculate Conception. Roman Catholic doctrine, quite distinct from the teaching of the virgin birth, that Jesus' mother, Mary, was sinless from conception. This teaching was promulgated as official church dogma in 1854 by Pope Pius IX and is part of the Islamic tradition too.

inerrancy, biblical. Christian belief, common among fundamentalists, that the Bible is entirely without error, not only in theology and ethics but also in history, geography, and science. A less strict view of the Bible, held by many evangelicals, is that the Bible is simply inspired by God.

infallibility, papal. Roman Catholic doctrine, promulgated at the First Vatican Council (1869–70), that the pope can, under circumscribed circumstances, speak without error on matters of "faith or morals." Catholics, it should be noted, do not believe that this doctrine means that everything the pope says or does is infallible. And the pope can never speak infallibly on other matters, politics included.

intelligent design. See creationism.

Islam. The faith of over one billion people and the world's second largest religion after Christianity. *Islam* literally means "submission." Muslims exhibit their submission to Allah (God) by practicing the Five Pillars of Islam: by praying, fasting during the month of Ramadan, almsgiving, going on pilgrimage to Mecca, and testifying to the oneness of Allah and the prophethood of their founder, Muhammad (570–632). Their holy book, the Quran, speaks of caring for the poor, a day of judgment, and the bodily resurrection. Their holiest cities are Mecca, Medina, and Jerusalem (in that order). The religion is divided into two major branches: Sunnis (the majority) and Shiites.

Islam first came to the United States with African slaves. There are records of slaves refusing to eat pork, speaking Arabic, and calling God Allah. But Islam all but vanished in the colonies. Muslims began immigrating to the United States in significant numbers in the early twentieth century and those numbers jumped dramatically after the US Congress liberalized immigration in 1965. Many associate American Islam with the Black Muslims of the Nation of Islam, the controversial and heterodox group founded in Detroit by W. D. Fard, led after Fard's mysterious disappearance in 1934 by Elijah Muhammad, and later embraced by such notables as Malcolm X, Muhammad Ali, and Louis Farrakhan. But most American Muslims are of either Middle Eastern or Asian descent, and most African American Muslims, including Elijah Muhammad's son Warith Deen Muhammad are affiliated not with the Black Muslims but with more orthodox Sunni groups.

Today Islam is a major presence on the American religious landscape. Muslims have delivered prayers to open sessions of the US Congress, their holidays have appeared on postage stamps, and their leaders meet with US presidents. They are represented by a variety of pressure groups, including the Muslim Public Affairs Council (established 1988), the American Muslim Council (1990), the American Muslim Alliance (1994), and the Council on American-Islamic Relations (1994). After 9/11 Americans vigorously debated the nature of Islam. Was Islam, as President George W. Bush argued, a "religion of peace"? Or was it, as the conservative political activist Paul Weyrich insisted, "a religion of war"?

Estimates of the American Muslim population vary widely, in part because Islam is growing so rapidly here. There are over 1,200 mosques in the United States, and Islam is likely the religion of roughly 1 to 2 percent of the US population, or three to six million people. Worldwide, roughly one in every five people is a Muslim. Although the religion is often identified with the Middle East, the vast majority of the world's

Muslims live elsewhere. The country with the most Muslims is Indonesia, followed by Pakistan, Bangladesh, and India.

Islamism. Also known as "political Islam," Islamism refers to ultraconservative Islamic movements that use their religion to advance a political agenda. This term is typically pejorative, used as an epithet by critics of such movements as al-Qaeda and Wahhabism. It should not be confused with the term Islamicist, which is used in academic circles to refer to scholars specializing in Islam. Seizing on the popularity of the term *Islamist,* some critics of the Religious Right began in the early twenty-first century to refer to politically active conservative Christians as Christianists.

Jehovah's Witnesses. A Protestant denomination, officially known as the Watchtower Bible and Tract Society, rooted in the end-of-the-world teachings of Charles Taze Russell (1852–1916). This rapidly growing group claims about a million adherents in the United States but nearly seven million active members worldwide. Witnesses, as members are called, live up to their name. They are aggressive door-to-door evangelizers, and they publish their *Watchtower* magazine, which Russell began in the 1870s, in 152 languages. They became notorious in early twentieth-century America for refusing to salute the flag or serve in the military. Their unorthodox theological views extend to denying the Trinity and refusing blood transfusions. Witnesses have been quite active in the legal arena, taking dozens of cases to the Supreme Court—more than any other religious group. In *Minersville School District v. Gobitis* (1940), the Supreme Court ruled that Witnesses in public schools could be forced to salute the flag (which members understand as a form of idolatry). After that decision was interpreted by vigilantes as a warrant to attack Witnesses and burn down their Kingdom Halls, the Supreme Court quickly reversed itself in *West Virginia State Board of Education v. Barnette* (1943), upholding Witnesses' right not to salute the flag. The most influential case involving this group was *Cantwell v. Connecticut* (1940), which extended First Amendment protections from the federal to the local and state levels and vastly expanded the range of religious liberty for all minority religions in the United States.

Jerusalem. Known by Muslims as *al-Quds* ("The Holy") and mentioned more than 600 times in the Hebrew Bible, Jerusalem is a sacred place for Jews, Christians, and Muslims and a magnet for both pilgrimage and tourism. As much an idea as a reality, it is built on the metaphors of exile and return and on the blood of Jewish, Christian, and Muslim martyrs who fought to control it during the crusades of the Middle Ages. Its many holy places include: for Jews, the remains of the Western Wall of the Second Temple; and for Christians, the Via Dolorosa, along which Jesus walked to his crucifixion, and the Church of the Holy Sepulchre, on the site where according to tradition he was buried and resurrected. Muslims consider Jerusalem sacred because it is where the angel Gabriel took Muhammad on his famed "night journey"—from the mosque in Mecca to the Dome of the Rock in Jerusalem and then to the heavens to converse with prior prophets and to learn how to pray.

Conquered by King David, Jerusalem was the site of Solomon's Temple until the Babylonians sacked the city and destroyed that landmark in 586 BCE. The Second Temple was destroyed by the Romans in 70 CE. Since that time control over Jerusalem has passed back and forth between Christians, Muslims, and Jews. Today both Israelis and Palestinians claim Jerusalem as their capital, and this city's status remains a major sticking point in Middle East peace negotiations. Conflicting religious convictions remain a major reason why those negotiations are so difficult and the conflicts they seek to resolve so bitter.

Jesus. The central figure in Christianity and the second person in the Christian Trinity. According to the Christian tradition, Jesus was born to the Virgin Mary and raised as a carpenter by her husband, Joseph. After being baptized by John the Baptist, Jesus began his public ministry at roughly the age of thirty. He preached the kingdom of God, healed the sick, cast out demons, and gathered twelve apostles. The Passion— the story of his suffering and death told in all four Gospels—begins with the Last Supper he celebrated with his followers. It includes charges brought by Jewish authorities, a trial before the Roman governor Pontius Pilate, and ultimately his scourging and crucifixion. Christians affirm, however, that after three days Jesus rose from the dead, appeared to his followers, and ascended to heaven. Through the centuries Christians developed many competing christologies, or theologies about Jesus. Some emphasized his humanity and others his divinity, but the view that he was both God and human prevailed. According to the Nicene Creed of the fourth century, which is accepted by Catholic, Protestant, and Orthodox Christians alike, Jesus was "the only-begotten Son of God, begotten of the Father before all worlds, God of God, Light of Light, Very God of Very God."

The New Testament describes Jesus as "the same yesterday, and today, and forever" (Hebrews 13:8), but in the United States he has changed dramatically over time. American Christians have portrayed him as "black and white, male and female, straight and gay, a socialist and a capitalist, a pacifist and a warrior, a Ku Klux Klansman and a civil rights agitator."[268] Non-Christians have embraced Jesus also. Buddhists revere him as a bodhisattva, Hindus as an avatar of God, and Jews as a great rabbi. Muslims do not believe that Jesus was crucified or resurrected, but they regard him as a prophet and affirm both the virgin birth and his ascension into heaven. American popular culture has celebrated Jesus too—in best-selling novels such as *The Man Nobody Knows* (1925), Broadway musicals such as *Jesus Christ Superstar* (1971), and blockbusters from Cecil B. DeMille's *King of Kings* (1927) to Mel Gibson's *The Passion of the Christ* (2004).

Today Jesus is a major presence in American politics also, widely invoked by politicians of both parties on a variety of public policy questions. "What would Jesus do?" was first asked over a century ago in the novel *In His Steps* (1897) by Congregationalist minister Charles Sheldon. But it remains a vital question for many Americans today on such matters as environmentalism, poverty, war, immigration, civil rights, and abortion.

jihad. The term *jihad* is derived from an Arabic word that means "to struggle" or "make an effort." So to participate in a jihad is to struggle on behalf of God. Muslims see two different types of jihads. The greater is the spiritual struggle of each believer against his or her lesser nature. The lesser is the physical struggle against enemies of Islam, a category that has traditionally included polytheists but not Jews or Christians (whom Muslims classically regard as fellow "people of the book"). In these physical struggles Muslims are enjoined to fight in accordance with strict regulations (including prohibitions against harming women, children, the old, the sick, and other noncombatants). Those who participate in such a jihad are called Mujahideen, a term popularized by opponents of the Soviet occupation of Afghanistan. Individuals who die in this sort of battle may be revered as martyrs who go straight to paradise without having to wait (as others must) for the final judgment. Recently some radical Muslims have tried to modify the strict rules governing the "jihad of the sword," particularly rules against injuring or killing women, children, civilians, and fellow Muslims. Others have tried to expand the Five Pillars to include a sixth: jihad. Still others have tried to break down the long-standing tradition between "holy wars" in defense of Islam, which have been widely accepted as legitimate, and offensive "holy wars," which have been seen as more dubious. Few Muslims, however, have accepted these reinterpretations. The only groups that stress jihad as "holy war" are Muslim extremists and extreme critics of Islam.

Joan of Arc (1412?–1431). Fifteenth-century French saint, martyr, and national hero. *Not* Noah's wife.

Judaism. Of the major world religions, the smallest in terms of adherents but one of the most historically influential. Judaism is a religion more of practice than belief; its adherents are knit together less by a shared worldview than by shared observances. Jews attempt to follow the Torah, or Law. They rest once a week on the Sabbath, which they celebrate from sundown on Friday to sundown on Saturday. They celebrate holidays such as Passover (which commemorates the Exodus of the Israelites from bondage to freedom), Rosh Hashanah (Jewish New Year), and Yom Kippur (Day of Atonement).

There is, however, something of a Jewish creed, called the *Shema,* which begins: "Hear, O Israel: The Lord our God is one Lord" (Deuteronomy 6:4). As this creed indicates, Judaism is monotheistic. It recognizes one God who is creator, lawgiver, and judge, whose words are recorded in the Torah ("law" or "teaching"). Judaism's scripture is called the Tanakh, an acrostic for: Torah (understood here as the five books of Moses: Genesis, Exodus, Leviticus, Numbers, Deuteronomy); Neviim (prophetic and historical books); and Ketuvim (other writings, including Psalms, Proverbs, Job, and the Song of Songs). In addition to recording God's commandments, the Tanakh tells the story of God's relationship with his "chosen people," the Jews, a relationship marked by covenants made, broken, and remade, and by the rhythms of exile and return.

Although this story goes back millennia, Judaism proper did not emerge until after the destruction of the Second Temple in Jerusalem in 70 CE transformed what had been a tradition of priests performing sacrifice in a temple into a more portable tradition of rabbis interpreting texts in synagogues. Today there are only about 15 million Jews worldwide, but Judaism gave birth to the two largest religions in the world—Christianity and Islam—which together with Judaism constitute the "Abrahamic" religions. There are roughly 5 million Jews in the state of Israel and over 5.2 million Jews in the United States. Reform Judaism accounts for 39 percent of the religiously affiliated US Jewish population, followed by Conservative Judaism (33 percent), Orthodox Judaism (21 percent), and Reconstructionist Judaism (3 percent). Because Judaism is as much a people as a religion, it is also possible to be a secular Jew.

Judas Iscariot. One of Jesus' twelve apostles, notorious for betraying Jesus with a kiss in exchange for thirty pieces of silver. In Dante's *Divine Comedy* Judas is one of the heads of a three-headed Satan, but the noncanonical Gospel of Judas, discovered in Egypt in the 1970s and published in English translation in 2006, tells a different story. According to this Gnostic gospel, Judas is a hero rather than a villain. He gave Jesus up to the authorities because Jesus asked him to assist his Lord in sloughing off "the man that clothes me" (in other words, his body).

Judeo-Christian. Neologism, dating to the 1930s, that describes Judaism and Christianity as sister faiths in a hybrid religious tradition undergirding the American way of life. Initially the term was used to distinguish American Jews and Christians from European Nazis and Fascists, who were appropriating the term *Christian* for themselves and their politics. After World War II Americans began to use this slogan to distinguish their "one nation under God" from the Soviet Union under godless Communism. This "triple melting pot" ideal informed the decision of the Reverend Jerry Falwell to open the doors of the Moral Majority to Catholics and Jews as well as Protestants. After 9/11 some have tried to redefine the United States as a country of Christians, Jews, and Muslims—a "Judeo-Christian-Islamic" nation. Meanwhile, Osama bin Laden drew on the Judeo-Christian tradition to denounce the US military and other "Judeo-Christian crusaders" for attacking Islam.

Judeo-Christian-Islamic. Neologism, dating to the 1980s, that describes Judaism, Christianity, and Islam as sister faiths in a hybrid religious tradition undergirding the American way of life. This model of America can be seen in presidential rhetoric, which since the turn of the twenty-first century has tended to refer when discussing religious congregations to "churches, synagogues, and mosques" rather than simply "churches and synagogues." It was championed by American Muslim groups during the 1990s and moved into broader circulation after 9/11. In 2003 groups such as the Council on American-Islamic Relations and the American Muslim Council argued that Americans should stop referring to the United States as "Judeo-Christian" and use "Judeo-Christian-Islamic" or "Abrahamic" instead. Liberal Christian groups such as the National Council of Churches welcomed this change in nomenclature, but more conservative organizations such as the National Association of Evangelicals dismissed it as political correctness run amok.

just-war theory. Catholic tradition, dating to Thomas Aquinas, describing both what makes a war just (*jus ad bellum*) and what conduct is justifiable during such a war (*jus in bello*). Concerning how to conduct a war, just war theorists often cite such principles as "discrimination" (which says that combatants should direct their aggression against other combatants rather than innocent civilians) and "proportionality" (which says that force cannot be out of proportion to the injury suffered). Just war theory also prohibits torture and mandates proper care for prisoners of war. Many of its tenets were codified in the Geneva Conventions of 1949. In recent years just war theory surfaced, implicitly or explicitly, in debates concerning suicide bombings in Israel, the treatment of prisoners detained at Guantanamo Bay in Cuba, and the alleged torture of terrorists overseas. This tradition of moral reasoning is opposed by pacifists, who believe that war can never be morally justifiable, and by "realists," who say that war is inherently immoral and should not therefore be called to the bar of justice.

Kabbalah. Jewish mystical teachings, rooted in the Zohar, a multivolume, thirteenth-century text offering mystical interpretations of Jewish law. Kabbalah (lit. "tradition"), which attends to such spiritual matters as angels and the afterlife, is supposed to be esoteric—that is to say, hidden—but in the early twenty-first century it went public. The Kabbalah Centre of Los Angeles disseminated Kabbalistic beliefs and practices to a wide variety of celebrities, including Demi Moore, Britney Spears, and Madonna, who were seen sporting its trademark red string bracelets. Critics decried the Kabbalah Centre as a "cult" and the teachings of its leader, Rabbi Philip Berg (b. 1929), as "McMysticism." But Berg defended his approach as a way to bring Kabbalah to people of other faiths (and none at all).

Kama Sutra. Hindu scripture popular in the West, originally intended as a sex manual for courtesans. Hindus recognize four goals of life: *kama* (pleasure), *dharma* (duty), *artha* (wealth), and *moksha* (spiritual liberation). The Kama Sutra, written by the Hindu thinker Vatsyayana around 400 CE, is an explicit treatise on sexual pleasure. Widely read and frequently translated, it discusses sixteen different types of kisses and a plethora of positions for sexual intercourse. The Sanskrit word *kama* should not be confused with the Sanskrit word *karma,* which means action.

karma. In Sanskrit, karma refers both to an action and its consequences, but the term connotes more broadly the ethical law of cause and effect that drives *samsara,* the never-ending cycle of birth, life, death, and rebirth in Hinduism, Jainism, Buddhism, Sikhism, and other Asian religions. According to this law, which like gravity operates without divine intervention, positive consequences follow from good actions and negative consequences from bad actions—either in this lifetime or in a future incarnation. One troubling corollary of this tradition is that all of us deserve the circumstances into which we are born. Thinkers disagree about whether "good karma" can be transferred from one person to another. Classically, the answer to that question is no. But as more devotional understandings of Asian religions developed, many came to believe that gods, Buddhas, and other supernatural beings can transfer to their devotees portions of the vast storehouses of merit they accrued over lifetimes of good deeds. Now an English word, karma refers in popular parlance to the tendency for "what goes around" to "come around," as in the bumper sticker: "My Karma Ran Over My Dogma."

King Jr., Martin Luther (1929–1968). African American Baptist minister and civil rights leader who creatively combined religion and politics. The son of a well-known preacher in Atlanta, Georgia, King rose to national prominence during the bus boycott in Montgomery, Alabama, in 1955. Inspired by the nonviolent direct action of Mohandas Gandhi and the neo-orthodox theology of Reinhold Niebuhr (1892–1971), King used nonviolent civil disobedience to bring an end to racial segregation. He won the Nobel Peace Prize in 1964 and was shot and killed by a white racist in Memphis, Tennessee, in 1968. King's "Letter from a Birmingham Jail," a classic in American literature, cannot be understood without grasping its many religious references—to Jesus, Paul, neo-orthodox theologian Reinhold Niebuhr, Jewish philosopher Martin Buber, Augustine, Thomas Aquinas, Martin Luther, the Nation of Islam, and Shadrach, Meshach, and Abednego of the Old Testament. Following the passage of the Civil Rights Act of 1964, King turned his attentions to fighting poverty and opposing the Vietnam War. In 1983 President Reagan signed a bill declaring the third Monday of every January Martin Luther King Day. This is the only federal holiday commemorating the life of an African American and the only such day commemorating the life of a clergyman.

kirpan. See 5 Ks.

Koran. See Quran.

Kwanzaa. Year-end festival held annually from December 26 through January 1 to commemorate the African heritage of African Americans. Each of this festival's seven days centers on a different principle—unity, self-determination, collective work and responsibility, cooperative economics, purpose, creativity, and faith—and features the lighting of a candle on a seven-branched candelabrum. An invention of black nationalist Maulana Karenga, Kwanzaa was first celebrated in 1966 in San Diego, California.

Lao-tzu. See Taoism.

Last Supper. Final meal (perhaps a Passover Seder) shared by Jesus with his disciples before his arrest, trial, and crucifixion. This event is commemorated each Sunday by Christians who drink wine (symbolizing the blood of Christ) and eat bread (symbolizing his body) in a sacramental reenactment of this last meal. Arguably the most famous scene in Christendom, the Last Supper has inspired legions of artists—from the pop artist Andy Warhol to the surrealist Salvador Dali—to try their hand at depicting Jesus and his twelve followers arrayed around a supper table. The most beloved of these images is Leonardo Da Vinci's *Last Supper* (1498).

Latter-day Saints, Church of Jesus Christ of. See Mormonism.

Lord's Prayer. Christianity's most popular prayer, taught by Jesus to his followers and widely recited by Christians today. Of the two New Testament versions (Matthew 6:9–13 and Luke 11:2–4), Matthew's is the most popular. It reads (in the King James Bible): "Our Father which art in heaven, Hallowed be thy name. Thy kingdom come, Thy will be done in earth, as it is in heaven. Give us this day our daily bread. And forgive us our debts, as we forgive our debtors. And lead us not into temptation, but deliver us from evil: For thine is the kingdom, and the power, and the glory, for ever. Amen."

Luther, Martin (1483–1546). German leader of the sixteenth-century Protestant Reformation and founder of Lutheranism. Martin Luther is best remembered for publishing his Ninety-five Theses on indulgences (1517), a bold action that prompted Pope Leo X to excommunicate him from the Roman Catholic Church. Central to Luther's thought are two key ideas: justification by grace through faith, which he found in the Pauline epistles and the writings of Saint Augustine; and *sola scriptura,* which asserts that the "Bible alone" is authoritative for Christians, not (as Catholics claimed) both the Bible and tradition. Luther's primary institutional legacies in the United States today are Lutheran colleges such as St. Olaf College in Northfield, Minnesota, and Lutheran denominations such as the Evangelical Lutheran Church in America and the Lutheran Church–Missouri Synod.

Lutheranism. Protestant denomination based on the teachings of the sixteenth-century German religious reformer Martin Luther. Lutherans follow their founder in stressing justification by grace through faith and the authority of the Bible alone (*sola scriptura*). Along with Episcopalianism, Lutheranism is one of the more liturgical Protestant groups. The largest Lutheran body in the United States (and the third largest Protestant denomination after the Southern Baptist Convention and the United Methodist Church) is the Evangelical Lutheran Church in America, a liberal Protestant group formed when smaller Lutheran groups merged in the late 1980s. It claims 5.1 million members. Far more conservative is the Lutheran Church–Missouri Synod, which claims 2.5 million members. This group, founded by German immigrants in the 1830s, supports a large network of parochial schools that inculcate a strict interpretation of the Lutheran confessions and a belief in biblical infallibility. Lutheranism is most prominent in the Midwest and among people of Scandinavian and German descent. Although Lutherans are overrepresented in governors' mansions, there has never been a Lutheran president.

Malcolm X. See Black Muslims.

martyr. In Judaism, Christianity, and Islam, a martyr (from the Greek word *martys* or "witness") is someone who dies, typically young and violently, for a sacred cause. According to popular Islam, the Muslim martyr, or *shahid* ("witness" in Arabic), is transported immediately to paradise rather than having to wait for the last judgment. Martyrdom is particularly emphasized among Shiites, whose identity has been profoundly shaped by the suffering and death of Muhammad's grandson Husayn (625–680) during a battle at Karbala on the banks of the Euphrates in

680, an event commemorated annually by Shiites in the festival of Muharram. During the late twentieth and early twenty-first centuries, martyrdom became a terrorist strategy for suicide bombers in Israel, Iraq, and other countries.

Martyrs are made by the circumstances of their lives and deaths, of course, but also and more significantly by the communities who memorialize them. In the United States devotees transformed President Lincoln and the Reverend Martin Luther King Jr. into American Christs. Over the last half century, adoring fans have elevated to martyr status James Dean, Jimi Hendrix, Janis Joplin, Tupac Shakur, and dozens of other celebrities who suffered early and violent deaths. Cassie Bernal, who died in the shootings at Columbine High School in Colorado in 1999, has also been embraced as a martyr, since according to evangelical admirers she testified to her belief in God just before she was killed.

Mary. Mother of Jesus and, after Jesus himself, the most popular figure in Christian history. In the Bible she figures prominently in stories about Jesus' birth, infancy, childhood, and death. Roman Catholics, among whom Marian devotions are most prominent, give the Blessed Virgin Mary, as they call her, a role in sacred history above the saints. In 1854 Pope Pius IX proclaimed that she was sinless from conception (the Immaculate Conception), and in 1950 Pope Pius XII promulgated the doctrine that she was assumed bodily into heaven (the Assumption). Among Catholics, Mary is an object of popular devotion on dozens of feast days and at such pilgrimage shrines as Our Lady of Guadalupe in Mexico and Our Lady of Lourdes in France. The most common act of Marian devotion is praying the rosary, which involves praying both the Lord's Prayer and the "Hail Mary," which reads: "Hail Mary, full of grace, the Lord is with thee. Blessed art thou among women, and blessed is the fruit of thy womb, Jesus. Holy Mary, Mother of God, pray for us sinners now, and at the hour of our death. Amen." Many Protestants reject such devotions as "Mariolatry."

Mary is also a major figure in Islam, where she is revered as Maryam and mentioned repeatedly in the Quran as the mother of Jesus. A Quranic chapter named after her, where the story of Jesus' miraculous birth is told, may be recited to women in labor. Some of the most bitter Bible translation disputes have concerned one Hebrew word used in Isaiah to describe the woman who will give birth to a son who shall be called Emmanuel. This term, *almah,* which Christians have typically translated as "virgin," has been used for centuries by the church to bolster the claim that Jesus came into the world via a miraculous virgin birth. Many insist, however, that this term's plain meaning in Hebrew is simply "young girl."

Mary Magdalene. Jesus' most famous female follower, an eyewitness to his death, and the first witness to his resurrection. The popular tradition that she was once a prostitute seems to be based on the identification of her with an unnamed "sinner" who anoints Jesus' feet in the Gospel of Luke. A more controversial tradition is that Mary Magdalene and Jesus married and had children. This view, which has no biblical warrant, informs the Martin Scorcese film *The Last Temptation of Christ* (1988) and is a major premise in Dan Brown's best-selling book, *The DaVinci Code* (2003).

Mass. See Holy Communion.

Mecca. The holiest city in the Islamic world, located in modern-day Saudi Arabia. Mecca is holy to Muslims because Muhammad was born there, because he received his earliest revelations in a cave outside the city, and because upon his triumphant return to Mecca in 630 CE he replaced polytheistic worship around the city's Kaaba shrine with monotheistic worship of the one true God. Muslims face Mecca when they pray, and mosques include a niche in the wall (*mihrab*) to orient them in that direction. Going at least once on the hajj, or pilgrimage, to Mecca is a sacred obligation for all Muslims who are physically and financially able. To keep Mecca pure, no non-Muslims are allowed in the city.

One of America's great spiritual memoirs, *The Autobiography of Malcolm X* (1965), turns on the pilgrimage to Mecca of this African American convert to the Nation of Islam. While on the hajj, Malcolm X comes to see himself not so much in racial as in religious terms—as a Muslim among Muslims. Osama bin Laden has indicated that he and al-Qaeda began their "holy war" against the United States because Americans put troops in the Muslim holy land in Saudi Arabia after the first Gulf War. *Mecca* has also become a generic term in American English, where it connotes the world center of something. For example, Moab, Utah, is described as a mecca for mountain bikers and Colorado Springs, Colorado, as an evangelical Christian mecca.

Medina. After Mecca, Islam's holiest city. Medina, which lies today in Saudi Arabia, is the place where Muhammad fled after leaving Mecca in

622 CE, where he founded the Islamic community (*ummah*), and where he established himself as not only a prophet but also a patriarch, politician, and military leader. It is also the city where he built the first mosque, where he died, and where he is buried. Muhammad's flight in 622 from Mecca to Medina—known as the *hijra*—is so important in Islam that Muslims date their lunar calendar from that moment. (Much of 2007 CE falls for them in 1427 AH—"in the year of the *hijra*.") During the 1990s some American Muslims began speaking of transforming the United States into a Medina, by which they meant it was time to establish an American *ummah*—an Islamic community that was both authentically American and authentically Islamic.

megachurch. A large congregation, typically Protestant and often evangelical, with a weekly worship service attendance measured in the thousands, an authoritative male pastor, and a wide array of social ministries and recreational activities. Few US megachurches are politically active, most are theologically conservative, and, while many are nondenominational, two-thirds carry a denominational affiliation. Worship services put a premium on good music, with live bands and song lyrics projected on large screens.

There are over 1,200 megachurches in the United States—up from only 350 in 1990. They cluster in the suburbs of rapidly growing cities, particularly in the southern "sunbelt," which stretches from Florida to California. The largest is Joel Osteen's Houston-based Lakewood Church, which typically draws thirty thousand to its Sunday services. Another is Rick Warren's Saddleback Valley Church in Lake Forest, California. Both pastors are also best-selling authors. Osteen's *Your Best Life Now* (2004) has sold millions of copies, and Warren's *The Purpose-Driven Life* (2002) is one of the best-selling nonfiction books in US history.

messiah. The long-awaited king who according to the Jewish tradition will come at the last days, restore the Jews to the Promised Land, rebuild the Temple, and inaugurate the just and peaceful "world to come." Christians believe that Jesus was this messiah (hence the title Christ, from *christos,* Greek for messiah), as do Jews for Jesus and other messianic Jewish groups. But Jews generally reject Jesus' messianic status. Messianism is not a major emphasis among Reform and Conservative Jews, but it is emphasized by the Orthodox. Among the Orthodox, Hasidic Jews are especially drawn to messianic thinking. For many other Jews, Zionism is a form of messianism too.

Methodism. Mainline Protestant denomination founded in eighteenth-century England by John Wesley (1703–1791) and his brother Charles (1707–1788) and, after the Baptists, the largest Protestant family in the United States. The "Methodist" moniker, like many in religious history, derives from opponents who used the term derisively, but the Wesleys wore it with pride to refer to their methodical pursuit of Christian holiness. One of the Methodists' distinctive teachings concerns the Christian doctrine of sanctification. According to John Wesley, sanctification culminated in a second work of grace—the first was salvation—which perfected the believer in love. This idea of Christian perfectionism helped to fuel many nineteenth-century social reform movements, including the campaign to abolish slavery.

Methodism spread rapidly in the United States during the Second Great Awakening of the nineteenth century, thanks to the Methodists' willingness to send unlettered "circuit riders" into the frontier and the determination of these missionaries to preach in the vernacular of ordinary people. By the 1840s Methodism was the largest Christian group in the United States.

The Wesleyan tradition is carried forward in contemporary America by the United Methodist Church, whose 10.4 million members make it the second largest American Protestant denomination after the Southern Baptist Convention. The largest African American Methodist bodies are the African Methodist Episcopal (established 1816) and the African Methodist Episcopal Zion (1820), which together number about 5 million. Although Methodists initially believed that an educated clergy produced flaccid faith, they went on to establish seminaries at Boston University, Vanderbilt, Emory, Duke, Drew, and other institutions of higher learning. Additional Methodist legacies include the Holiness movement, which emphasized sanctification and perfectionism even more than the Methodists, and Pentecostalism, which extended Wesley's two-step formula of salvation and sanctification into a third step: baptism of the Holy Spirit.

millennialism. See dispensational premillennialism.

monotheism. Belief shared by Jews, Christians, Muslims, and others that there is only one god. (By contrast, polytheism affirms the existence of multiple gods and atheism denies them all.) In 1954 the US Congress inserted the phrase "under God" into the Pledge of Allegiance, suggesting that the United States is officially monotheistic—a view reinforced after 9/11 by repeated public references to the country as a Judeo-Christian-Islamic nation and by the Supreme Court's refusal to take "under God" out of the pledge in *Elk Grove Unified School District v. Newdow* (2004). Opponents of monotheism include Buddhists who typically affirm no divinity and Hindus who typically affirm many, though it should be noted that many Hindus call themselves monotheists.

Moral Majority. The most visible and powerful instrument of the Religious Right during the Reagan Revolution of the 1980s. This pressure group was founded in 1979 by the Reverend Jerry Falwell (b. 1933), a fundamentalist Baptist pastor, Liberty University chancellor, and televangelist. The group defined itself not in narrowly Baptist or even Christian terms but as a Judeo-Christian organization open to Protestants, Catholics, and Jews committed to promoting "family values" by opposing pornography, homosexuality, abortion, feminism, and secular humanism. After helping to send California's governor, Ronald Reagan, to the White House in 1980, the group drew fire from the Secular Left for ostensibly violating the separation of church and state. From the right, *Faith for the Family* magazine of Bob Jones University criticized the Moral Majority for selling Jesus out to politics, blasting the group as "one of Satan's devices to build the world church of Antichrist."[269] With the Religious Right a fixture on the American political scene, Falwell dissolved the organization in 1989, the same year that another religious broadcaster, Pat Robertson, established a like-minded but more narrowly Christian pressure group called the Christian Coalition. Since that time Falwell has continued to stir the pot of the culture wars, particularly on matters of sexual ethics. On September 13, 2001, Falwell pinned blame for 9/11 on "the pagans, and the abortionists, and the feminists, and the gays and lesbians ... who have tried to secularize America."

Mormonism. Religious movement founded in New York in the 1820s by Joseph Smith Jr. (1805–1844). According to Smith, an angel revealed to him the location of gold tablets buried in the fifth century in modern-day upstate New York. Smith found the tablets, used two seer stones to translate their "Reformed Egyptian" into English, and published the resulting Book of Mormon in 1830. In that book, which Mormons view as scripture, Jesus visits the New World after his resurrection and before his ascension, founding his true church among Native Americans.

Widely persecuted for their distinctive beliefs and practices (which came to include polygamy), Mormons moved westward from New York to Ohio and Missouri before settling in Illinois, where Smith was arrested, jailed, and then killed by a mob in 1844. Mormons later migrated under the direction of Brigham Young (1801–1877) to Utah, where they established something of a theocratic state. After the Church of Jesus Christ of Latter-day Saints (the official name of the largest Mormon church) renounced polygamy in 1890, Utah was admitted into the Union as the forty-fifth state.

Mormons recognize four scriptures: the Bible ("as far as it is translated correctly"), the Book of Mormon, Pearl of Great Price, and Doctrine and Covenants. But they also believe in ongoing revelation, investing in their successive presidents the power of prophecy. In 1978 President Spencer Kimball announced a revelation that lifted a prior ban on African American men becoming priests. Today Mormons' distinctive practices include baptism for the dead and marriage for eternity, and their distinctive beliefs include the corporeality of God and the eternal progression of humans into godhood. Mormons also follow a health code called the Word of Wisdom, which prohibits the ingestion of tobacco, alcohol, and caffeine.

Mormonism was widely discussed in the United States during the 2002 Winter Olympics, held in the shadow of LDS international headquarters in Salt Lake City, Utah. Although once seen as un-American, Mormons are now viewed by many as quintessentially American. The LDS Church reports over 4 million members in the United States and 12 million worldwide and is one of the world's fastest growing religious movements. Some have predicted that Mormonism is well on its way to becoming the first great world religion since Islam. It has already become an American political force. Mormons were overrepresented relative to their total population in the 109th Congress, and in 2006 the governors of both Utah and Massachusetts were LDS members.

Moses. The most important figure in the history of Judaism and, according to Muslims and Christians, a great prophet. Moses is remembered today as the man who received the Ten Commandments on Mount Sinai and led the Israelites on the Exodus out of bondage in Egypt. According to the Pentateuch, the five books of the Hebrew Bible attributed to Moses, he was born in Egypt, hidden in reeds in the Nile River after Pharaoh ordered the slaughter of all male Israelite babies, and discovered by Pharaoh's daughter, who raised him in luxury as her son. After Moses fled his life as an adopted prince, God spoke to him from a burning bush, commanding him to lead the Israelites out of slavery and into the Promised Land. Moses then appealed to Pharaoh to "let my people go." When Pharaoh refused, God sent ten plagues against Egypt. Pharaoh finally relented, but when Moses led his people out of Egypt Pharaoh's armies pursued them. At the Red Sea God miraculously parted the waters, allowing Moses and the Israelites to cross onto dry land, but as Pharaoh's armies pursued them God ordered the waters to return and the soldiers drowned. At Mount Sinai God gave Moses the Torah, or Law. For forty years Moses led the Israelites through the wilderness and to the edge of the land promised by God to Abraham's descendants. But he died at the age of 120 before he could enter into Canaan.

Moses's afterlife in the United States—where he has figured in films such as *The Ten Commandments* (1956) and *The Prince of Egypt* (1998) and novels such as Zora Neale Hurston's *Moses, Man of the Mountain* (1939) and William Faulkner's *Go Down, Moses* (1942)—is almost as extensive as that of Jesus. In the African American tradition, notably in slave spirituals, Jesus is a Black Moses who saves his people from sin and delivers them from bondage. Many have seen the Reverend Martin Luther King Jr. as a Moses figure, particularly after he yoked the story of the Exodus to his hope for freedom for all Americans in his 1963 "I Have a Dream" speech.

mosque/masjid. A place where Muslims assemble for congregational prayer on Fridays is called a mosque in English or a *masjid* ("place of prostration") in Arabic. Classically, mosques have a minaret from which a call to prayer is issued five times a day. They also feature fountains equipped with running water for ritual ablutions, a niche in the wall facing Mecca called a *mihrab,* and, near the *mihrab,* an elevated pulpit from which a sermon is given during Friday worship. Mosques also function as educational centers, where students come for instruction in the Quran, hadith, and Islamic law. The three most important mosques in the Muslim world are in Mecca, Medina, and Jerusalem.

Muhammad (570–632 CE). The founder and last prophet of Islam, and the vehicle through whom God revealed the Quran. Muhammad was born in Mecca in 570 CE, raised as an orphan, and buried in Medina in 632. He received his first revelation from God at roughly the age of forty, when the angel Gabriel appeared to him in a cave outside Mecca and commanded him to "recite." The words he subsequently recited were memorized by his followers and eventually written down as the Quran. As a trader, Muhammad was exposed both to indigenous polytheistic traditions and to monotheistic Christians and Jews. The revelations he received emphasized the oneness of God (*tawhid*). So did his subsequent preaching, which earned him not only his first followers (including his wife Khadijah) but also opponents in polytheistic Mecca. Hostility to his preaching there prompted Muhammad to flee with his followers to Medina, where they established the Muslim community (*ummah*). This flight (*hijra*) from Mecca happened in 622, which now serves as the first year in the Muslim lunar calendar. In 630 Muhammad and his army conquered Mecca and cleansed the area around the ancient Kaaba shrine of idol worshippers. He died two years later in 632.

During his lifetime Muhammad established himself as not only a prophet but also a patriarch—after Khadijah's death he took multiple wives—and a political, legal, and military leader. He was also a diplomat, embracing Jews and Christians not as mortal enemies but as "people of the book" with legitimate, though corrupted, revelations delivered through prophets by the one true God. Muslims also see Muhammad as a spiritual and moral exemplar. The hadith, a Muslim textual tradition second in importance only to the Quran, records his sayings and actions so that Muslims might imitate both. Although often compared with Jesus in Christianity, he is actually more comparable to the Virgin Mary, since it was through him (by tradition an illiterate man) that God delivered his revelation (the Quran in this case) to the world.

In 1987 a book called *The 100: A Ranking of the Most Influential Persons in History* tapped Muhammad as the most influential person ever, chiefly because (unlike Jesus) he was both a spiritual and a political man, the founder of a new religion and its first leader. American televangelists have a much lower opinion of Muhammad. After 9/11 televangelist Jerry Falwell called him "a man of war" and "a terrorist." Pastor Jerry Vines, former president of the Southern Baptist Convention, called him "a demon-possessed pedophile." Muslims, however, continue to recall Muhammad as the final prophet and "a beautiful example," as he is called in the Quran. In Islamic speech, the phrase "peace be upon him" follows any mention of his name.

Nation of Islam. See Black Muslims.

nativity. The birth of Jesus in a Bethlehem stable. A number of Supreme Court rulings on the First Amendment's establishment clause have concerned the constitutionality of nativity scenes (or crèches) on public property. These cases have not produced particularly clear general guidelines, so some legal scholars have read into them a principle called the "Three-Reindeer Rule." According to this oft-cited (and ridiculed) rule, a nativity scene passes constitutional muster as long as it incorporates sufficient symbols from other religions (Hanukkah menorahs or dreidels, for example) or from secular life (Santas, candy canes, and reindeers) to signal to any "reasonable observer" that the purpose of the display is something other than endorsing Christianity.

New Testament. The second portion of the Christian Bible (after the Old Testament), canonized by Christians in the fourth century. The New Testament consists of twenty-seven different books: four Gospels (Matthew, Mark, Luke, and John); a narrative of the early church (Acts); twenty-one letters, many attributed to Paul; and an apocalyptic text called Revelation. The New Testament has conveyed to the world not only Christianity but also a vast inventory of characters, places, sayings, and stories—from Doubting Thomas to Calvary to "The truth shall make you free" to the Parable of the Mustard Seed—which in turn have supplied artists, novelists, filmmakers, and politicians with an endless supply of inspiration.

nirvana. The ultimate goal of Buddhism, variously described as the extinction of suffering, emancipation from ignorance, and liberation from the cycle of birth, life, death, and rebirth (*samsara*). Mahayana Buddhists believe that the apparent distinction between nirvana and *samsara* is illusory; this world of suffering is itself nirvana. Nirvana, which literally means "blowing out," was also the name of the grunge band headlined by Kurt Cobain (1967–1994) and is a generic term in American English for paradise.

Noah. Righteous man ridiculed for building an ark on dry land but vindicated when a great flood came. According to Genesis 6–9, God decides to destroy the world because it has become so corrupt. But he warns Noah, commanding him to build a great ship for himself and his family and to stock it with a male and a female of all the animals. After many days of rain, Noah sends out birds in search of land. A dove returns with an olive leaf, indicating that the waters are receding. As Noah leaves the ark, God promises never to destroy the world again by water and seals the covenant with a rainbow. This story, which has sparked a series of Bible-believing adventurers to search for the lost ark, is paralleled in flood stories in other cultures, including Mesopotamia's Gilgamesh epic.

nonviolence. See ahimsa.

Old Testament. The first portion of the Christian Bible, preceding the New Testament. Protestant Bibles divide the twenty-four books of the Hebrew Bible into thirty-nine books. Catholic Bibles include seven additional books regarded by Protestants as noncanonical Apocrypha, for a total of forty-six. Jews, who do not accept the New Testament or Apocrypha as scripture, do not refer to these books as the Old Testament. The Old Testament narrates the adventures of the Israelites, including a series of covenants made by God with Adam, Noah, Abraham, and Moses. Christians understand the Old Testament to prophesy and foreshadow the birth and death of Jesus. The Old Testament has inspired countless artists, novelists, and filmmakers with characters such as Samson and Delilah, stories such as the Tower of Babel and the Flood, and passages of wisdom and prophecy in books such as Proverbs and Isaiah.

Orthodox Christianity. Along with Protestantism and Roman Catholicism, one of Christianity's three main branches. Orthodoxy split from Roman Catholicism in 1054 over the now arcane matter of whether the Holy Spirit proceeds from the Father alone (the Orthodox position) or from both the Father and Son (as the Catholics claimed). Orthodox Christianity is led today by patriarchs with authority in their own nations yet in communion with one another. (There is no Orthodox pope.) Of all the dimensions of religion, Orthodox piety emphasizes ritual, more specifically the celebration of the Eucharist—the "mystery of mysteries"—which is done in a high style, complete with incense, sacred music, and colorful clerical vestments. When it comes to priests and marriage, the Orthodox split the difference between Protestantism and Catholicism, allowing parish priests to marry but insisting on celibacy for bishops (who are recruited from the monastic ranks). Orthodox Christians practice baptism by immersion and call confirmation chrismation (because of its use of holy oil, or *chrism*). Finally, this tradition makes considerable use of icons, so much so that Orthodoxy can be described as Christianity conveyed through sight.

Orthodox Christians arrived in North America as early as a 1794 Russian mission to Alaska, but their numbers remained small until immigration from Greece, Russia, and other Orthodox countries picked up in the late nineteenth and early twentieth centuries. There are roughly 100 million Orthodox Christians in the world, with perhaps 5 million in the United States. The largest Orthodox group in the United States is the Greek Orthodox Archdiocese of America.

Orthodox Judaism. One of three main branches in Judaism—alongside Reform and Conservative—and the most traditional. Although the term *orthodox* refers to "correct doctrine," what really distinguishes Orthodox Judaism from other forms is orthopraxy, or correct practice, more specifically strict adherence to both oral and written Law, which it regards as divinely inspired. So, for example, Orthodox Jews strictly observe the Sabbath and eat only kosher food. This community is divided into Modern Orthodox Jews and Haredi Jews (including Hasidic Jews). Of these two groups, the Modern Orthodox are more open to secular influences and Haredis most zealous about separating themselves from non-Jewish influences. Orthodox Jews arrived in the New World as early as 1654, and they came in significant numbers from Eastern Europe between the 1880s and the 1920s. Orthodox institutions in the United States include New York's Yeshiva University and the Union of Orthodox Jewish Congregations of America.

Paul. First-century church leader, author of many New Testament epistles, and according to some the real founder of Christianity. Born Jewish, Paul (whose given name was Saul) was a Pharisee and a persecutor of Christians. According to Acts 9:1–19, he saw the resurrected Christ on the road to Damascus and converted to Christianity. He then traveled widely, preaching the gospel as he understood it to Jews and Gentiles alike. According to church tradition, he was arrested, tried, and executed under the Roman emperor Nero in roughly 65 CE. Scholars typically regard seven of the letters attributed to Paul as authentically his; the other six are disputed. His authentic letters, which date from the fifties, are earlier than the Gospels, and their theology profoundly shaped both ancient and modern Christianity.

Martin Luther's reading of Paul's Letter to the Romans as a brief for "justification by grace through faith" set the Protestant Reformation in motion, but Paul has long been a contested figure in American life. Many Americans perceive a yawning gap between the ideals of Jesus and the realities of institutional Christianity, and some blame Paul for turning Jesus' faith into "Churchianity." Some African Americans, noting Paul's insistence that slaves obey their masters, have even refused to read the letters of Paul aloud in their churches. Still, Paul remains a towering figure in Christian history, second in importance only to Jesus.

Pentecostalism. Protestant movement that affirms that the gifts of the Holy Spirit manifested among the apostles on the first day of Pentecost (in Acts 2) are still available today. Pentecostals emphasize experience and downplay doctrine. Like evangelicals, they affirm the centrality of conversion, but in addition they insist on the importance of a second experience of grace, which they refer to as baptism in the Spirit. This "second baptism" can instill such charismatic gifts as glossolalia (speaking in tongues), prophecy, and healing. Modern Pentecostalism, which grew out of the Methodist and Holiness traditions, dates from the Asuza Street Revival, which saw speaking in tongues and other charismatic gifts break out among a mixed-race group in Los Angeles in 1906. It came into the national spotlight through the ministrations of Aimee Semple McPherson (1890–1944)—"Sister Aimee" to her fans—whose radio ministry and flamboyant preaching at the five-thousand-seat Angelus Temple in Los Angeles in the 1920s made her the most famous female preacher in American history.

Controversy has followed Pentecostalism almost from the start. In 1926, at the height of her popularity, McPherson disappeared, reportedly the victim of a kidnapping. But many believe that McPherson ran off with a lover and that she died of a drug overdose. In the late 1980s sex scandals involving two Pentecostal preachers—Jim Bakker (b. 1939), the founder of the PTL ("Praise the Lord") television network, and another televangelist, Jimmy Swaggart (b. 1935)—rocked the movement. Still, Pentecostalism is one of the fastest growing religious movements in the world.

Though Pentecostalism was originally a movement of the dispossessed, it has increasingly attracted middle-class Americans. Worldwide, however, this "third force in Christianity" continues to appeal to the poor. Because Pentecostalism is fractured into tens of thousands of denominations, membership figures are hard to come by. An estimate of 20 million members in the United States and at least 100 million worldwide seems reasonable, though some sources have fixed the global figure as high as 600 million. The largest white Pentecostal denomination in the United States, the Assemblies of God, claims 2.6 million members. America's largest black Pentecostal group is the Church of God in Christ.

Pharisees. After Democrats in Georgia and Alabama started agitating for Bible classes in the public schools in the early twenty-first century, Republicans denounced them as "modern-day Pharisees" on the grounds that they were exploiting religion for political gain. This term originally referred to Jews around the time of Jesus who were known for their openness to oral traditions and their belief in the bodily resurrection. The

Sadducees, by contrast, were wary of oral traditions and rejected the resurrection of the body. Jesus criticizes the Pharisees in the New Testament for being overly legalistic on such matters as the observation of the Sabbath. The apostle Paul was a Pharisee who joined the early Christian movement and eventually came to believe that God's grace trumps law.

polytheism. Belief in multiple gods. Hinduism is typically described as polytheistic, though many Hindus insist that behind the myriad manifestations of divinity is one Absolute Reality.

pope. This title, which derives from the Greek term for "father," refers to the bishop of Rome, who simultaneously serves as the leader of the Roman Catholic Church and the head of state of Vatican City. Catholics believe that the authority of the pope derives from apostolic succession—an unbroken line of Christian leaders going back to the apostle Peter, whose authority was vested in him by Jesus himself. Since the First Vatican Council of 1870, Catholics have affirmed that the pope can speak infallibly on matters of faith and morals. One long-standing concern in American political life has been that Catholic politicians would take their marching orders not from the people who elected them but from the pope. Responding to this concern, Massachusetts senator John Kennedy pledged during his 1960 presidential campaign that he would neither request not accept political advice or instructions from any pope. "I am not the Catholic candidate for president," Kennedy said, but a candidate "who happens also to be a Catholic."

predestination. Belief that God has predetermined the eternal destiny of each individual, assigning the elect to heaven and (in the case of "double predestination") the damned to hell. This view, which accents God's sovereignty at the expense of human free will, characterized the theology of the Swiss theologian John Calvin and, through him, Puritanism and other expressions of Reformed theology. The most famous opponent of predestination was the Dutchman Jacob Arminius (1559–1609), whose "Arminian" theology insisted that human beings were free to cooperate with God in their salvation or damnation. Divine sovereignty trounced free will at the Synod of Dort (1618–1619) and in the Westminster Confession (1647), both of which affirmed predestination, but Arminianism routed Calvinism during the Second Great Awakening and predominates among American Christians today.

Presbyterianism. Two distinguishing marks, one doctrinal and the other ecclesiastical, distinguish Presbyterianism (from the Greek term *presbuteros,* or elder) from other mainline Protestant denominations. In terms of doctrine, Presbyterians adhere to the Reformed theology of John Calvin as expressed in the Westminster Confession (1646). In terms of church governance, Presbyterians distinguish themselves from both Episcopalian polity (which has bishops) and Congregational governance (where local churches are sovereign) by maintaining a system of congregations, presbyteries (geographical units comprising many congregations), synods (composed of clergy and lay leaders elected by presbyteries), and a general assembly (composed of synods). American Presbyterians split over revivalism, slavery, and fundamentalism but managed to grow into one of the country's leading Protestant families. Their largest denomination, with 3.1 million members, is the Presbyterian Church (USA). Although Presbyterians make up less than 3 percent of the current US population, they held nearly 10 percent of the seats in the 109th Congress and have accounted for nearly one-quarter of all US presidents. This denomination's long-standing commitment to education is evident in many theological schools, including Princeton Theological Seminary (established 1812).

Prodigal Son. Character in one of the most popular parables of Jesus (Luke 15:11–32). This son leaves his home and family with money his father has given him. But he soon squanders it all. Returning home, he begs for his father's forgiveness, and surprisingly his father welcomes him back with a grand celebration. Allusions to this story, which also features a good son convinced that his father's mercy is unjust, recur in the works of Shakespeare and throughout Western art.

Promised Land. In the Hebrew Bible, the land of Canaan promised by God to Abraham and claimed by the people of Israel following their exile. The longing for this "land flowing with milk and honey" (Exodus 3:8) contributed mightily to Zionism and the creation of the state of Israel, but the Promised Land is also a recurring image in American history. The Pilgrims saw the New World as a Promised Land, African slaves saw the North as their Canaan, and Mormons saw Utah as theirs. Many American spirituals and hymns conflate heaven with the Promised Land. The most famous use of this phrase in American public life occurs in the "I've Been to the Mountaintop" speech the Reverend Martin Luther King Jr. delivered on April 3, 1968, one day before his assassination. "It really doesn't matter what happens now," King said. "Like anybody, I would like to live a long life. Longevity has its place, but I'm not concerned about that now. I just want to do God's will. And He's allowed me to go up to the mountain. And I've looked over, and I've seen the Promised Land. I may not get there with you. But I want you to know tonight, that we, as a people, will get to the Promised Land."

Protestantism. One of Christianity's three main branches, along with Orthodoxy and Roman Catholicism, and the dominant form of American Christianity. As the name implies, Protestantism began as a protest. In sixteenth-century Europe, thinkers such as Martin Luther and John Calvin harshly criticized the Roman Catholic Church, and, thanks to advances in literacy and print technology, these criticisms reached a large and ready audience. Whereas Catholics had long argued that salvation results from both faith and works, these reformers insisted on *sola fide* ("faith alone"). Whereas Catholics had based their tradition on the authority of both the Bible and tradition, Protestants insisted on the authority of the Bible alone (*sola scriptura*). Protestants also whittled the Catholics' seven sacraments down to two: baptism and Holy Communion. Other distinctive beliefs of the Reformation included "the priesthood of all believers," an egalitarian posture that elevated the status of the laity at the expense of priests.

As Protestantism broke with the pope and set off on its own, it formed four main branches: Lutheranism, Calvinism, Anglicanism, and Anabaptism. Lutherans followed the lead of Luther and were particularly strong in Germany and Scandinavian countries. The Calvinist or Reformed tradition looked for leadership to Calvin and the Swiss theologian Ulrich Zwingli. It produced the Puritan impulse as well as three key denominational families: Presbyterians, Baptists, and Congregationalists. The Anglican tradition emerged when King Henry VIII set himself up as the head of the Church of England in 1534. It later gave birth to Methodism, which gestated the Holiness and Pentecostal movements. The most radical wing of the Reformation, the Anabaptists (or "rebaptizers"), insisted on adult rather than infant baptism, the strict separation of church and state, and pacifism. Groups such as the Mennonites and the Amish developed out of this Anabaptist branch.

Puritanism. Sixteenth-century Protestant movement to "purify" the Church of England of unscriptural beliefs and practices, particularly lingering vestiges of Roman Catholicism (including the celebration of

Christmas). The most radical Puritans—the Pilgrims among them—separated from the Church of England, which they regarded as apostate; nonseparating Puritans sought to change the Church of England from within. Many immigrants to the British colonies were Puritans, and Puritanism became the dominant theology in New England in the seventeenth and eighteenth centuries. Puritans came to the New World in search of religious freedom, but they did not extend that courtesy to others. Separation of church and state was unknown to them; they sought to create "Holy Commonwealths"—in Massachusetts Bay, Plymouth, Connecticut, and New Haven—that dealt strictly, sometimes lethally, with Quakers, Baptists, and other dissenters who did not share their understanding of scripture.

American Puritanism was dominated by Calvinism, or Reformed theology, which originated with the thought of the Swiss theologian John Calvin. Much of the dynamism of Puritan thought derived from two Calvinist emphases: the absolute sovereignty of God and the total depravity of human beings. Given God's power and human sinfulness, Puritans were convinced that salvation was not a matter of individual free will; God had predestined all human beings either to heaven or to hell. Although Puritans have often been described as priggish and prudish—hence the term *puritanical*—they were not killjoys. Regarding alcohol as the "good creature of God," they drank liberally at weddings, ordinations, and funerals. Their religion, moreover, was not as pure as many Puritan thinkers would have liked. Few Puritans took their Calvinist theology neat. They told folktales, read the stars for signs and portents, dabbled in magic, and heeded the dreams and visions of "cunning folk."

Along with evangelicalism, Puritanism is one of the two most influential religious movements in American history. It profoundly influenced the Presbyterians and the Congregationalists. It also bequeathed to evangelicalism an emphasis on experience, particularly the experience of conversion, and on *sola scriptura,* or "scripture alone." But far more than evangelicals, Puritans valued the doctrinal and narrative dimensions of religion, believing that learning was a matter of the head as well as the heart.

Quakers. Pacifist Protestant group founded in England in the 1650s by George Fox (1624–1691). Officially known as the Religious Society of Friends, Quakers believe that individuals should follow their God-given "Inner Light" rather than external authorities. Their name may derive from an exchange between Fox and a British judge; after Fox instructed the judge to "tremble at the Word of the Lord," the judge reportedly called him "a quaker." Friends, as Quakers are also called, are best known for their opposition to war and for their refusal to take oaths. Their distinctive services, which forgo both clergy and sacraments, emphasize silence and spontaneity.

Quakers played an important role in early American history. Quaker William Penn (1644–1718) founded Pennsylvania in 1681 as a safe haven for Quakers and granted liberty of conscience to all but atheists. Quakers also played key roles in nineteenth-century social reform movements, including the campaign for woman's suffrage. Their belief in the equality of all human beings before God—a belief manifested in their refusal to tip their hats to monarchs—propelled them to the forefront of the abolitionist movement. The American Friends Service Committee, founded by Quakers in 1917, remains a key voice on issues of peace, justice, and human rights. Both President Nixon and President Herbert Hoover were Friends (though of the "fighting Quaker" sort). Today the Religious Society of Friends is a small denomination with roughly one hundred thousand American members.

Quran (lit. "recitation"). The holy book of Islam, the final revelation of Allah, and the ultimate authority for Muslims in law, religion, and ethics. Muslims affirm that this scripture was miraculously revealed by Allah via the angel Gabriel to Muhammad, recited by Muhammad, memorized by his companions, written down by scribes, and later compiled into a codex. The first revelation came in 610 CE, and the official version was canonized (in Arabic) decades after Muhammad's death in 632. While Muslims affirm that the Hebrew and Christian Bibles were revealed by God, they believe that both scriptures have been corrupted over time. The Quran, by contrast, exists today just as it was originally delivered. It is authoritative only in the Arabic original; translations are understood to be human products.

The Quran, which is about as long as the New Testament, consists of 114 chapters or suras, which vary in length from 3 to 286 ayas (verses), organized largely from longest to shortest. Commentators divide these chapters into recitations received by Muhammad in Mecca (Meccan suras) and those received by him after his flight to Medina (Medinan suras). The Quran's first sura is the Fatihah ("The Opening"):

In the name of Allah, the Beneficent, the Merciful.
Praise be to Allah, Lord of the Worlds,

The Beneficent, the Merciful.
Master of the Day of Judgment,
Thee (alone) we worship; Thee (alone) we ask for help.
Show us the straight path,
The path of those whom Thou hast favored; Not the (path) of those
    who earn Thine anger nor of those who go astray.

The best way for newcomers to read the Quran is not from front to back but from back to front. Start with the Fatihah, but then skip to the shorter, more theological suras in the back. Then read the narratives of the prophets (toward the middle) before concluding with the legalistic content of the long suras at the front.

In addition to the unity of God and the prophethood of Muhammad, the Quran teaches the bodily resurrection and a coming judgment. It requires prayers and almsgiving and fasting and pilgrimage. It portrays a world in which one God repeatedly reveals his will to human beings through prophets and messengers that stretch from Moses to Jesus to Muhammad. Jesus is mentioned nearly one hundred times in the Quran, where he is hailed as both miracle worker and messiah. Though Muslims affirm the virgin birth of Jesus, they do not believe that he was killed on a cross or raised from the dead. They believe instead that he ascended into paradise.

After 9/11, and particularly after it was learned that one of the hijackers had a Quran in his suitcase, interest in the Quran skyrocketed in the United States. "Anyone concerned with what's happening in our world ought to spend some time reading the Quran," CBS commentator Andy Rooney said, and for months after 9/11 Qurans outsold Bibles in many bookstores. Although awareness of the Quran is new to the United States, controversies about this scripture are not unknown. In 2002 conservative Christian groups protested after the University of North Carolina at Chapel Hill assigned a book on the Quran to its incoming students. In 2005 the US military admitted to mishandling the Quran at its prison at Guantanamo Bay, Cuba. And some Muslims testifying in US courts have asked judges to allow them to swear in on the Quran rather than the Bible.

Ramadan. Period of obligatory fasting from dawn to sunset, observed by Muslims during the ninth month of the Islamic year. This month, which ends with Eid al-Fitr, the feast of the breaking of the fast, commemorates the first revelation of the Quran to Muhammad. A significant minority of

NBA basketball players are observant Muslims, and the decisions of Hakeem Olajuwon, Shareef Abdur-Rahim, and others to fast during Ramadan have called public attention to the holiday, just as Sandy Koufax's decision, as a Jew, not to pitch in a 1965 World Series game on Yom Kippur focused public attention on that Day of Atonement. It is now traditional for US presidents to send greetings to Muslims and to host fast-breaking dinners at the White House during Ramadan. Travelers, the sick, the elderly, children, and pregnant and nursing women are generally exempt from fasting during Ramadan.

Reform Judaism. One of the three main branches in Judaism—alongside Orthodox and Conservative—and the most liberal. Like liberal Protestantism, Reform Judaism is in part a product of the eighteenth-century Enlightenment. It achieved clear expression in the United States in the Pittsburgh Platform (1885), in which Reform rabbis referred to Judaism as "a progressive religion, ever striving to be in accord with the postulates of reason" and accepted as binding only the moral (as opposed to the ritual and dietary) laws of their tradition. Unlike Orthodox Jews, Reform Jews ordain women and worship in vernacular languages. And while Orthodox Jews trace Jewish identity through the mother only, Reform Jews typically view a child as Jewish if either parent was. Reform Judaism is represented in the United States in Hebrew Union College–Jewish Institute of Religion and the Union of American Hebrew Congregations. It is the largest branch of American Judaism, claiming 39 percent of America's religious Jews.

Reformation. Movement in sixteenth-century Europe that intended to reform the Roman Catholic Church but instead gave birth to Protestantism. Sparked in 1517 in Wittenberg, Germany, when Martin Luther published his Ninety-five Theses against indulgences (payments for the remission of sins), the Reformation spread across Europe, producing four types of Protestantism: the Lutheran, Reformed, Anglican, and Anabaptist traditions. The key slogans of the Reformation were "justification by grace through faith," "the priesthood of all believers," and *sola scriptura* (Bible alone). Its key impulse was rejection of papal and priestly authority in the name of individual conscience—an impulse that would produce thousands of different Protestant denominations and redraw the map of Europe.

Reformed theology. See Calvinism.

reincarnation. Belief, common among Hindus, that souls take on new bodies after death as part of a never-ending cycle of birth, death, life, and rebirth known as *samsara*. Buddhists also affirm reincarnation, but because they deny the existence of an eternal soul, they typically contend that it is one's consciousness that is reborn. Most of those who affirm reincarnation understand this process to be driven by karma, or the law of actions and their consequences. According to this law, the rebirth you get is the rebirth you deserve. Although reincarnation derives from Asian religions, roughly one-quarter of US Christians believe in it too. However, while Asian religious practitioners typically understand reincarnation to be undesirable—their ultimate goal is to escape from *samsara* (and thus from rebirth)—Americans who affirm reincarnation typically see it as a welcome opportunity to do things in the next life that they could not do in this one.

Religious Right. Religiously inspired political movement, dating from the late 1970s, of conservative Christians groups seeking to revive "family values" and ransom the nation from moral bankruptcy. These groups included the Moral Majority, founded by televangelist Jerry Falwell in 1979, and the Christian Coalition, founded by religious broadcaster Pat Robertson in 1989. The Religious Right's formidable grassroots power derived from widespread antipathy among many evangelicals and fundamentalists to a series of culture shocks delivered in the 1960s and 1970s. These shocks included Supreme Court rulings banning school prayer and devotional Bible reading in the early 1960s, the *Roe v. Wade* decision legalizing abortion in 1973, and an obscure 1978 IRS ruling that stripped tax-exempt status from Christian schools that discriminated on the basis of race. Together these developments signaled to conservative religious activists that "secular humanism" was becoming America's unofficial religious establishment.

For the most part, the Religious Right focuses its political efforts on bedroom issues such as homosexuality, pornography, and abortion. It works through a vast network of state and local groups, many led by Christian ministers who use their pulpits, membership rolls, and church buses to get out the vote. The Religious Right has been credited with helping to elect presidents from Ronald Reagan to George W. Bush. It has also been widely criticized by liberal groups such as Norman Lear's People for the American Way, who contend that its faith-based political activism violates the separation of church and state.

resurrection. Belief that the dead will rise on some future day to stand for final judgment. This doctrine, which foresees the reunion of souls with the bodies lost to them at death, is closely associated with the Jewish, Christian, and Islamic conviction that a person is an indivisible combination of body and soul. Resurrection belief appears in Judaism fairly late— in such apocalyptic texts as 2 Maccabees, written a century before the life of Jesus. It was later adopted and adapted by Christians, for whom the resurrection of Jesus, celebrated on Easter, is a central affirmation. Bodily resurrection is also a Muslim belief. Today Orthodox Jews continue to affirm this doctrine, but many Reform Jews either believe simply in the immortality of the soul or prefer not to speculate about the afterlife. The Apostles' Creed of the Christians affirms "the resurrection of the body," but Christians disagree about what shape this body will take in heaven. (1 Corinthians 15:44 says the "natural body," which is buried, will become a "spiritual body.") Belief in the resurrection is closely tied to the tradition of martyrdom, whose logic demands that God mete out rewards and punishments in the afterlife. Like the doctrine of the bodily resurrection, martyrdom is a Jewish development that makes its way into Christianity and Islam.

revivalism. Revivals are Christian worship services that produce mass conversions and intensify the commitments of existing Christians, often through ecstatic sermons and emotional songs. Revivalism, therefore, is the impulse to affirm and produce such revivals. This impulse was most visible in the Great Awakening of the early eighteenth century and the Second Great Awakening of a century later. It also manifested in the great urban revivals of Dwight Moody, Billy Sunday, and Billy Graham, which drew on many of the "new measures" promoted in the 1830s by the master of American revivalism, Charles Grandison Finney. Although some revivals have proceeded on a Calvinist basis, most have been informed by Arminianism, the view that every human being is free to accept or reject the saving grace offered by Jesus' death upon the cross. Revivals have been most popular among evangelicals and fundamentalists and among Methodist, Baptist, Holiness, and Pentecostal groups. Because revivalism typically appeals to the heart rather than the head, its techniques have drawn fire from Lutherans, Episcopalians, and other confessional Christians who believe that revivals produce believers with little or no real understanding of what they are supposed to believe.

Roman Catholicism. See Catholicism, Roman.

Sabbath. The seventh day of the week, designated by Jews as a day of rest because according to Genesis God worked to create the world for six days and then rested on the seventh. According to the Ten Commandments, work is forbidden on this day, and over time this day of rest also became a day for worship. Jews traditionally observe the Sabbath on Saturday and Christians on Sunday. Seventh-Day Adventists, however, observe a Saturday Sabbath. Blue laws, which restrict activities on Sundays (notably the sale of alcohol), are one example of the enduring force of the Sabbatarian ideal on American culture.

sacraments. See 7 sacraments.

Sadducees. See Pharisees.

Satan. The personification of evil and God's primary antagonist in Judaism, Christianity, and Islam. Also known as Lucifer and the devil and widely described as a fallen angel, Satan (from the Hebrew word for "adversary") has had a long life in the United States. Witches in seventeenth-century New England were accused of sidling up to him. Rock musicians claimed to have sold their souls to him in exchange for artistic greatness. And he appeared as a character in dozens of feature films and television shows, including *The Exorcist* (1973) and *South Park*. There is even a Church of Satan, founded in San Francisco in 1966 by Anton LaVey (1930–1997), who was also the author of *The Satanic Bible* (1969). Ayatollah Khomeini, the Shiite cleric who led the Iranian Revolution of 1979, famously referred to the United States as "the Great Satan."

Scientology. One of the most successful new religious movements of the twentieth century, founded in 1953 by science fiction writer L. Ron Hubbard (1911–1986) and outlined in his best seller, *Dianetics: The Modern Science of Mental Health* (1950). Like Buddhism, Scientology seeks to uproot suffering, which is caused according to Scientologists when one's "engrams" (ingrained records of past experiences, including those in past lives) cause one's "reactive mind" to repeat destructive behaviors. Scientologists who are able to accomplish this task are called "Clears." Conservative Christian groups have denounced Scientology as a "cult of greed," but the movement has attracted many prominent celebrities, including actors John Travolta and Tom Cruise.

Scopes Trial. Trial of John Scopes for violating a law forbidding the teaching of evolution in public schools, held in Dayton, Tennessee, in 1925. This "Monkey Trial" featured two famous lawyers: the skeptic Clarence Darrow and the fundamentalist politician William Jennings Bryan. Scopes was convicted, but Darrow trounced Bryan in the court of public opinion, which mercilessly ridiculed fundamentalists as ignorant rubes. Fundamentalists responded to this humiliation by withdrawing from public view for decades, focusing during the 1930s, 1940s, and 1950s on building their own subculture of Bible schools, seminaries, radio stations, and publishing houses. They reemerged in the late 1970s as a powerful political force, intent on introducing "creationism" to public school students. The Scopes Trial, which served as something of a dress rehearsal for the contemporary culture wars, was fictionalized on Broadway in 1955 and on celluloid in 1960 as *Inherit the Wind.*

Second Coming. Belief that Jesus will return to judge the world at the end of time. Christians have expended considerable efforts calculating just when the Second Coming will occur and reading the signs of the times for evidence of Jesus' impending return. Shakers view their prophetess Ann Lee (1736–1784) as the Second Coming of Jesus, while Bahais attribute this status to Bahaullah (1817–1892) and Rastafarians to Haile Selassie (1892–1975). In popular parlance the term *second coming* is used to signal both greatness and similitude, as in the oft-repeated claim that the NBA sensation LeBron James is the second coming of Michael Jordan.

Second Great Awakening. A series of revivals that took place throughout the United States during the first few decades of the nineteenth century. The dominant figure here was Charles Grandison Finney, who introduced to American revivalism many controversial "new measures." Whereas Jonathan Edwards, a leader of the Great Awakening of a century earlier, saw a revival as "a surprising work of God," Finney understood it to be a human technique. A "revival is not a miracle," he wrote in his *Lectures on Revivals* (1835), but simply "the right use of the constituted means." In this way Finney and his followers paved the way for contemporary American revivalism.

The effects of the Second Great Awakening are hard to overestimate. It injected ecstasy and emotion into American Protestantism, particularly in frontier camp meetings. It secured the victory of Arminian theology, which accented human free will, over Calvinist theology, which accented

God's sovereignty. It solidified the position of evangelicalism at the center of American religious life. And it motivated Protestants nationwide to work for a wide variety of social reforms in nondenominational organizations such as the American Anti-Slavery Society and the American Temperance Society. Inside these organizations Protestants learned to subordinate their particular theological convictions to the greater moral good of temperance or peace or abolitionism. In this way the Second Great Awakening contributed mightily to the decline of religious literacy in the United States.

Second Vatican Council. The second great council of the Roman Catholic Church (the first was held in 1869–1870), convened in 1962 by Pope John XXIII in an effort to effect an *aggorniamento* (updating) of the church in the modern world. One important outcome of this council, which concluded in 1965 under Pope Paul VI, was a more democratic understanding of the church itself, which was redefined as the entire "people of God" rather than a hierarchy of popes, bishops, and priests. Another outcome was an affirmation of religious freedom and the separation of church and state. Yet another was a greater openness to other forms of Christianity and other religions—an openness that extended to a repudiation of both anti-Semitism and the long-standing dogma that "there is no salvation outside the Church." In terms of politics, this council condemned the nuclear arms race in the name of peace and supported in the name of justice the right of workers to organize. Its affirmation of "the dignity of the human person" contributed, particularly in Latin America, to the legitimation of liberation theology and its "preferential option for the poor." Vatican II also called for greater attention to the Bible in private piety, church services, and theology, but there is little evidence that this reorientation made American Catholics more biblically literate. Following this council American Catholics applied the *aggorniamento* dictum to catechesis, by dropping rote memorization of the Baltimore Catechism in CCD (Confraternity of Christian Doctrine) classes and introducing more experiential approaches to faith, including an emphasis on social service. In terms of the daily lives of American Catholics, the key outcomes were a lifting of the ban on eating meat on Fridays and the decision to allow Mass to be celebrated in vernacular languages rather than Latin only.

secular humanism. More an epithet of the Religious Right than a self-designation, secular humanism refers to the view that human beings can get along just fine without God. As such, it stands in stark opposition to the Judeo-Christian tradition, both theologically (because it does not affirm God) and morally (because it denies God-given moral absolutes). In *Torcaso v. Watkins* (1961), Supreme Court Justice Hugo Black referred in a footnote to "Buddhism, Taoism, Ethical Culture, Secular Humanism" as "religions in this country which do not teach what would generally be considered a belief in the existence of God." Pointing to this dictum, some conservative Christians and Jews have argued that secular humanism, which they view as the villain behind America's moral degradation, has replaced Christianity (or Judeo-Christianity) as the de facto religion of America's public schools. In the early 1990s a science teacher in California brought a federal lawsuit claiming that his school district, by insisting that he teach evolution, was unconstitutionally forcing him to teach the "religion" of secular humanism. "We reject this claim," wrote the Ninth Circuit Court of Appeals, "because neither the Supreme Court, nor this circuit, has ever held that evolutionism or secular humanism are 'religions' for Establishment Clause purposes." Religion or not, this viewpoint has its supporters, who are represented by the Council for Secular Humanism.

separation of church and state. See First Amendment.

Sermon on the Mount. Christianity's most famous sermon, delivered by Jesus in the Gospel of Matthew. It begins with the Beatitudes (from the Latin word *beatus,* meaning "blessed"), starting in Matthew 5:3 with "Blessed are the poor in spirit: for theirs is the kingdom of heaven"—a line that takes on a more socioeconomic cast in Luke 6:20 as "Blessed are ye poor: for yours is the kingdom of God." The Sermon on the Mount also includes the most popular Christian prayer, the Lord's Prayer, as well as the Golden Rule, which many believe to be Jesus' central moral teaching. President George W. Bush referred to the Sermon on the Mount in his January 2005 inaugural address, and the *Congressional Record* contains hundreds of distinct references to this sermon over the last two decades.

Serpent. See Garden of Eden.

Seven Deadly Sins. See 7 deadly sins.

seven sacraments. See 7 sacraments.

Seventh-Day Adventism. Protestant group rooted in the teachings of William Miller (1782–1849), who predicted the end of the world and the

Second Coming of Jesus on various dates in 1843 and 1844. When Jesus did not return and the world did not end, many Adventists lost their faith. Those who did not formed a variety of splinter groups. The largest was led by Ellen Gould White (1827–1915), who learned in a vision that Jesus' second advent had been delayed because believers were not keeping the Sabbath. Seventh-Day Adventists, as her followers are now called, distinguish themselves from other Protestants by their belief that the Second Coming is imminent, by their observation of the Sabbath on Saturday instead of Sunday, and by their strict diet (which eschews meat, alcohol, coffee, and tobacco). The group claims just under a million members in the United States and 10 million worldwide.

Like Jehovah's Witnesses, Seventh-Day Adventists have played a role in First Amendment jurisprudence far out of proportion to their numbers. Their most important legal case, *Sherbert v. Verner* (1963), concerned unemployment benefits for an Adventist dismissed from her job because she refused to work on Saturdays. In this case, which the Adventist won, the Supreme Court promulgated its "Sherbert Test," which governed free exercise cases from 1963 until a much narrower test was promulgated in *Employment Division v. Smith* (1990).

Shahadah. See 5 Pillars of Islam.

Shariah. This term refers in Arabic to a path to water worn by camels. So *Shariah* is the Islamic path—the body of divinely inspired laws for individual and social life rooted in the Quran and the hadith. Muslims distinguish between *Shariah* and *fiqh*. The former term refers to divine law proper. The latter refers to jurisprudence, or human efforts to interpret that law, and is much more open to debate. Different Shiite groups recognize different schools of legal interpretation. Sunnis recognize four: Hanafi, Maliki, Shafii, and Hanbali. The Hanbali school, which currently predominates in Saudi Arabia and the wider Arabian Peninsula, is often described as the most conservative since it favors literal interpretation of the Quran.

Shiite Islam. Along with Sunni Islam, one of the two main divisions in the Muslim tradition, and the smaller of the two. After the death of Muhammad in 632, the Muslim community split over the question of succession. One party, which became the Sunni majority, determined his successors by election, referring to them as caliphs. Another party insisted that Muhammad's successors be drawn from his family. They followed

Muhammad's son-in-law Ali, referring to him as their imam and calling themselves Shiites or Shias (lit. "partisans" of Ali). Unlike Sunnis, who invest only political authority in their caliphs (leaving spiritual authority in the Muslim community as a whole), Shiites invest both political and spiritual authority in their imams. They view as authoritative not only the Quran and the hadith but also the teachings of their imams, whom they see as intercessors between themselves and Allah. Shiites disagree on how many imams followed Ali, but the largest Shiite faction affirms a line of twelve and believes that the final imam, who went into hiding, will return at the end of time to restore peace and justice on earth. One key moment in Shiite history was the murder at Karbala in 680 of Husayn, Muhammad's grandson and the third Shiite imam. This event, remembered every year by Shiites in the festival of Muharram, has made Shiites more receptive to the tradition of martyrdom than their Sunni counterparts. Shiism is the most popular form of Islam in Iran and Iraq, and there are large Shiite populations in Pakistan, India, Azerbaijan, Lebanon, Syria, and Afghanistan. Roughly 15 percent of the world's Muslims are Shiites.

shirk. See *tawhid.*

Sikhism. Religious tradition founded by Guru Nanak (1469–1538) in the Punjab region of northwestern India. The term *Sikh* means "learner" or "disciple," so Sikhs are disciples of the one God and those who learn from its gurus. Sikhs refer to God as Sat Guru ("True Teacher") and respect ten gurus. They also refer to their scripture, the Adi Granth, as a guru of sorts—Guru Granth Sahib—and view both its language (Punjabi) and its script (Gurmukhi) as sacred. Under Guru Gobind Singh (1666–1708), their tenth guru, Sikhs established a community of committed believers called the Khalsa ("The Pure"). Men in this group practice the Five Ks, wearing five symbols of Sikh belief.

Sikhism emerged out of a culture steeped in both Hinduism and Islam, and early Sikhs attempted to reconcile the two, in part by focusing on heartfelt devotion to God rather than rites and doctrines. "There is no Hindu and no Muslim, so whose path shall I follow?" asked Guru Nanak. "I shall follow the path of God." Like Muslims, Sikhs are strict monotheists who emphasize divine sovereignty. They reject the view that God incarnates in human form, believing instead in a formless God that can be known through singing and meditation. Sikhs too have a sacred center, in this case the Golden Temple of Amritsar, India. Like Hindus, Sikhs believe in karma and reincarnation.

Although Sikhs have been coming to the United States for roughly a century, they were largely invisible until after 9/11, when many Sikh leaders were invited to participate in interfaith services. Shortly after September 11, 2001, a Sikh man named Balbir Singh Sodhi was shot and killed in Mesa, Arizona, by a bigot who thought the man's turban marked him as a Muslim. Since that time Sikhs have worked to educate Americans about the differences between Sikhism and Islam. Sikhism received more positive recognition after Manmohan Singh was sworn in as the first Sikh prime minister of India in 2004. There are currently roughly 20 million Sikhs worldwide (the vast majority of them in the Punjab in India) and roughly 250,000 in the United States.

Social Gospel. Protestant theological movement that sees sin and salvation as social and seeks to apply Jesus' teachings to socioeconomic problems. Inspired by Old Testament prophets and led by Baptist theologian Walter Rauschenbusch (1861–1918), the Social Gospel movement emerged in the late nineteenth and early twentieth centuries. Its goal was to ameliorate the social ills brought on by capitalism, industrialization, and urbanization. Leaders repeatedly asked themselves, "What would Jesus do?"—a query popularized in Charles Sheldon's 1897 novel *In His Steps.* In the early twentieth century the Social Gospel helped to precipitate the fundamentalist/modernist controversy, which pitted those who emphasized helping the poor here and now against those who emphasized helping sinners gain eternal life. This movement also set the stage for the New Deal, which made many of the Social Gospelers' proposals official US government policy. Today many Democrats seeking to rediscover the religious roots of progressive politics look back for inspiration to the writings of Rauschenbusch and other Social Gospel leaders. Meanwhile, the Social Gospel can be found in any contemporary congregation—Christian or otherwise—that uses its resources to feed the poor or shelter the homeless.

Sodom and Gomorrah. Cities destroyed by God for their sinfulness. In Genesis 18 and 19 people from Sodom and Gomorrah demand that Lot give over two angels staying with him so that they might "know" them. After Lot refuses, these people attack his home but are thwarted by God, who strikes them blind and destroys their cities. Many Christians have understood this story as a condemnation of homosexuality; in fact, the term *sodomy* derives from this text. But others argue that the theme here is hospitality to strangers rather than gay sex. This narrative has been widely invoked in recent debates about homosexuality in general and gay marriage in particular. Ironically, a significant minority of Americans believe that Sodom and Gomorrah were husband and wife.

stations of the cross. Fourteen images, found in some Roman Catholic and Episcopal churches, depicting the Passion of Jesus, intended as devotional aids for Christians seeking to walk with Jesus through his last hours. These stations are: Jesus is tried and condemned to death; he picks up the cross; he falls; he meets his mother; Simon of Cyrene helps him carry the cross; Veronica wipes his face; he falls again; he speaks to the women of Jerusalem; he falls a third time; he is stripped of his clothes; he is nailed to the cross; he dies; his body is taken off the cross; his corpse is laid in a tomb. Mel Gibson structured his movie *The Passion of the Christ* (2004) on the stations of the cross—a fact lost on Protestants (and Catholics) unfamiliar with this tradition.

Sunni Islam. Along with Shiite Islam, one of two main divisions in the Muslim tradition, and the larger of the two. Sunnis get their name from *sunna* ("custom" or "tradition" in Arabic), which refers to the religious and ethical model set by Muhammad. Sunni Muslims, therefore, are those who adhere strictly to the traditions of the Quran and the exemplary sayings and actions of Muhammad—"the way of the prophet"—as recorded in the hadith. Sunnis split from Shiites after Muhammad's death, when Sunnis said that the prophet's successor should be elected by the *ummah,* or Muslim community, rather than coming (as Shiites insisted) from Muhammad's bloodline. Sunnis invest less authority in their leaders than do Shiites. They view Shiite prayers uttered in the name of Ali or Husayn or other imams as violations of the principle of divine oneness (*tawhid*). Roughly 85 percent of the world's Muslims are Sunnis. Countries where Sunni Islam predominates include Afghanistan, Algeria, Egypt, Indonesia, Pakistan, Saudi Arabia, and Turkey.

Taliban. Islamic militants, many of them students—*talib* means "student" in Arabic—who were trained in *madrasahs* (Islamic schools) in Pakistani refugee camps during the Russo-Afghan war. Led by Mullah Mohammad Omar (b. 1959), the Taliban took control of much of Afghanistan in 1994, running it as a theocratic state with rigid gender segregation, severe restrictions on female schooling, strict punishments (stoning for adultery and amputations for theft), and bans on television, music, and sports. In 2001 the Taliban destroyed two giant Buddhas carved in the third century CE into the cliffs in Afghanistan's Bamiyan valley. Because the Taliban had provided shelter to Osama bin Laden and his al-Qaeda network, they were attacked and defeated by American and other forces after 9/11. During the Taliban's short reign only three of the world's fifty-three Muslim-majority countries officially recognized their government.

Tanakh. See Bible.

Tao Te Ching. See Taoism.

Taoism. Alongside Buddhism and Confucianism, one of the three "Great Teachings" of China. Taoism (also spelled "Daoism") began with Lao Tzu (570–490 BCE), the author of the Tao Te Ching ("The Classic of the Way and Its Power"), which has seen more translations in the United States than any scripture other than the Bible. Taoism was later advanced by Chuang Tzu (370–290 BCE), who published a Taoist classic that bears his name. These early Taoists criticized Confucianism as a tradition of meaningless etiquette, empty ritual, and hyperformality. They commended instead a way of self-cultivation that emphasized naturalness, spontaneity, and freedom. Their ideal human being hungered after intuitive wisdom rather than the book learning of the Confucian sage. He acted not so much in keeping with civilization as in accordance with the Tao, which is variously translated as "The Way," "Ultimate Reality," or "The Source." A later form of Taoism, called "religious Taoism" (to distinguish it from the "philosophical Taoism" of Lao Tzu and Chuang Tzu), seeks health and physical immortality through meditation techniques and dietary practices.

Taoism first came to the United States with Chinese immigrants in the 1840s, and Taoist temples were built in California as early as the 1850s. This tradition owes much of its current popularity, however, to a vast network of martial arts academies, which inculcate in Americans not only the skills of karate or tai chi but also such Taoist concepts as *yin/yang* (complementarity of opposites), *qi* (vital energy), and *wu-wei* (nonaction). Taoism has also been popularized via books such as *The Tao of Pooh* (1983) and television shows such as *The Simpsons,* where the precocious daughter, Lisa, is known to utter Taoist maxims.

tawhid. Arabic for the oneness and uniqueness of God. Expressed in the first half of the Muslim creed the *Shahadah*—"There is no god but

God ..."—*tawhid* is the central teaching of Islam and of the Quran. This doctrine of radical monotheism denies not only atheism and polytheism but also the Christian Trinity, which Muslims condemn as *shirk,* or ascribing partners to God. *Tawhid* has been used throughout Islamic history as a call for unity among the world's Muslims. It has been particularly stressed by Wahhabis, who denounce popular devotions to saints as violations of *tawhid.*

Ten Commandments. See 10 Commandments.

Torah. This term ("teaching" in Hebrew) refers most broadly to Jewish Law, both oral and written. More narrowly, it refers to the Hebrew Bible, which Jews call the Tanakh. More narrowly still, it refers to the Pentateuch, the first five books of the Hebrew Bible, and to the synagogue scrolls on which these holy books are written. The most famous effort to distill the Torah down to one simple formulation comes from the famed rabbi Hillel, a rough contemporary of Jesus. When asked to summarize the Torah while standing on one leg, Hillel answered: "What is hateful to you, do not do to your neighbor. That is the whole Torah; the rest is commentary. Go and study it."

Tower of Babel. Hebrew Bible story about prideful people who try to build a tower to heaven. The story, which appears in Genesis 11, ends when God thwarts these people's arrogance (and their construction project) by causing them to speak many different languages. Unable to communicate, they abandon their tower and scatter across the globe, carrying their languages with them. The name of the tower derives from two Hebrew words—*Babel* or Babylon and *balal* or confuse—and it contributed to English the word *babble.* Cultural conservatives who insist that English should be the only official language of the United States use this story to argue that a nation divided against itself linguistically cannot stand. If we start singing the national anthem in Spanish, this argument goes, we will soon devolve into a multiculturalist Babel.

Trinity. The Christian doctrine that the one God exists in a community of three divine persons—the Father, the Son (Jesus), and the Holy Spirit—who share one divine substance. Although Christians call themselves monotheists, some outsiders see at least a hint of polytheism in this belief. (As one author put it, the persons of the Trinity are "triplets perched on the fence between polytheism and monotheism."[270]) Unitarianism, which came to the United States from England in the late eighteenth century, rejects Trinitarianism on the grounds that this doctrine, which was first codified in the Council of Constantinople in 381, cannot be found in the Bible.

Unitarianism. Unitarians get their name from their rejection of the divinity of Jesus and therefore the doctrine of the Trinity—there is one God, not three, they argue—but the most distinctive teaching of this nineteenth-century offshoot from Congregationalism is the belief that human beings are born good. Unitarianism is now institutionalized in the United States in the Unitarian Universalist Association, America's most theologically and politically liberal denomination. Some Muslims refer to Wahhabis as Unitarians because of their emphasis on the unity of God (*tawhid*).

Upanishads. Hindu scriptures, dating to the first millennium BCE, containing philosophical and theological reflections on divinity, the soul, karma, and reincarnation. According to the Upanishads, human beings can achieve *moksha,* or liberation from the cycle of birth, life, death, and rebirth, by realizing that Atman (the essence of the human soul) is the same as Brahman (Ultimate Reality).

Vatican II. See Second Vatican Council.

Vedas. The oldest and most authoritative Hindu scriptures, regarded as *shruti* (that which is heard: revelation), as opposed to *smrti* (that which is remembered: tradition). Most narrowly, the term *Vedas* (from the Sanskrit for "knowledge") refers to four collections of hymns, dating as early as the second millennium BCE and used in ancient Indian sacrificial rituals: the Rig Veda, the Sama Veda, the Yajur Veda, and the Atharva Veda. More broadly, the Vedas refer to four types of sacred literature: the four Vedas just mentioned; the Brahmanas, or priestly commentaries on these hymns; the Aranyakas, meaning "forest books" or esoteric teachings; and the Upanishads, or philosophical and mystical treatises. The first major Hindu organization in the United States, the Vedanta Society, took its name from the Vedas; *Vedanta* means "the end of the Vedas."

virgin birth. Christian teaching that Jesus was conceived by Mary without a human father. The New Testament Gospels refer to Mary becoming pregnant without having sexual intercourse with her husband, Joseph, and the Apostles' Creed refers to Jesus being "conceived by the power of the Holy Spirit" and "born of the Virgin Mary." In addition to affirming Mary's virginity at Jesus' conception and birth, some Christians believe that Mary was a virgin her entire life. The doctrine of the virgin birth, which is accepted by Muslims as well as Protestant, Catholic, and Orthodox Christians, should not be confused with the Catholic doctrine of the immaculate conception, which states that Mary herself was born without sin.

Vishnu. The most popular Hindu deity. Vishnu is said to have ten different incarnations, including the Buddha. He appears as Rama and Krishna, respectively, in the Hindu epics the Ramayana and Mahabharata. Images of these incarnations have on occasion become a matter of public controversy in the United States. The album cover for *Axis: Bold as Love* (1967), which depicted Jimi Hendrix as a multiarmed Hindu deity, failed to cause a stir, but when the rock band Aerosmith released a CD in 1997 with a cover image of Krishna with breasts, many Hindus cried foul. American Hindus Against Defamation, a group modeled after the Anti-Defamation League, protested, and Sony/Columbia (Aerosmith's label) responded by publicly apologizing and changing the cover art.

Wahhabism. Ultraconservative Sunni Muslim revitalization movement that aims to reverse the moral decline of the Muslim world by returning to the pure Islam of the Quran and Muhammad. Opponents gave Wahhabis their name, which derives from founder Muhammad ibn Abd al-Wahhab (1703–1792), a scholar of the Sunnis' conservative Hanbali school. But Wahhabis often refer to themselves either as *Muwahhidun* (upholders of divine unity) or as Salafis, a broader but closely related school that denounces as apostates Muslims who deviate from the beliefs and practices of the first three generations of Muslims (the righteous "predecessors": *Salaf*). Wahhabism, which has been compared with both Unitarianism and Puritanism, rejects as corruptions of the pure faith virtually all medieval and modern accretions to Islam, including popular devotions to saints and Sufi mysticism. Wahhabis are particularly zealous about strict adherence to Shariah, or Islamic law. They reject the separation of church and state, and they regard Muslims who do not accept their views as heretics. This movement, which dates to the 1740s in Arabia, won the support of the Bedouin chief Muhammad ibn Saud in 1747 and became dominant in modern-day Saudi Arabia (though many Wahhabis criticized the House of Saud when it opened the nation up to Western influences after the discovery of oil in the 1930s). In recent decades

Wahhabism spread to Afghanistan under the Taliban regime and, thanks to an aggressive mosque-building program funded by Saudis, into mosques in Europe and the United States. Osama bin Laden and al-Qaeda are both influenced by Wahhabism, but the greater influence on each seems to be the thought of the Egyptian radical Sayyid Qutb.

yin/yang. Two opposite yet complementary forces in the cosmos, important in Confucianism, Taoism, and Chinese popular religion. These terms originally referred to the shady and sunny sides of a mountain, respectively. Yin is dark, passive, female, cool. Yang is bright, active, male, warm. The ancient Chinese art of feng shui ("the way of wind and water"), popularized in the United States in the late twentieth century, relies on the complementarity of yin and yang to create harmonious spaces for living and working.

yoga. Although *yoga* has in recent years come to refer to India-derived body postures and stretching exercises, this Sanskrit term originally meant "discipline." In Hinduism (from which yoga derives), there are many yogas, including the discipline of knowledge (*jnana* yoga) and the discipline of devotion (*bhakti* yoga). The contemporary craze for yoga as exercise derives from *hatha* yoga or the discipline of force, which was itself originally a mode of *raja* yoga (the discipline of royalty). Its key elements, which go back thousands of years in India, are bodily postures (*asana*) and breath control (*pranayama*). Its ultimate aim is nothing less than to "yoke"—the term *yoga* is related to the English word *yoke*—one's true self (Atman) with Ultimate Reality (Brahman). In other words, classic yogis did not separate yogic techniques from Hindu religion and philosophy.

Americans' interest in yoga dates to the arrival of Swami Vivekananda, the first Hindu missionary to the United States, at the World's Parliament of Religions in Chicago in 1893. But neither Vivekananda nor the Vedanta Society that he founded one year later emphasized what we now know as yoga. That practice first took off in the United States in the 1950s and 1960s, when such teachers as Indra Devi took the Hinduism out of it, stressing physical fitness and mental health instead. Yoga went mainstream in the 1990s, when pop stars such as Sting became associated with it. In 1999 Madonna won a Grammy for her *Ray of Light* CD, which included a Sanskrit track praising Patanjali, the ancient author of the *Yoga Sutras*. In 2001 *Time* magazine put the yoga craze on its cover, as did the *New Yorker* two years later. Today secularized forms of yoga, severed almost entirely from its Hindu roots, are offered in many health clubs, university gyms, and even churches. A Christian version of yoga, known as PraiseMoves, is popular among evangelicals.

Zen. The Japanese term *Zen* derives from the Sanskrit term *dhyana,* meaning meditation. So Zen is a meditation school of Buddhism. More specifically, it is a Mahayana Buddhist school that uses various techniques to attain *satori* (enlightenment). It was popularized in the United States by the Zen layman D. T. Suzuki (1870–1966) and by Jack Kerouac and other members of the Beat generation, who together helped to kick off a Zen vogue in 1950s America. The popularity of Robert Pirsig's bestseller, *Zen and the Art of Motorcycle Maintenance* (1974) prompted authors to write hundreds of "Zen and" titles—from *Zen and the Art of Poker* to *Zen and the Art of Happiness.*

Zionism. Movement to create a Jewish nation in the land of Zion, namely Israel/Palestine. This movement, rooted in the Jewish hope for a messiah who would fulfill God's promise of a land for Abraham's descendants, dates to the destruction of the First Temple in 586 BCE and the subsequent scattering of the Jews into the diaspora. It took political form in 1897 when Theodor Herzl convened in Basel, Switzerland, the First Zionist Congress, which aimed to create "for the Jewish people a home in Palestine secured by public law." Zionism was initially opposed on the right by Orthodox Jews who thought that this task belonged to God alone and on the left by Reform Jews who did not want to be accused of having mixed loyalties to their homelands. Following the Holocaust, however, a new consensus emerged among Jews and non-Jews alike for a Jewish state, which became a reality in 1948. Today some "Christian Zionists" support the state of Israel because of their belief that the New Testament book of Revelation describes a Jewish state as a prerequisite for the Second Coming of Jesus.

Appendix

The quiz that follows appears in chapter 1 but is reprinted here along with the answers. To figure out how you did, add up your total points then multiply by two to get your score on a standard 100-point scale. An A is 90 points or higher. B is 80–89. C is 70–79. A passing grade is 60 points or more.

Religious Literacy Quiz

1. Name the four Gospels. List as many as you can.

2. Name a sacred text of Hinduism.

3. What is the name of the holy book of Islam?

4. Where according to the Bible was Jesus born?

5. President George W. Bush spoke in his first inaugural address of the Jericho road. What Bible story was he invoking?

6. What are the first five books of the Hebrew Bible or the Christian Old Testament?

7. What is the Golden Rule?

8. "God helps those who help themselves": Is this in the Bible? If so, where?

9. "Blessed are the poor in spirit, for theirs is the kingdom of God": Does this appear in the Bible? If so, where?

10. Name the Ten Commandments. List as many as you can.

11. Name the Four Noble Truths of Buddhism.

12. What are the seven sacraments of Catholicism? List as many as you can.

13. The First Amendment says two things about religion, each in its own "clause." What are the two religion clauses of the First Amendment?

14. What is Ramadan? In what religion is it celebrated?

15. Match the Bible characters with the stories in which they appear. Draw a line from one to the other. Hint: Some characters may be matched with more than one story or vice versa:

Adam and Eve	Exodus
Paul	Binding of Isaac
Moses	Olive Branch
Noah	Garden of Eden
Jesus	Parting of the Red Sea
Abraham	Road to Damascus
Serpent	Garden of Gethsemane

Answers (and Grading)

1. Name the four Gospels. List as many as you can. (1 point each.)

   Matthew, Mark, Luke, and John.

2. Name a sacred text of Hinduism. (1 point.)

   There are many possibilities here. They include: the Vedas, Brahmanas, Aranyakas, Upanishads, Puranas, Mahabharata, Bhagavad Gita, Ramayana, Yoga Sutras, Laws of Manu, and the Kama Sutra.

3. What is the name of the holy book of Islam? (1 point.)

   Quran.

4. Where according to the Bible was Jesus born? (1 point.)

   Bethlehem.

5. President George W. Bush spoke in his first inaugural address of the Jericho road. What Bible story was he invoking? (1 point.)

> The Good Samaritan.

6. What are the first five books of the Hebrew Bible or the Christian Old Testament? (1 point each.)

> Genesis, Exodus, Leviticus, Numbers, Deuteronomy.

7. What is the Golden Rule? (1 point.)

> "Do unto others as you would have them do unto you" (Matthew 7:12), or a similar sentiment from Rabbi Hillel or Confucius. ("Love your neighbor as yourself" is *not* the Golden Rule.)

8. "God helps those who help themselves." Is this in the Bible? If so, where? (2 points.)

> No, this is not in the Bible. In fact, it is contradicted in Proverbs 28:26: "He who trusts in himself is a fool." The words are Ben Franklin's.

9. "Blessed are the poor in spirit, for theirs is the kingdom of God": Does this appear in the Bible? If so, where? (2 points.)

> Yes, in the Beatitudes of Jesus' Sermon on the Mount (Matthew 5:3).

10. Name the Ten Commandments. List as many as you can. (10 points.)

> The Protestant, Catholic, and Jewish versions of the Ten Commandments differ. Give yourself credit for any ten of the following twelve commandments, each of which appears in at least one of those three versions:
>
> 1. I the Lord am your God who brought you out of the land of Egypt, the house of bondage.
>
> 2. You shall have no other gods before me.
>
> 3. You shall not make yourself a graven image.
>
> 4. You shall not take the name of the Lord your God in vain.
>
> 5. Remember the Sabbath day and keep it holy.

6. Honor your father and your mother.

7. You shall not kill/murder.

8. You shall not commit adultery.

9. You shall not steal.

10. You shall not bear false witness against your neighbor.

11. You shall not covet your neighbor's wife.

12. You shall not covet your neighbor's goods.

11. Name the Four Noble Truths of Buddhism. List as many as you can. (4 points.)

1. Life is suffering.

2. Suffering has an origin.

3. Suffering can be overcome (nirvana).

4. The path to overcoming suffering is the Noble Eightfold Path.

12. What are the seven sacraments of Catholicism? List as many as you can. (7 points.)

1. Baptism

2. Eucharist/Mass/Holy Communion

3. Reconciliation/Confession/Penance

4. Confirmation

5. Marriage

6. Holy Orders

7. Anointing of the Sick/Last Rites

13. The First Amendment says two things about religion, each in its own "clause." What are the two religion clauses of the First Amendment? (1 point each.)

"Congress shall make no law respecting an establishment of religion, or prohibiting the free exercise thereof." The words before the comma are referred to as the establishment clause; the words that follow constitute the free exercise clause.

14. What is Ramadan? In what religion is it celebrated? (2 points.)

    Ramadan is a Muslim holiday characterized by a month of fasting.

15. Match the Bible characters with the stories in which they appear by drawing a line from one to the other. Some characters may be matched with more than one story or vice versa. (7 points.)

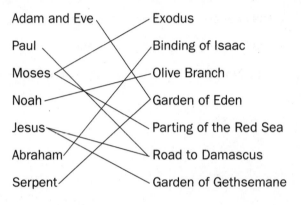

Adam and Eve	Exodus
Paul	Binding of Isaac
Moses	Olive Branch
Noah	Garden of Eden
Jesus	Parting of the Red Sea
Abraham	Road to Damascus
Serpent	Garden of Gethsemane

Further Reading

The World's Religions

Whenever I speak on religious literacy, people come up to me and ask about an accessible book they can read on the religious traditions of the world. I refer them to Huston Smith's *The World's Religions: Our Great Wisdom Traditions* (HarperSanFrancisco, 1991). Originally published as *The Religions of Man,* this well-written and succinct book includes short chapters on Hinduism, Buddhism, Confucianism, Taoism, Islam, Judaism, and Christianity. The author believes—wrongly in my view—that all these religions are essentially the same, so readers should be aware of that key bias. But if you are going to read just one book on the world's religions, this is the one.

Christianity

Here Sandra S. Frankiel's *Christianity: A Way of Salvation* (HarperSanFrancisco, 1985) provides an excellent mix of beliefs, practices, and history. *Mere Christianity* (HarperSanFrancisco, 2001) by the British writer C. S. Lewis is something of a second Bible for American evangelicals, and provides quick and easy access to the evangelical mind.

Islam

The starting point on Islam is Carl W. Ernst, *Following Muhammad: Rethinking Islam in the Contemporary World* (University of North Carolina Press, 2004). The best way into the Quran is via Michael Sells, *Approaching the Qur'an: The Early Revelations* (White Cloud Press, 1999). As its subtitle implies, Sells's book focuses on the Quran's early suras, leaving out many of the more controversial (and violent) passages revealed after Muhammad moved from Mecca to Medina. Nonetheless, it is the best introduction available. Jane Smith's *Islam in America* (Columbia University Press, 1999) is the place to go for Islam in the United States.

Judaism

Start here with Michael Fishbane, *Judaism: Revelation and Traditions* (HarperSanFrancisco, 1987). Hasia R. Diner's *Jews in America* (Oxford University Press, 1999) offers an accessible introduction to American Judaism.

Buddhism

When it comes to this hard-to-understand tradition, the easiest place to begin is *What the Buddha Taught* (Grove Press, 1974) by the scholar-monk Walpola Rahula. This book covers the basics from a Theravada Buddhist perspective and includes some famous sermons of the Buddha. Donald S. Lopez Jr.'s *The Story of Buddhism: A Concise Guide to Its History and Teachings* (HarperSanFrancisco, 2001) focuses more on practices than beliefs and covers the Theravada, Mahayana, and Vajrayana schools. The best introduction to American Buddhism is Richard Seager, *Buddhism in America* (Columbia University Press, 1999).

Hinduism

A delightful introduction to Hinduism, written in a chatty style as a dialogue between father and son, is Ed Viswanathan's *Am I a Hindu? The Hinduism Primer* (Halo Books, 1992). Organized in question-and-answer style, this book is widely read in immigrant Hindu circles, especially by young people. A more scholarly but still accessible book is Gavin Flood, *An Introduction to Hinduism* (Cambridge University Press, 1996). For Hinduism (and other Asian religions) closer to home, see *Buddhists, Hindus, and Sikhs in America* (Oxford University Press, 2002) by Gurinder Singh Mann, Paul David Numrich, and Raymond B. Williams.

Acknowledgments

The genesis of this project goes back to two workshops convened in 1998 by Lynn Szwaja of the Rockefeller Foundation on "The Changing Role of Religion in American Life." The purpose of these gatherings, which were led by Laurie Maffly-Kipp of the University of North Carolina, Chapel Hill, was to make recommendations to the Rockefeller Foundation concerning funding in the study of religion. I don't know whether anyone ever heeded whatever recommendations we made, but I remember having great fun batting ideas around with Nancy Ammerman, Gail Bederman, Rudy Busto, Betty DeBerg, Kate Joyce, Laurie Maffly-Kipp, John McGreevy, Joel Martin, Don Mathews, Deborah Dash Moore, Keith Naylor, Timothy Tseng, and Thomas Tweed. Repeatedly over the course of two weekends, we returned as a group to the idea of religious literacy— what it meant, why it mattered, and how it might be cultivated.

I also want to acknowledge the dedicated students and faculty I work with at Boston University. Dietmar Winkler is the Austrian colleague whose off-the-cuff remarks about European and American undergraduates helped to clarify the paradox that stands at the center of this project. Students in my Spring 2006 "Death and Immortality" course took my Religious Literacy Quiz and offered useful comments on it. I have also discussed various twists and turns in this book with colleagues in BU's Department of Religion and School of Theology, including Gina Cogan, David Eckel, Peter Hawkins, Tariq Jaffer, Jonathan Klawans, Deeana Klepper, Frank Korom, Diana Lobel, Dana Robert, and Michael Zank. Eric Baldwin, a fine young scholar of American religious history, did expert work as my research assistant and helped me shape my historical arguments. Scott Girdner, another graduate student, assisted with the dictionary. My dean, Jeffrey Henderson, who unlike many deans is an active scholar himself, supported unfailingly my efforts to juggle a writing career with obligations as chairman of BU's Department of Religion and director of its Division of Religious and Theological Studies. In these units Karen Nardella and Neil O'Callaghan covered for me when I was home at my computer writing.

Colleagues farther afield in education, history, and religious studies read portions of the book and offered helpful criticisms. They include David Chappell, Donna Freitas, Khyati Joshi, Gary Laderman, Gerald McDermott, Doug Winiarski, and Lauren Winner. Bruce Grelle and Betty DeBerg discussed recent developments in religion and public education. Other scholars who provided assistance include David Hall, James Davison Hunter, Franklin Lambert, Tom Long, John McGreevy, David Morgan, Harry Stout, and Jay Wexler.

Closer to home, I am also grateful to neighbors, friends, and family members who discussed this book with me. My friend Patrick Ramage read part of the manuscript. My wife, Edye Nesmith, and my daughters, Molly and Lucy Prothero, endured my long absences at the computer and my prodding questions. Edye also read and commented astutely on much of the book.

I am grateful to Susan Brenneman of the *Los Angeles Times* for allowing me to try out my arguments in an op-ed piece in her newspaper, and to the dozens of editors across the country and as far away as Qatar, India, and China who, by reprinting the piece, convinced me that there might be a wide audience for this topic. I also want to thank Boston University's School of Theology, Bates College, and Southern Methodist University's Perkins School for Laity for allowing me to address this topic in formal lectures in 2005 and 2006.

Finally, I would like to acknowledge both my San Diego–based agent, Sandy Dijkstra, and my San Francisco–based editor, Roger Freet, who together demonstrate that living roughly three thousand miles away from New York can actually be an asset when it comes both to working on books and to working with writers.

Notes

1. On faith and unbelief in the United States and Europe, see results of the World Values Survey (2000), posted at http://www.religionstatistics.net/gendaten.htm. America's most famous Jesus-loving politician is, of course, President George W. Bush, who, when asked to name the political philosopher he most admired (during a December 13, 1999, debate in Des Moines, Iowa, with five other Republican candidates for president), responded, "Christ, because he changed my heart." Republican presidential hopefuls Gary Bauer and Orrin Hatch also tapped Jesus as their favorite political philosopher during that campaign, and Al Gore was later quoted (by Sally Quinn of the *Washington Post* on MSNBC's *Hardball* on December 14, 2000) as saying, "I never make a political decision that I don't ask myself what would Jesus do."

2. Two years later the bloodshed continued when Timothy McVeigh, who traveled to Waco to witness the siege firsthand, chose the second anniversary of the end of that siege, April 19, 1995, to bomb the Murrah Federal Building in Oklahoma City. The best academic book on Waco is James D. Tabor and Eugene V. Gallagher, eds., *Why Waco? Cults and the Battle for Religious Freedom in America* (Berkeley and Los Angeles: University of California Press, 1995). Nancy T. Ammerman's "Waco, Federal Law Enforcement, and Scholars of Religion," http://religiousmovements.lib.virginia.edu/nrms/davidians/ammerman.html, provides a succinct analysis of how ignorance of religion proved deadly in this case. For two very different views of government complicity in the tragedy, see the documentary film *Waco: The Rules of Engagement,* and John C. Danforth, "Final Report to the Deputy Attorney General Concerning the 1993 Confrontation at the Mt. Carmel Complex, Waco, Texas," November 8, 2000, http://www.waco93.com/Danforth-finalreport.pdf.

3. "'Islam is Peace' Says President, Remarks by the President at Islamic Center of Washington, D.C.," White House press release, September 17, 2001, http://www.whitehouse.gov/news/releases/2001/09/20010917-11.html; Jerry Falwell in *60 Minutes* interview, October 6, 2002, CBS-TV; Nicholas D. Kristof, "Bigotry in Islam—And Here," *New York Times,* July 9, 2002, A21. The Kristof piece includes two additional

widely quoted remarks: the Reverend Jerry Vines, past president of the Southern Baptist Convention, describing Muhammad as "a demon-possessed pedophile," and the Reverend Franklin Graham calling Islam "a very evil and wicked religion."

4. E. D. Hirsch Jr., *Cultural Literacy: What Every American Needs to Know* (Boston: Houghton Mifflin, 1987), xv, 113, 12. On "core knowledge," see the Web site of Hirsch's Core Knowledge Foundation: http://www.coreknowledge.org. See also Hirsch's *The Knowledge Deficit: Closing the Shocking Education Gap for American Children* (Boston: Houghton Mifflin, 2006). Critics contend that Hirsch's approach is elitist and biased toward dead, white, Western men.

5. Madeleine Albright, *The Mighty and the Almighty: Reflections on America, God, and World Affairs* (New York: HarperCollins, 2006), 75. "In the future, no American ambassador should be assigned to a country where religious feelings are strong unless he or she has a deep understanding of the faiths commonly practiced there" (75), Albright writes. "The State Department should hire or train a core of specialists in religion to be deployed both in Washington and in key embassies overseas" (76).

6. Richard John Neuhaus, *The Naked Public Square: Religion and Democracy in America* (Grand Rapids, MI: Eerdmans, 1984).

7. Harold Bloom, *The American Religion: The Emergence of the Post-Christian Nation* (New York: Simon and Schuster, 1992); Jay D. Wexler, "Preparing for the Clothed Public Square: Teaching About Religion, Civic Education, and the Constitution," *William and Mary Law Review* 43.3 (February 2002): 1161–62, 1163.

8. George Gallup Jr. and Jim Castelli, *The People's Faith: American Faith in the 90's* (New York: Macmillan, 1989), 60. Echoing Gallup and Castelli, researcher George Barna concludes that "the Christian body in America is immersed in a crisis of biblical illiteracy"; see "Religious Beliefs Vary Widely by Denomination," The Barna Update, June 25, 2001, http://www.barna.org/FlexPage.aspx?Page=BarnaUpdate&Barna UpdateID=92. On naming the four Gospels: Gallup and Castelli, *People's Religion,* 60. I have not been able to find the original source for the survey of high school seniors on Sodom and Gomorrah as husband and wife, but see Albert Mohler, "Sodom and Gomorrah Lived Happily Ever After?" http://www.crosswalk.com/news/1223338.html.

9. Marie Wachlin and Byron R. Johnson, *Bible Literacy Report* (Fairfax, VA: Bible Literacy Project, 2005), 48.

10. "Profile: Diana Eck," *Religion and Ethics Newsweekly,* June 22, 2001, http://www.pbs.org/wnet/religionandethics/week443/profile.html. On knowledge of the world's religions: Wachlin and Johnson, *Bible Literacy Report,* 31. The figures were Buddhism (54 percent), Judaism (47 percent), Islam (41 percent), and Hinduism (36 percent).

11. Danièle Hervieu-Léger, *Religion as a Chain of Memory,* trans. Simon Lee (New Brunswick, NJ: Rutgers University Press, 2000). On Oliver Sacks, memory, and "theological amnesia," see Craig Dykstra, "Memory and Truth," *Theology Today* 44.2 (July 1987): 159–63, http://theologytoday.ptsem.edu/jul1987/v44-2-editorial1.htm.

12. Many advocates for religious studies in secondary and higher education refer to religion as "the Fourth R." See Joan DelFattore, *The Fourth R: Conflicts over Religion in America's Public Schools* (New Haven, CT: Yale University Press, 2004).

13. Will Herberg, *Protestant-Catholic-Jew: An Essay in American Religious Sociology* (Garden City, NY: Doubleday, 1955), 15, 282, 286. I disagree with Herberg's extrapolation from these facts that America was in 1955 "one of the most religious and most secular of nations" (286). Ignorance of your own religion doesn't make you secular. It just makes you religious in a peculiar way.

14. Herberg, *Protestant-Catholic-Jew,* 251.

15. Peter Cobb, "Teaching in an Age of Religious Pluralism, Skepticism, Resurgence, and Ambivalence," *Independent School Magazine* (Summer 2003), http://www.nais.org/publications/ismagazinearticle.cfm?Itemnumber=144312&snItemNumber=145956&tn.ItemNumber=145958.

16. Warren A. Nord, *Religion and American Education: Rethinking a National Dilemma* (Chapel Hill: University of North Carolina Press, 1995), 8.

17. The Barna Group, "Discipleship Insights Revealed in New Book by George Barna," November 28, 2000, http://www.barna.org/FlexPage.aspx?Page=BarnaUpdate&BarnaUpdateID=76. Seventy-five percent of Americans and 68 percent of born-again Christians believe that this saying is in the Bible; see the Barna Group, "Americans' Bible Knowledge is in the Ballpark, but Often Off Base," July 12, 2000, http://www.barna.org/FlexPage.aspx?Page=BarnaUpdate&BarnaUpdateID=66.

18. Two recent books—Philip Jenkins, *The New Anti-Catholicism* (New York: Oxford University Press, 2003), and Mark S. Massa, *Anti-Catholicism in America* (New York: Crossroad, 2003)—bear the subtitle *The Last Acceptable Prejudice.* I disagree. Criticizing Catholic teachings on abortion or contraception is not anti-Catholic, and anti-Catholicism is no longer socially acceptable. Antifundamentalism, by contrast, is.

19. See *Engel v. Vitale,* 370 U.S. 421 (1962) and *Abington v. Schempp* 374 U.S. 203 (1963). Sam Ervin, a Democratic senator from North Carolina, said of *Engel:* "The Supreme Court has held that God is unconstitutional." The Democratic representative from South Carolina Lucius Mendel Rivers was even more incensed about the Supreme Court's "disbelief in God Almighty": "I know of nothing in my lifetime that could give more aid and comfort to Moscow," he said, "than this bold, malicious, atheistic, and sacrilegious twist of this unpredictable group of uncontrolled despots" (*Congressional Record,* June 26, 1962, 11709, 11732, quoted in DelFattore, *Fourth R,* 79–80). The Supreme Court reinforced these rulings when it banned moments of silence in 1985, prayer at school graduations in 1992, and public prayer before football games in 2000; see *Wallace v. Jaffree,* 472 U.S. 38 (1985), *Lee v. Weisman,* 505 U.S. 577 (1992), and *Santa Fe Independent School District v. Doe,* 530 U.S. 290 (2000).

20. Francis X. Clooney, SJ, "Reading the World Religiously: Literate Christianity in a World of Many Religions," in *Theological Literacy for the Twenty-First Century,* ed. Rodney L. Petersen and Nancy M. Rourke (Grand Rapids, MI: Eerdmans, 2002), 250.

21. "Religious Affiliation of U.S. Congress," http://www.adherents.com/adh_congress.html#109. In 2006, 494 out of 535 members of Congress and 47 out of 50 governors self-identified as Christians.

22. At Ellis Island President Bush said, "Ours is the cause of human dignity; freedom guided by conscience and guarded by peace. This ideal of America is the hope of all mankind. That hope drew millions to this harbor. That hope still lights our way. And the light shines in the darkness. And the darkness will not overcome it." John 1:5 reads: "The light shines in the darkness, and the darkness hasn't overcome it" (World English Bible translation). For the text of the two presidential speeches, see "Statement by the President in his Address to the Nation," September 11, 2001, http://www.whitehouse.gov/news/releases/2001/09/20010911-16.html; and "President's Remarks to the Nation," September 11, 2002, http://www.whitehouse.gov/news/releases/2002/09/20020911-3.html.

23. Osama bin Laden, "Declaration of War Against the Americans Occupying the Land of the Two Holy Places," 1996, http://www.pbs.org/newshour/terrorism/international/fatwa_1996.html.

24. Other dimensions of religion doubtless play a role in religious literacy, which is created and sustained through (among other things) rituals and spiritual experiences. But the most important components of religious literacy in America are in my view the doctrinal and the narrative, so I emphasize them here.

25. Here I have been influenced by David D. Hall, who defines basic literacy as "not a fixed term or condition but a practice that was mediated by different frames of meaning and social circumstances"; see his introduction to *The Colonial Book in the Atlantic World,* ed. Hugh Amory and David D. Hall, *A History of the Book in America 1* (New York: Cambridge University Press, 2000), 10.

26. Dean R. Hoge, William D. Dinges, Mary Johnson, and Juan L. Gonzales Jr., *Young Adult Catholics: Religion in the Culture of Choice* (Notre Dame, IN: University of Notre Dame Press, 2001), 162.

27. Center for Civic Education, "CIVITAS: A Framework for Civic Education," http://www.civiced.org/civitasexec.html.

28. Telephone interview with Yvana Peery, February 2005. Peery is an independent theater producer from lower Manhattan and a self-described secular humanist.

29. Bill O'Reilly, "Christmas Under Siege: The Big Picture," December 24, 2004, http://www.foxnews.com/story/0,2933,140742,00.html; "The Debate over the L.A. County Seal," *The O'Reilly Factor,* June 28, 2004, transcript; Hendrik Hertzberg, "Bah Humbug," *New Yorker,* December 26, 2005, 43; Jerry Falwell, "The Impending Death of Christmas?" December 11, 2004, http://www.worldnetdaily.com/news/article.asp

?ARTICLE_ID=41877; Patrick J. Buchanan, "Christianophobia," December 13, 2004, http://www.worldnetdaily.com/news/article.asp?ARTICLE_ID=41900. See too John Gibson, *The War on Christmas: How the Liberal Plot to Ban the Sacred Christian Holiday Is Worse Than You Thought* (New York: Sentinel, 2005).

30. "Treaty of Tripoli, 1796, 1806," http://candst.tripod.com/tripoli1.htm; *Church of the Holy Trinity v. U.S.*, 143 U.S. 266 (1892).

31. Richard Rorty, "Religion as a Conversation Stopper," in Richard Rorty, *Philosophy and Social Hope* (New York: Penguin Books, 1999), 168–74; John Rawls, *Political Liberalism* (New York: Columbia University Press, 1993), 212–54; *Address of the General Executive Committee of the American Republican Party of the City of New-York, to the People of the United States* (New York: J. F. Trow, 1845), 9–10, quoted in Philip Hamburger, *The Separation of Church and State* (Cambridge: Harvard University Press, 2002), 228; Stephen Macedo, "Liberal Civic Education and Religious Fundamentalism: The Case of God v. John Rawls?" *Ethics* 105.3 (April 1995): 470. On "public reason," see also John Rawls, *The Law of Peoples: With "The Idea of Public Reason Revisited"* (Cambridge: Harvard University Press, 1999). For a rebuttal of Rawls and Rorty, see Jeffrey Stout, *Democracy and Tradition* (Princeton, NJ: Princeton University Press, 2004), 63–91.

32. Bill Broadway, "Use of 'Jesus' in Inaugural Prayers Breeds Some Worry," *Washington Post,* January 27, 2001, B9; G. K. Chesterton, *The Collected Works of G. K. Chesterton* (San Francisco: Ignatius Press, 1990), 21:41–45. See also Sidney E. Mead, *The Nation with the Soul of a Church* (New York: Harper and Row, 1975). On the 1997 Clinton inauguration: *Congressional Record* 143, S119–22.

33. On belief in God: Linda Lyons, "Religiosity Compass Points South," Gallup Poll, January 14, 2003, http://poll.gallup.com. On religion as personally important: "Economic Values Survey, 1992," the Association of Religion Data Archives, http://www.thearda.com/Archive/Files/Descriptions/ECON.asp. On daily prayer: George Gallup Jr. and D. Michael Lindsay, *Surveying the Religious Landscape: Trends in U.S. Beliefs* (Harrisburg, PA: Morehouse Publishing, 1999), 46. On giving to houses of worship: Giving USA Foundation press release, "Charitable Giving Rises 5 Percent to Nearly $250 Billion in 2004," http://www.aafrc.org/gusa/GUSA05_Press_Release.pdf.

34. Peter Berger, "Religion and the West," in *National Interest* 80 (Summer 2005): 113; Michael Hout and Claude S. Fischer, "Why More Americans Have No Religious Preference: Politics and Generations," *American Sociological Review* 67.2 (April 2002): 175. On doubling of the nation's "Nones" and "Nones" who pray, see the same source, 165, 176. On teenager "Nones": Christian Smith with Melinda Lundquist Denton, *Soul Searching: The Religious and Spiritual Lives of American Teenagers* (New York: Oxford University Press, 2005), 43. See also Ariela Keysar, Egon Mayer, and Barry A. Kosmin, "No Religion: A Profile of America's Unchurched," *Public Perspective* 14.1 (January/February 2003): 44. Hout and Fischer, in "No Religious Preference," argue that the most important factor behind the rise in "unchurched believers" is likely political. With the

Religious Right's ascent, Americans have increasingly come to associate terms such as *church* and *Christianity* and *religion* with conservative politics, leading some liberals to eschew "organized religion" for political reasons. "Holding no religious preference in the late 1990s," Hout and Fischer conclude, "was a political act, a dissent from the affinity that had emerged between conservative politics and organized religion" (188).

35. On percentages of Protestants, Catholics, and other Christians: Linda Lyons, "Tracking U.S. Religious Preferences over the Decades," May 24, 2005, Gallup Poll, http://poll.gallup.com. On Mormons in Utah (66 percent of the population): "State Membership Report," the Association of Religion Data Archives, http://www.thearda .com/mapsReports/reports/state/49_2000.asp. On Jews in Israel (76 percent of the population): Central Bureau of Statistics, "Statistical Abstract of Israel 2005," http:// www1.cbs.gov.il/shnaton56/st02_01.pdf. On church membership: Linda Lyons, "Religiosity Compass Points South," Gallup Poll. On church attendance: Gallup News Service, "Eastern Season Finds a Religious Nation," Gallup Poll, April 13, 2001, http://poll .gallup.com. Some researchers have argued that Americans attend church far less frequently than they say they do; see C. Kirk Hadaway, Penny Long Marler, and Mark Chaves, "What the Polls Don't Show: A Closer Look at U.S. Church Attendance," *American Sociological Review* 58.6 (December 1993): 741–52; C. Kirk Hadaway, Penny Long Marler, and Mark Chaves, "Overreporting Church Attendance in America: Evidence That Demands the Same Verdict," *American Sociological Review* 63.1 (February 1998): 122–30.

36. On self-identification as born-again: Frank Newport and Joseph Carroll, "Another Look at Evangelicals in America Today," Gallup Poll, December 2, 2005, http://poll.gallup.com. On having a born-again experience: Albert L. Winseman, "U.S. Evangelicals: How Many Walk the Walk?" Gallup Poll, May 31, 2005, http://poll .gallup.com. On biblical literalism at home and abroad: Jennifer Robison, "In the Beginning Was the Word," Gallup Poll, February 5, 2002, http://poll.gallup.com.

37. Since 1995 *Time* magazine alone has run cover stories on Jesus, Mary, Abraham, Moses, Pope John Paul II, Billy and Franklin Graham, Roman Catholicism, Buddhism, Mormonism, heaven—at least fifteen in all; see "Hail, Mary" (March 21, 2005), "Abraham" (September 30, 2002), "Can the Catholic Church Save Itself?" (April 1, 2002), "What Jesus Saw: Jerusalem Then and Now" (April 16, 2001); "The Pope in the Holy Land" (April 3, 2000); "Jesus at 2000" (December 6, 1999); "Who Was Moses?" (December 14, 1998); "The Shroud of Turin" (April 20, 1998); "America's Fascination with Buddhism" (October 13, 1997); "Mormons, Inc." (August 4, 1997); "Does Heaven Exist?" (March 24, 1997); "Jesus Online" (December 16, 1996); "And God Said . . ." (October 28, 1996); "The Prodigal Son" (May 13, 1996); "The Search for Jesus" (April 8, 1996). On Christian music sales: Mark Allan Powell, "Jesus Climbs the Charts," *Christian Century* 119.26 (December 18, 2002): 20–26.

38. Stephen Prothero, *American Jesus: How the Son of God Became a National Icon* (New York: Farrar, Straus and Giroux, 2003), 290.

39. Diana L. Eck, *A New Religious America: How a "Christian Country" Has Become the World's Most Religiously Diverse Nation* (San Francisco: HarperSanFrancisco, 2001), 4; R. Scott Hanson, "City of Gods," The Pluralism Project, http://www.pluralism.org/affiliates/shanson/index.php. On Buddhism's reach: Robert Wuthnow and Wendy Cadge, "Buddhists and Buddhism in the United States: The Scope of Influence," *Journal for the Scientific Study of Religion* 43.3 (September 2004): 363–80. On mosques in America: Ihsan Bagby, Paul M. Perl, and Bryan T. Froehle, *The Mosque in America: A National Portrait* (Washington, DC: Council on American-Islamic Relations, 2001). On Singapore: "Singapore Census of Population, 2000, Advance Data Release No. 2: Religion," http://www.singstat.gov.sg/papers/c2000/adr-religion.pdf. Warren A. Nord and Charles C. Haynes also call the United States "the most religiously diverse country on earth," in *Taking Religion Seriously Across the Curriculum* (Alexandria, VA: Association for Supervision and Curriculum Development and Nashville, TN: First Amendment Center, 1998), 68.

40. Jon Butler, *Awash in a Sea of Faith: Christianizing the American People* (Cambridge: Harvard University Press, 1990); R. Laurence Moore, *Selling God: American Religion in the Marketplace of Culture* (New York: Oxford University Press, 1994), 10.

41. Henry David Thoreau, *Walden* (New York: C. E. Merrill, 1910), chap. 3, http://xroads.virginia.edu/~hyper/WALDEN/hdt03.html; Ralph Waldo Emerson, *The Letters of Ralph Waldo Emerson,* ed. Ralph L. Rusk (New York: Columbia University Press, 1939–1995), 3:290; *ISKCON v. Houston,* 689 F. 2d 541, 549 (1982); Gary Rosen, "God Is So Not Dead," *New York Times,* October 2, 2005, BR 34.

42. Only 11 percent of my students passed this exam with a grade of 60 (out of 100) or higher. The rest failed. The average score was 43.

43. On religious illiteracy at UNC and Wheaton, respectively: W. A. Nord, *Religion and American Education,* 199–200; Gary M. Burge, "The Greatest Story Never Read," *Christianity Today* 43.9 (August 9, 1999): 45–49. On the demography of American Baptists, Aroostook County (Maine), Catholicism, Southern Baptists, and Mormons: see the Association of Religion Data Archives, http://www.thearda.com. On women and men, angels and witches: Linda Lyons, "Paranormal Beliefs Come (Super)Naturally to Some," Gallup Poll, November 1, 2005, http://poll.gallup.com. On political beliefs and haunted houses: Linda Lyons, "One-Third of Americans Believe Dearly May Not Have Departed," Gallup Poll, July 12, 2005, http://poll.gallup.com. On evangelicals and reincarnation: Gallup and Lindsay, *Surveying the Religious Landscape,* 40. On evangelicals and women: "Southern Baptists Pass New Statement of Faith Based on Literal Interpretation of Bible: Where Do Americans Stand?" Gallup Poll, June 15, 2000, http://poll.gallup.com.

44. Karen R. Long, "Bible Knowledge at Record Low, Pollster Says," *National Catholic Reporter,* July 15, 1994, 9. On the decline of Bible reading and the Bible answering life's questions: Alec Gallup and Wendy W. Simmons, "Six in Ten Americans Read Bible at Least Occasionally," Gallup Poll, October 20, 2000, http://poll.gallup.com. On the Bible in homes: Jennifer Robison, "The Word on Bible-Buying," Gallup Poll, June 18, 2002, http://poll.gallup.com. On annual Bible sales and the Gideons: David Gibson, "America's Favorite Unopened Text," http://www.beliefnet.com/story/57/story_5746_1.html. On twice-a-month Bible reading: Gallup and Lindsay, *Surveying the Religious Landscape,* 50.

45. "Jay Walking with Jay Leno," http://www.bibleliteracy.org/Site/PressRoom/press_lenovideo.htm.

46. George Gallup Jr., *The Role of the Bible in American Society* (Princeton, NJ: Princeton Religion Research Center, 1990), 17.

47. David Gibson, "We Revere the Bible ... We Don't Read It," *Washington Post,* December 9, 2000, B9.

48. David Gibson, "America's Favorite Unopened Text," http://www.beliefnet.com/story/57/story_5746_1.html.

49. "Economic Values Survey, 1992," The Association of Religion Data Archives, http://www.thearda.com/Archive/Files/Descriptions/ECON.asp.

50. "Economic Values Survey, 1992," the Association of Religion Data Archives, http://www.thearda.com/Archive/Files/Descriptions/ECON.asp.

51. George Barna, *The Index of Leading Spiritual Indicators* (Dallas: Word Publishing, 1996), 79.

52. Barna, *Leading Spiritual Indicators,* 79.

53. "Harper's Index for December 2005," http://www.harpers.org/HarpersIndex2005-12.html; Charles Colson, "Reversing Memory Loss," *Christianity Today* 45.10 (August 6, 2001): 88. On the religious knowledge of journalists, see Christian Smith, "Religiously Ignorant Journalists," *Books and Culture,* January 1, 2004, http://www.ctlibrary.com/bc/2004/janfeb/2.06.html.

54. "Barna Reviews Top Religious Trends of 2005," Barna Update, December 20, 2005, http://www.barna.org/FlexPage.aspx?Page=BarnaUpdate&BarnaUpdateID=214; Marie Wachlin and Byron R. Johnson, *Bible Literacy Report* (Fairfax, VA: Bible Literacy Project, 2005), 5. On the downward trend, see the same source, 15.

55. Wachlin and Johnson, *Bible Literacy Report,* 48, 42, 50.

56. Rodney Stark and Charles Y. Glock, *American Piety: The Nature of Religious Commitment* (Berkeley and Los Angeles: University of California Press, 1968), 150–51; "Economic Values Survey, 1992," the Association of Religion Data Archives, http://www.thearda.com/Archive/Files/Descriptions/ECON.asp. In this 1992 survey Jews also fared better than evangelicals when asked whether the book of Acts is in the Old Testa-

ment: 28 percent of the evangelicals surveyed wrongly answered yes while only 16 percent of the Jewish respondents made that error.

57. On teachers who teach about the Bible: M. G. Wachlin, "The Place of Bible Literature in Public High School English Classes," *Research in the Teaching of English* 31 (February 1997): 18–19. On students whose schools teach about the Bible: Wachlin and Johnson, *Bible Literacy Report,* 23. Predictably, private schools are, according to Wachlin and Johnson, far more likely than public schools to offer courses in the Bible, religious studies, and the world's religions (23).

58. David Van Biema et al., "The 25 Most Influential Evangelicals in America," *Time,* February 7, 2005, 34–45. On not knowing what evangelicalism means: Barna, *Leading Spiritual Indicators,* 78. On congregations doing "an excellent job" (27 percent) or "a fairly good job" (33 percent) teaching teens: Smith and Denton, *Soul Searching,* 66.

59. Smith and Denton, *Soul Searching,* 27. On naming religious founders: Stark and Glock, *American Piety,* 161. "Exploring Religious America," a 2002 survey conducted for *U.S. News and World Report* and *Religion and Ethics Newsweekly,* found that most Americans know little about Islam, Hinduism, and Buddhism. Fully 65 percent said that they were either "somewhat unfamiliar" or "very unfamiliar" with Islam, a figure that rose to 73 percent for Buddhism and 85 percent for Hinduism (http://www.pbs.org/wnet/religionandethics/week534/specialreport.html). This same survey found that 71 percent of Americans did not know a Muslim, 81 percent did not know a Buddhist, and 82 percent did not know a Hindu.

60. John C. Cavadini, "Ignorant Catholics: The Alarming Void in Religious Education," *Commonweal* 131.7 (April 9, 2004): 14; James D. Davidson, "Challenging Assumptions About Young Catholics," *National Catholic Reporter,* September 30, 2005, http://natcath.org/NCR_Online/archives2/2005c/093005/093005r.htm. A renewed emphasis on the Bible, instigated by Vatican II and expressed in the church's new catechism (published in English in 1994), seems to have done little to close the Bible-reading gap between Protestants and Catholics. As poorly as Protestants do on Bible literacy quizzes, Catholics fare even worse.

61. Hoge, Dinges, Johnson, and Gonzales, *Young Adult Catholics,* 25, 28, 134–35. On the shifts from sacraments to Jesus and from religion to morality, see 168 and 171 in the same book.

62. John C. Cavadini, "Ignorant Catholics," 13; "Catholic Group Hails Bernardin Call for New Unity," press release, Association for the Rights of Catholics in the Church, August 14, 1996, http://astro.temple.edu/~arcc/press.htm; Martin E. Marty, "Declining Catechesis," *Sightings,* October 16, 2000, http://marty-center.uchicago.edu/sightings/archive_2000/sightings-101600.shtml; "Department of Theology Strategic Planning," Department of Theology, University of Notre Dame, http://al.nd.edu/resources-for/faculty-and-staff/documents/StrategicPlan_Theology.pdf; "Catholics Read,"

http://www.catholicsread.org. On converting Catholics to Catholicism, see also William J. O'Malley, "Plow Before You Plant," *America* 183.7 (September 16, 2000), http:// www.americamagazine.org/gettext.cfm?articleTypeID=1&textID=2184&issueID= 380. On the Bible-reading gap, see "The State of the Church, 2000," Barna Update, March 21, 2000, which indicates that, while Catholics are slightly more likely than Protestants to have attended church in the last week (49 percent to 47 percent), they are far less likely (25 percent to 53 percent) to have read the Bible during that same time period (http://www.barna.org/FlexPage.aspx?Page=BarnaUpdate&BarnaUpdate ID=49). In fact, Catholic youth are far more likely to meditate in any given year than they are to attend a Bible study group. See Hoge, Dinges, Johnson, and Gonzales, *Young Adult Catholics,* 156.

63. Johannes G. Vos, "Roadblocks Limiting Church Effectiveness—Part 1," *Ordained Servant* 9.3 (July 2000): 57; Mark A. Noll, *The Scandal of the Evangelical Mind* (Grand Rapids, MI: Eerdmans, 1994), 3; Os Guinness, "Persuasion for the New World: An Interview with Dr. Os Guinness," *Crucible* 4.2 (Summer 1992): 15, quoted in Noll, *Scandal of the Evangelical Mind,* 23; Burge, "Greatest Story Never Read," 48; David F. Wells, *No Place for Truth, or Whatever Happened to Evangelical Theology?* (Grand Rapids, MI: Eerdmans, 1993), 4; Burge, "Greatest Story Never Read," 45–49.

64. *Revolve: The Complete New Testament* (Nashville, TN: Thomas Nelson Bibles, 2003), 167; *Refuel: The Complete New Testament for Guys* (Nashville, TN: Thomas Nelson Bibles, 2004), 189; "Biblezines," http://www.thomasnelson.com/consumer/dept.asp ? dept_id=190900&TopLevel_id=190000.

65. Joseph Telushkin, *Jewish Literacy: The Most Important Things to Know About the Jewish Religion, Its People, and Its History* (New York: William Morrow, 1991), 9; Jewish Literacy Foundation, "About JLF," http://www.leviathanpress.com/JLF_about_0.htm.

66. Weststar Institute, Jesus Seminar Forum, http://virtualreligion.net/forum/ westar.html.

67. Alicia Caldwell and Felisa Cardona, "Lisl Auman Wins New Trial," *Denver Post,* March 29, 2005. The majority decision in *People v. Harlan* appears at http://www.cobar .org/opinions/opinion.cfm?OpinionID=5061.

68. On the God gap: *Religion and Public Life: A Faith-Based Partisan Divide* (Washington, DC: Pew Forum on Religion and Public Life, 2005); John C. Green, "Religion Gap Swings New Ways," *Religion in the News* 7.3 (Winter 2005): 2–3.

69. Harold Bloom, *The American Religion: The Emergence of the Post-Christian Nation* (New York: Simon & Schuster, 1992); Peter L. Berger, "The Desecularization of the World: A Global Overview," in *The Desecularization of the World: Resurgent Religion and World Politics,* ed. Peter L. Berger (Grand Rapids, MI: Eerdmans, 1999), 2. More recently Berger has written that secularization theory "fails spectacularly in explaining the difference between America and Europe"; see "Religion and the West," *National Interest* 80 (Summer 2005): 112. See also Roger Finke and Rodney Stark, *The Churching of*

America, 1776–2005: Winners and Losers in our Religious Economy (New Brunswick, NJ: Rutgers University Press, 2005).

70. Samuel P. Huntington, *The Clash of Civilizations and the Remaking of World Order* (New York: Simon and Schuster, 1996). For a new take on Huntington's thesis, see Thomas L. Friedman, "War of the Worlds," *New York Times,* February 24, 2006, A23: "The world is drifting dangerously toward a widespread religious and sectarian cleavage—the likes of which we have not seen for a long, long time."

71. Jon Butler, "Jack-in-the-Box Faith: The Religion Problem in Modern American History," *Journal of American History* 90.4 (March 2004): 1357–78. On railroads and religion in textbooks: Nord and Haynes, *Taking Religion Seriously,* 79. In "Religion-Free Texts: Getting an Illiberal Education," *Christian Century* 116.20 (July 14–21, 1999): 711–15, Warren A. Nord reports searching in vain for an American history textbook that devotes more ink to postbellum religion than to the Watergate scandal.

72. O. L. Davis, Gerald Ponder, Lynn Burlbaw, Maria Garza-Lubeck, and Alfred Moss, *Looking at History: A Review of Major U.S. History Textbooks* (Washington, DC: People for the American Way, 1986), quoted in Association for Supervision and Curriculum Development, "Religion in the Curriculum," *Journal of the American Academy of Religion* 55.3 (Autumn 1987): 581.

73. Joe Loconte, "A Textbook Case," *Wall Street Journal,* August 13, 1999, W11; Gerhard Lenski, *The Religious Factor* (Garden City, NY: Doubleday, 1961).

74. Alexis de Tocqueville, *Democracy in America,* vol. 2, chap. 1, http://xroads.virginia .edu/~HYPER/DETOC/ch1_01.htm.

75. Max Weber, *The Protestant Ethic and the Spirit of Capitalism,* trans. Talcott Parsons (New York: Scribner, 1930). In addition to President Reagan's repeated evocations of America as a "shining city on the hill," President Clinton's promise of a "New Covenant" between the US government and its people was inspired by Puritan sermons. See Ronald Reagan, "Address to the Nation on the Eve of the Presidential Election," November 5, 1984, http://www.reagan.utexas.edu/archives/speeches/1984/110584e .htm; Bill Clinton, "1992 Democratic National Convention Acceptance Address," July 16, 1992, http://www.americanrhetoric.com/speeches/billclinton1992dnc.htm.

76. J. C. D. Clark, *The Language of Liberty, 1660–1832: Political Discourse and Social Dynamics in the Anglo-American World* (New York: Cambridge University Press, 1994), 305, cited in Gordon S. Wood, "Religion and the American Revolution," in *New Directions in American Religious History,* ed. Harry S. Stout and D. G. Hart (New York: Oxford University Press, 1997), 180; Abraham Keteltas, *God Arising and Pleading His People's Cause* (Newburyport, 1777), in "Religion and the Founding of the American Republic," Library of Congress, http://www.loc.gov/exhibits/religion/rel03.html. On the "moderate Enlightenment," see Henry F. May, *The Enlightenment in America* (New York: Oxford University Press, 1976).

77. Nathan O. Hatch, *The Democratization of American Christianity* (New Haven, CT: Yale University Press, 1989), 35, 125–61; Elias Smith, *The Loving Kindness of God Displayed in the Triumph of Republicanism in America* (Massachusetts, 1809), 27, quoted in Gordon S. Wood, "Religion and the American Revolution," 194.

78. Abraham Lincoln, "Second Inaugural Address," March 4, 1865, http://www.bartleby.com/124/pres32.html; "Address to all Churches of Christ," in *The Collected Writings of James Henley Thornwell, D.D., LL.D.,* ed. John B. Adger and John L. Girardeau (Richmond, n.p.: Presbyterian Committee of Publication, 1873), 4:460; Frederick Douglass, *Narrative of the Life of Frederick Douglass, an American Slave* (Boston: Anti-Slavery Office, 1845), 118.

79. Andrew Carnegie, "Wealth," *North American Review* 148.391 (June 1889): 653–64; Russell H. Conwell, "Acres of Diamonds," http://www.materialreligion.org/documents/apr97doc.html; Charles M. Sheldon, *In His Steps,* http://www.kancoll.org/books/sheldon.

80. On Jesus as "sweet Savior" and "manly Redeemer," see Prothero, *American Jesus,* 43–86, 87–123. The best book on "muscular Christianity" is Clifford Putney, *Muscular Christianity: Manhood and Sports in Protestant America, 1880–1920* (Cambridge: Harvard University Press, 2001).

81. Patrick Allitt, *Religion in America Since 1945: A History* (New York: Columbia University Press, 2003), xv.

82. George Washington, "First Inaugural Address," April 30, 1789, in *Inaugural Addresses of the Presidents of the United States: From George Washington 1789 to George Bush 1989* (Washington, DC: United States Government Printing Office, 1989), 4; Thomas Jefferson, "First Inaugural Address," March 4, 1801, in *Inaugural Addresses of the Presidents,* 17; Franklin Steiner, *The Religious Beliefs of Our Presidents* (Girard, KS: Haldeman-Julius Publications, 1936), 146. On the Republicans as a "party of theocracy": Paul Krugman, "An Academic Question," *New York Times,* April 5, 2005, A23; and Kevin Phillips, *American Theocracy: The Peril and Politics of Radical Religion, Oil, and Borrowed Money in the 21ˢᵗ Century* (New York: Viking, 2006). The most balanced treatment of presidential piety is Edwin S. Gaustad, *Faith of Our Fathers: Religion and the New Nation* (San Francisco: Harper and Row, 1987). John Sutherland Bonnell's *Presidential Profiles: Religion in the Life of American Presidents* (Philadelphia: Westminster Press, 1971) bends over backward to demonstrate the heartfelt faith of even Ulysses Grant, arguably the least religious US chief executive, while Steiner's *Religious Beliefs of Our Presidents* turns dozens of believers into doubters, all in the service of free thought.

83. Edwin S. Gaustad, "American History: With and Without Religion," *Magazine of History* 6.3 (Winter 1992): 17, quoted in Paul Boyer, "In Search of the Fourth 'R': The Treatment of Religion in American History Textbooks and Survey Courses," *History Teacher* 29.2 (February 1996): 210. On atheists and the presidency: Peter Steinfels,

"Some Surprising Commonalities in the Status of Believers and Nonbelievers in American Society," *New York Times,* March 24, 2001, B6.

84. Gaustad, "American History: With and Without Religion," 15; On Nord's observations on Islam in textbooks: First Amendment Center and the Pew Forum on Religion and Public Life, *Teaching About Religion in Public Schools: Where Do We Go From Here?* 2004, http://pewforum.org/publications/reports/TeachingAboutReligion.pdf, 9.

85. Carleton W. Young, "Religion in United States History Textbooks," *History Teacher* 28.2 (February 1995): 265; Association for Supervision and Curriculum Development, "Religion in the Curriculum," *Journal of the American Academy of Religion* 55.3 (Autumn 1987): 571. On the disappearance of the Holocaust from textbooks: Glenn S. Pate, *Treatment of the Holocaust in U.S. History Textbooks* (New York: Anti-Defamation League of New York, 1970); Michael Kane, *Minorities in Textbooks: A Study of Their Treatment in Social Science Texts* (Chicago: Quadrangle Books, 1970).

86. Paul C. Vitz: *Censorship: Evidence of Bias in Our Children's Textbooks* (Ann Arbor, MI: Servant Books: 1986), 18; "Top Ten Most Embarrassing Moments in the History of the Textbook (in No Particular Order)," *Stay Free!* 18 (May 1, 2001), http://www.stayfreemagazine.org/archives/18/topten.html. The Tennessee case is *Mozert v. Hawkins County,* 827 F.2d 1058 (6th Cir. 1987); the Alabama case is *Smith v. Board of School Commissioners,* 827 F.2d 684 (11th Cir. 1987).

87. On homeschooling: US Department of Education, National Center for Education Statistics, "1.1 Million Homeschooled Students in the United States in 2003," July 2004, http://nces.ed.gov/pubs2004/2004115.pdf. On conservative Christian schools, which are the fastest growing segment in private schooling: US Department of Education, National Center for Education Statistics, "The Condition of Education 2005: Indicator 2: Trends in Private School Enrollments," 2005, http://nces.ed.gov/programs/coe/2005/pdf/02_2005.pdf. On the evils of erasing religion from the public square, two classics are: Neuhaus, *Naked Public Square,* and Stephen L. Carter, *The Culture of Disbelief: How American Law and Politics Trivialize Religious Devotion* (New York: Basic Books, 1993).

88. Vitz, *Censorship,* 1; Timothy Smith, "High School History Texts Adopted for Use in the State of Alabama: The Distortion and Exclusion of Religious Data," *Religion and Public Education* 15 (Spring 1988): 178. For a response to these criticisms by a religion-friendly textbook author, see Boyer, "In Search of the Fourth 'R,'" 195–216.

89. Barbara Vobejda, "Why Censor Religion? Left and Right Agree It Belongs in Textbooks," *Washington Post,* April 19, 1987, D1.

90. *Abington v. Schempp;* Warren A. Nord, "Religion-Free Texts: Getting an Illiberal Education," *Christian Century* 116.20 (July 14–21, 1999): 713. On Christmas without Jesus: Nord and Haynes, *Taking Religion Seriously,* 61.

91. *Abington v. Schempp.*

92. *Abington v. Schempp.*

93. Frances Fitzgerald, *America Revised: History Schoolbooks in the Twentieth Century* (Boston: Little, Brown, 1979), 27.

94. On biblical names: Gloria L. Main, "Naming Children in Early New England," *Journal of Interdisciplinary History* 27.1 (Summer 1996): 1–27. According to Main, 66 percent of the girls born in New England between 1620 and 1794 and not named after family members were given biblical names; that figure was higher (75 percent) for boys (16).

95. Harold A. Buetow, *Of Singular Benefit: The Story of U.S. Catholic Education* (New York: Macmillan, 1970), 3; David D. Hall, "Readers and Writers in Early New England," in *Colonial Book,* ed. Amory and Hall, 120.

96. Madison to W. T. Barry (August 4, 1822), in *The Writings of James Madison,* ed. Gaillard Hunt (New York: G. P. Putnam's Sons, 1910), 9:103, quoted in Lawrence A. Cremin, *The American Common School: An Historic Conception* (New York: Bureau of Publications, Teachers College, Columbia University, 1951), 30.

97. John Adams diary, February 21, 1765, Adams Family Papers, Massachusetts Historical Society, http://www.masshist.org/digitaladams/aea/cfm/doc.cfm?id=D10, quoted in David D. Hall, *Cultures of Print: Essays in the History of the Book* (Amherst: University of Massachusetts Press, 1996), 167; David Paul Nord, *Faith in Reading: Religious Publishing and the Birth of Mass Media in America* (New York: Oxford University Press, 2004), 14; *Analectic Magazine* (April 1817), quoted in William J. Gilmore, *Reading Becomes a Necessity of Life: Material and Cultural Life in Rural New England, 1780–1835* (Knoxville: University of Tennessee Press, 1989), 118. The 1710–1795 data come from Edward E. Gordon and Elaine A. Gordon, *Literacy in America: Historic Journey and Contemporary Solutions* (Westport, CT: Praeger, 2003), xvi; the later data come from Gilmore, *Reading Becomes a Necessity,* 119. The broader literature on literacy is voluminous. The classic study is Kenneth A. Lockridge, *Literacy in Colonial New England: An Enquiry into the Social Context of Literacy in the Early Modern West* (New York: Norton, 1974), though Lockridge's data, which is based on the portion of will makers who signed their wills, significantly undercount reading literacy. An earlier study, also flawed, is Samuel Eliot Morison, *The Puritan Pronaos: Studies in the Intellectual Life of New England in the Seventeenth Century* (New York: New York University Press, 1936), which likely overstates literacy rates. The best recent corrective is E. Jennifer Monaghan's exhaustive *Learning to Read and Write in Colonial America* (Amherst: University of Massachusetts Press, 2005), which offers in its first appendix (384–85) the best compilation of data from various sources on "signature literacy" between 1650 and 1810. For an informed discussion, see Carl F. Kaestle, "Studying the History of Literacy," in Carl F. Kaestle et al., *Literacy in the United States: Readers and Reading since 1880* (New Haven, CT: Yale University Press, 1991), 3–32.

98. Monaghan, *Learning to Read and Write,* 89. The DuBois estimate can be found in W. E. B. Du Bois's *Black Reconstruction* (1935), quoted in Lawrence A. Cremin, *American*

Education: The National Experience, 1783–1876 (New York: Harper and Row, 1980), 229. Slave literacy is the subject of Janet Cornelius, *"When I Can Read My Title Clear": Literacy, Slavery, and Religion in the Antebellum South* (Columbia: University of South Carolina Press, 1991). Monaghan, *Learning to Read and Write,* devotes one chapter to blacks and two to Native Americans: 241–72, 46–80, 166–88. Douglas L. Winiarski discusses Indian literacy in "Native American Popular Religion in New England's Old Colony, 1670–1770," *Religion and American Culture* 15.2 (Summer 2005): 147–86; he finds Native American reading literacy rates ranging from 20 percent to 47 percent in different areas of southeastern New England (160).

99. Literacy rates for women trailed those of men, but literacy was an accomplishment, at least in New England, for virtually all women born in the decade before the Revolution. By 1850 literacy rates for white men and women as reported to the US Census were basically equivalent: 90 percent. Here I am rejecting the much more modest figures of Lockridge, siding instead with Joel Perlmann and Dennis Shirley, who found (among other things) that Lockridge undercounted the numbers of wills signed by women in both rural and urban Massachusetts. See Lockridge, *Literacy in Colonial New England;* and Joel Perlmann and Dennis Shirley, "When Did New England Women Acquire Literacy?" *William and Mary Quarterly* 48.1 (January 1991): 50–67. On female literacy, see also E. Jennifer Monaghan, "Literacy Instruction and Gender in Colonial New England," *American Quarterly* 40.1 (March 1988): 18–41; and Gloria L. Main, "An Inquiry into When and Why Women Learned to Write in Colonial New England," *Journal of Social History* 24.3 (Spring 1991): 579–89.

100. Hugh Amory, "Printing and Bookselling in New England, 1638–1713," in *Colonial Book,* ed. Amory and Hall, 109. On Bibles in homes, see Gilmore, *Reading Becomes a Necessity,* 447.

101. Mather's estimate regarding the catechisms appears in Lawrence A. Cremin, *American Education: The Colonial Experience, 1607–1783* (New York: Harper and Row, 1970), 130. The source for the Rye, New York, data is Monaghan, *Learning to Read and Write,* 150–51.

102. Harry S. Stout, *The New England Soul: Preaching and Religious Culture in Colonial New England* (New York: Oxford University Press, 1986), 4, 3; Kenneth P. Minkema, "The Lynn End 'Earthquake' Relations of 1727," *New England Quarterly* 69.3 (September 1996): 480. As Minkema notes, these relations changed over time. In the seventeenth century many "applicants would have to make a relation of their spiritual experience and a separate profession of Reformed dogma" (480).

103. David D. Hall, *Worlds of Wonder, Days of Judgment: Popular Religious Belief in Early New England* (Cambridge: Harvard University Press, 1989), 49. On the relative importance of books on religion: Gilmore, *Reading Becomes a Necessity,* 26, 285–343; on half of the colonial imprints being religious: Cremin, *American Education: The Colonial Experience,* 40–41; on Bibles as popular works and ministers as popular authors: Hugh

Amory, "A Note on Statistics," in *Colonial Book,* ed. Amory and Hall, 511; on the portion of religious books in rural New Englanders' family libraries: Gilmore, *Reading Becomes a Necessity,* 208. This last estimate would have been much higher if Gilmore had not included popular readers and spellers, many of which were feverishly religious, in the category of "secular works" (206).

The closest thing to a colonial J. K. Rowling was Cotton Mather, whose books accounted for 16 percent of all North American imprints in the 1701–1710 period, 15 percent in 1711–1720, and 8 percent in 1721–1730. Other leading eighteenth-century authors include the hymnist Isaac Watts (with ninety-eight books), the revivalist George Whitefield (also ninety-eight), and the Puritan divine Increase Mather (seventy-four)—all well ahead, it might be noted, of Thomas Paine, with only fifty-six. See David D. Hall and Russell L. Martin, "Appendix Two: Popular and Durable Authors and Titles," in *Colonial Book,* ed. Amory and Hall, 520.

104. John K. Nelson, *A Blessed Company: Parishes, Parsons, and Parishioners in Anglican Virginia, 1690–1776* (Chapel Hill: University of North Carolina Press, 2001), 190–91. Scholars have typically characterized colonial Virginia as spiritually moribund. In *Awash in a Sea of Faith,* Butler writes that seventeenth-century Virginia is "better known for irreligion and indifference than piety" (40). Nelson's exhaustively researched book undercuts such stereotypes, arguing that perceptions of the vast differences between pious New Englanders and secular Virginians are based more in styles of recordkeeping—New England churchgoers kept records in both senses of that verb, Virginians in neither—than in actual religious experiences.

105. Hall, *Cultures of Print,* 120–21; Anne Hulton, *Letters of a Loyalist Lady* (Cambridge: Harvard University Press, 1927), 105, quoted in Cremin, *American Education: The Colonial Experience,* 521. Hall discusses the differences between "intensive" and "extensive" reading in his *Cultures of Print,* 87–88.

106. Daniel Webster, "The First Bunker Hill Monument Oration" (1825), http://www.bartleby.com/268/9/2.html; Gilmore, *Reading Becomes a Necessity,* 355.

107. Benjamin Franklin, *Benjamin Franklin, His Autobiography, 1706–1757,* Harvard Classics (New York: P. F. Collier and Son, 1909–14), http://www.bartleby.com/1/1/1.html.

108. Here the new school was pioneered by Bernard Bailyn, who argued in *Education in the Forming of American Society: Needs and Opportunities for Study* (Chapel Hill: University of North Carolina Press, 1960) that education should be understood "not only as formal pedagogy but as the entire process by which a culture transmits itself across the generations" (14). Its greatest exemplar is Lawrence A. Cremin, who followed Bailyn's lead in seeing the household, the church, and the community as sites for education too. See, for example, his trilogy: *American Education: The Colonial Experience; American Education: The National Experience;* and *American Education: The Metropolitan Experience, 1876–1980* (New York: Harper and Row, 1988). For a representative of the

old school, which restricted the concept of education to formal schooling, see Ellwood P. Cubberley, *Public Education in the United States: A Study and Interpretation of American Educational History* (Boston: Houghton Mifflin, 1919).

109. Cremin, *American Education: The Colonial Experience,* 124.

110. Historian Linda K. Kerber coined the term. See her *Women of the Republic: Intellect and Ideology in Revolutionary America* (Chapel Hill: University of North Carolina Press, 1980), 229.

111. Quoted in Paul Leicester Ford, ed., *The New England Primer: A Reprint of the Earliest Known Edition* (New York: Dodd, Mead, 1899), 83–84.

112. Joseph T. Buckingham *Personal Memoirs and Recollections of Editorial Life,* 2 vols. (Boston: Ticknor, Reed and Fields, 1852), quoted in Hall, *Cultures of Print,* 55.

113. Cremin, *American Education: The Colonial Experience,* 155; Monaghan, *Learning to Read and Write,* 86.

114. Winiarski, "Native American Popular Religion," 161.

115. Cremin, *American Education: The Colonial Experience,* 162. On Paaonut and T'hayendanegea: Monaghan, *Learning to Read and Write,* 70, 188.

116. On the feats of Sturgeon's students: Monaghan, *Learning to Read and Write,* 259.

117. Cremin, *American Education: The Colonial Experience,* 181.

118. Cremin, *American Education: The Colonial Experience,* 184; Monaghan, *Learning to Read and Write,* 191; W. A. Nord, *Religion and American Education,* 63.

119. George B. Cheever, *Right of the Bible in Our Public Schools* (New York: R. Carter, 1854), 112, quoted in Cremin, *American Common School,* 47. On public school enrollments in 1850, see the same source, 126, 180. Of course, public education was available long before it was mandatory. Massachusetts was the first state to require school attendance (in 1852); Mississippi (in 1918) was the last.

120. James Gordon Carter, *The Schools of Massachusetts in 1824* (Boston: Directors of the Old South Meetinghouse, n.d.), 216, quoted in William Kailer Dunn, *What Happened to Religious Education? The Decline of Religious Teaching in the Public Elementary School, 1776–1861* (Baltimore: Johns Hopkins Press, 1958), 101.

121. Monaghan, *Learning to Read and Write,* 13, 83.

122. Wilberforce Eames, review of Ford, ed., *The New England Primer,* in *American Historical Review* 3.2 (January 1898): 372; Cremin, *American Common School,* 183.

123. Unless otherwise stated, all references to the *New England Primer* are to a 1777 edition available online at http://www.sacred-texts.com/chr/nep/1777/index.htm.

124. Paul Leicester Ford, "Introduction" to *New England Primer,* ed. Ford, 99.

125. Ross W. Beales and E. Jennifer Monaghan, "Part One: Literacy and Schoolbooks," in *Colonial Book,* ed. Amory and Hall, 384. As Beales and Monaghan note, other examples of these "denominational texts" included *A New Primmer or Methodical Directions To Attain the True Spelling, Reading and Writing of English* (1698), by the

Pietist Francis Daniel Pastorius, and *Instructions for Spelling* (1702), by the Quaker George Fox.

126. On the Vermont editions of Webster's speller, see Gilmore, *Reading Becomes a Necessity,* 53. The most careful examination of overall sales figures can be found in E. Jennifer Monaghan, *A Common Heritage: Noah Webster's Blue-Back Speller* (Hamden, CT: Archon Books, 1983), 215–28, 233. A widely cited source speculates that Webster's spelling book ranks third on a list of all-time best-selling books. See Russell Ash, *The Top 10 of Everything* (New York: DK Publishing, 1996), 112–13, reproduced at http://www.ipl.org.ar/ref/QUE/FARQ/bestsellerFARQ.html.

127. Henry Steele Commager, "Schoolmaster to America," in *Noah Webster's American Spelling Book* (New York: Bureau of Publications, Teachers College, Columbia University, 1962), 5, 1. This volume reproduces Noah Webster, *The American Spelling-Book* (Middletown, CT: William H. Niles, 1831). For an earlier version online (likely 1800), see http://www.merrycoz.org/books/spelling/SPELLING.HTM.

128. Monaghan, *Common Heritage,* 37; *Noah Webster's American Spelling Book,* 55. Webster's opener borrowed from Dilworth, whose first lesson (as cited in Monaghan, *Common Heritage,* 34) reads:

No man may put off the Law of God.
The Way of God is no ill Way.
My joy is in God all the Day.
A bad man is a Foe to God.

129. *Noah Webster's American Spelling Book,* 55; "Noah Webster 1828 Dictionary," The Foundation for American Christian Education, http://www.face.net/websters1828. htm; *Noah Webster's American Spelling Book,* 169.

130. *Noah Webster's American Spelling Book,* 115. On pronunciation, consider this footnote from an 1800 edition of Webster's speller: "In almost all scripture names of the Old Testament, *t* retains its proper sound, as in *Peletiah; ch* sounds like *k* as in *Chaldean, g* is generally hard before *i,* as in *Gibeon.* The letters *ai,* which represent the Hebrew *ain,* are generally pronounced like the first sound of *a.* In the New Testament *tia* and *cia* are pronounced as *she,* as in *Galatia*" (http://www.merrycoz.org/books/spelling/pages/amer104.jpg). Note how even this explanation assumes familiarity not only with Bible names but also with their pronunciation.

131. For estimates on the religious content of Webster's speller, see Oscar Tinglestad, "The Religious Element in American School Readers up to 1830; a Bibliographical and Statistical Study" (PhD diss., University of Chicago, 1925), which fixed the religious content at 33 percent for 1783–1804 editions and 47 percent for the 1804–1829 period.

132. Herbert Quick, *One Man's Life* (Indianapolis: Bobbs-Merrill, 1925), 156, quoted in Carol Kammen, "The McGuffey Readers," in *Children's Literature, Volume 5, Annual of the Modern Language Association Group on Children's Literature and the Children's Literature Association* (Philadelphia: Temple University Press, 1976), 62. On total sales figures and geographic reach: John H. Westerhoff, *McGuffey and His Readers: Piety, Morality, and Education in Nineteenth-Century America* (Knoxville, TN: Abingdon, 1978), 14–15.

133. Westerhoff, *McGuffey and His Readers,* 40; George M. Marsden, *The Soul of the American University: From Protestant Establishment to Established Nonbelief* (New York: Oxford University Press, 1994), 90.

134. D. A. Saunders, "Social Ideas in McGuffey Readers," *Public Opinion Quarterly* 5.4 (Winter 1941): 588.

135. Elliott J. Gorn, ed., *The McGuffey Readers: Selections from the 1879 Edition* (Boston: Bedford Books, 1998), 116–17.

136. Gorn, ed., *McGuffey Readers,* 28; William H. McGuffey, *The Eclectic Fourth Reader* (Cincinnati, OH: Truman and Smith, 1838), 143, reprinted in Westerhoff, *McGuffey and His Readers,* 151.

137. Gilmore, *Reading Becomes a Necessity,* 436; Charles W. Sanders, *The School Reader: First Book* (New York: Ivison, Phinney, Blakeman, 1858), 88–90, 114–16, 101, 59; S. G. Goodrich, *The Third Reader for the Use of Schools* (Louisville, KY: Morton and Griswold, 1839), 11–12; Charles H. Carpenter, *History of American Schoolbooks* (Philadelphia: University of Pennsylvania Press, 1963); Gorn, ed., *McGuffey Readers,* 13; M. B. Moore, *The First Dixie Reader* (Raleigh, NC: Branson, Farrar, 1868), 12. According to Gilmore, the 1783–1810 period saw "160 editions of the *New England Primer* in editions of 2,000–4,000 copies; 124 editions of Webster's and 45 similar editions of Dilworth's speller; and another 100 editions of other spellers and primers averaging perhaps 500 copies each. This amounts to 1,137,000 copies in circulation, or probably enough for every nonslave household in America during these 28 years" (436).

138. This discussion draws on Rt. Rev. Richard Gilmour, *The Sixth Reader* (New York: Benziger Brothers, 1877); and Rt. Rev. Richard Gilmour, *The New Fourth Reader* (New York: Benziger Brothers, 1886). Gilmour warns in the earlier book about the dangers of "godless education" in the public schools (xiii).

139. Ruth Miller Elson, *Guardians of Tradition: American Schoolbooks of the Nineteenth Century* (Lincoln: University of Nebraska Press, 1964), 41, 42, 55. A handful of studies have tried to quantify the religious content in early American schoolbooks. One author deemed 85 percent of the content in the readers he examined before 1775 religious while another fixed the religious content of colonial readers at 92 percent. For an overview of such studies, see John A. Nietz, *Old Textbooks* (Pittsburgh: University of Pittsburgh Press, 1961), 51–57.

140. Anne Boylan, *Sunday School: The Formation of an American Institution, 1790–1880* (New Haven, CT: Yale University Press, 1988), 133. This discussion of American

Sunday schools draws extensively on Boylan's work. For British Sunday schools, see Thomas W. Laqueur, *Religion and Respectability: Sunday Schools and Working Class Culture, 1780–1850* (New Haven, CT: Yale University Press, 1976). According to Gilmore, in *Reading Becomes a Necessity* (123), the most popular Sunday school book was George Fisher's *The Instructor, or The American Young Man's Best Companion* (London: Printed for the Booksellers, 1792). Like other schoolbooks of its time, this one was shot through with subtle and not-so-subtle religion lessons, such as: "Add to your faith virtue, and to virtue knowledge"; see Fisher, *The Instructor,* 34.

141. Boylan, *Sunday School,* 10. On the portion of school-age children in ASSU schools: Boylan, *Sunday School,* 11; on total enrollment and total Sunday schools: Candy Gunther Brown, *The Word in the World: Evangelical Writing, Publishing, and Reading in America, 1789–1880* (Chapel Hill: University of North Carolina Press, 2004), 36. Of the 8,268 Sunday schools reported by the ASSU in 1832, 70 percent were in the New England and Mid-Atlantic states; only 6 percent were in the South (Boylan, *Sunday School,* 31).

142. Horace Bushnell, *Discourses on Christian Nurture* (Boston: Massachusetts Sabbath School Society, 1847); Brown, *Word in the World,* 105. Sunday schools accounted for 30,000 of the country's 50,890 libraries and roughly 6 million of its 12,720,686 volumes. See William J. Rhees, *Manual of Public Libraries, Institutions, and Societies, in the United States and British Provinces of North America* (1859), cited in Cremin, *American Education: The National Experience,* 306–7.

143. Boylan, *Sunday School,* 163.

144. Boylan, *Sunday School,* 160, 40.

145. D. P. Nord, *Faith in Reading,* 4, 138, 79, 137.

146. D. P. Nord, *Faith in Reading,* 118. Another reason to question this literature of lament is the fact that, where books are scarce, they are also influential. Colporteur letters from the midnineteenth century told of many Americans who read their sacred books with considerable care and wrote them onto their hearts. In these days before radio, television, and the Internet, books were read and reread until they were falling apart into leaves, and then the leaves themselves were passed around repeatedly. Americans read their spiritual classics so often and with such care that some of them started speaking in the style of their favorite authors. "I have sometimes thought one might nearly tell what book was in the house by the tone of the remark," one colporteur wrote. "Where they have Bunyan, they use his language, and so with Baxter, Doddridge, Payson, and others. Where they have but few books, the impression is deep" (D. P. Nord, *Faith in Reading,* 146).

147. D. P. Nord, *Faith in Reading,* 9. On distribution statistics for the SPGNA and the Massachusetts Society for Promoting Christian Knowledge: D. P. Nord, *Faith in Reading,* 31–32, 35. According to a massive survey of some 8 million homes conducted by American Tract Society colporteurs, 94 percent of American families had a Bible,

and 91 percent had at least one religious book other than a Bible in the two decades preceding the Civil War. The situation was grimmer on the frontier, but even in such states as Kentucky and Tennessee ATS researchers found that only one in four families were "destitute" of religious books (D. P. Nord, *Faith in Reading,* 136).

148. Jonathan Edwards, *Some Thoughts Concerning the Present Revival of Religion in New England* (1742), quoted in Richard Hofstadter, *Academic Freedom in the Age of the College* (New York: Columbia University Press, 1955), 160.

149. Cremin, *American Education: The Colonial Experience,* 321, 213; Hall, "Readers and Writers in Early New England," 131. On works of divinity in Harvard's library: Cremin, *American Education: The Colonial Experience,* 397. On Harvard graduates becoming ministers: Hofstadter, *Academic Freedom in the Age of the College,* 192.

150. Lawrence R. Veysey, *The Emergence of the American University* (Chicago: University of Chicago Press, 1965), 21.

151. Gilmore, *Reading Becomes a Necessity,* 37.

152. "The Yale Report of 1828: Part II," http://collegiateway.org/reading/ yale-report-1828/curriculum; John H. Roberts and James Turner, *The Sacred and the Secular University* (Princeton, NJ: Princeton University Press, 2000), 165; William A. Scott, "The Religious Situation in State Universities," *Biblical World* 26.1 (July 1905): 26. The data on college graduates and the ministry appears in Bailey B. Burritt, "Professional Distribution of College and University Graduates," *Bulletin (United States Bureau of Education)* 19 (1912): 74–83, 142–44, cited in Walter P. Metzger, *Academic Freedom in the Age of the University* (New York: Columbia University Press, 1955), 21–22. Concerning state universities in the era before strict separatism overtook the U.S. Supreme Court, Marsden notes in *The Soul of the American University* that two-thirds of state college presidents in 1840 were ministers (81).

153. H. I. Gourley and J. N. Hunt, *The Modern Third Reader* (New York: Taintnor and Co., 1882), 196, quoted in Ruth Miller Elson, "American Schoolbooks and 'Culture' in the Nineteenth Century," *Mississippi Valley Historical Review* 46.3 (December 1959): 417.

154. Martin Marty, "Blessed Ignorance," *Christian Century* 119.5 (February 27, 2002): 55.

155. O. R. Sellers, "New Problems for the Biblical Instructor," *Journal of Bible and Religion* 19.3 (July 1951): 141, 113–14.

156. George Whitefield, *George Whitefield's Journals* (London: Banner of Truth Trust, 1960), 165; Nord, *Faith in Reading,* 31, 36.

157. Rufus Rockwell Wilson, ed., *Intimate Memories of Lincoln* (Elmira, NY: Primavera Press, 1945), 243. Books on the Second Great Awakening are legion. Here I rely particularly on Nathan O. Hatch, *The Democratization of American Christianity* (New Haven, CT: Yale University Press, 1989).

158. Jefferson to John Adams, May 5, 1817, in Lester J. Cappon, ed., *The Adams-Jefferson Letters: The Complete Correspondence between Thomas Jefferson and Abigail and John Adams* (Chapel Hill: University of North Carolina Press, 1959), 2:512; Butler, *Awash in a Sea of Faith,* 225–56. On the mixture of revivalism and republicanism, see Mark A. Noll's discussion of "Christian republicanism" (12) throughout *America's God: From Jonathan Edwards to Abraham Lincoln* (New York: Oxford University Press, 2002).

159. Albert J. Raboteau, *African-American Religion* (New York: Oxford University Press, 1999), 24. On church membership rates: Roger Finke and Rodney Stark, *The Churching of America, 1776–1990: Winners and Losers in Our Religious Economy* (New Brunswick, NJ: Rutgers University Press, 1992), 16.

160. Hatch, *Democratization of American Christianity,* 15. On evangelical publishing, see Brown, *Word in the World.*

161. *The New Schaff-Herzog Encyclopedia of Religious Knowledge,* vol. 2 (Grand Rapids, MI: Baker Book House, 1952), s.v. "Bible Societies," http://www.ccel.org/ccel/schaff/encyc02.bible_societies.html; Stephen Marini, "Hymnody as History: Early Evangelical Hymns and the Recovery of American Popular Religion," *Church History* 71.2 (June 2002): 284. As Marini notes, the most popular hymnbooks "crossed denominational lines" (285).

162. Ninian Smart, *Dimensions of the Sacred: An Anatomy of the World's Beliefs* (Berkeley and Los Angeles: University of California Press, 1996). Given how much has been written about the Puritans, there are bound to be disagreements about just how central the intellect was to them. Overturning generations of disdain for the Puritan mind, Perry Miller argued—in such volumes as *The New England Mind: The Seventeenth Century* (New York: Macmillan, 1939) and *The New England Mind: From Colony to Province* (Cambridge: Harvard University Press, 1953)—that the Puritans were among the greatest American intellectuals. John Morgan isn't so sure. See his *Godly Learning: Puritan Attitudes Towards Reasoning, Learning, and Education, 1560–1640* (New York: Cambridge University Press, 1986).

163. Cremin, *American Education: The National Experience,* 498.

164. John Dewey, *A Common Faith* (New Haven, CT: Yale University Press, 1934); Anson Phelps Stokes, *Church and State in the United States* (New York: Harper, 1950), 2:53.

165. George B. Cheever, *Right of the Bible in Our Public Schools* (New York: R. Carter, 1854), 112, cited in Cremin, *American Common School,* 47.

166. Horace Mann, *Lectures on Education* (Boston: Ide and Dutton, 1855), 73, quoted in Cremin, *American Education: The National Experience,* 146; "Report of a Committee of the Convention of Delegates from the Several Associations of Orthodox Congregational Churches of Massachusetts at Roxbury, June 26, 1849, on the Connection Between Common School Education and Religion," *Common School Journal* 11 (1849): 43–44, cited in Cremin, *American Common School,* 68; R. B. Culver, *Horace Mann and*

Religion in the Massachusetts Public Schools (New Haven, CT: Yale University Press, 1929), 170; Nancy T. Ammerman, "Golden Rule Christianity: Lived Religion in the American Mainstream," in *Lived Religion in America: Toward a History of Practice,* ed. David D. Hall (Princeton, NJ: Princeton University Press, 1997), 196–216.

167. *Life and Works of Horace Mann* (Boston: Lee and Shepard, 1891), 4:311, 325, 326, 335, quoted in Robert Michaelsen, "Common School, Common Religion? A Case Study in Church-State Relations, Cincinnati, 1869–70," *Church History* 38.2 (June 1969): 213; *Twelfth Annual Report of the Board of Education, Together with the Twelfth Annual Report of the Secretary of the Board* (Boston: Dutton and Wentworth, 1849), 116–17, quoted in Cremin, *American Common School,* 70.

168. Scholars have not ignored this episode. See Carl F. Kaestle, *The Evolution of an Urban School System: New York City, 1750–1850* (Cambridge: Harvard University Press, 1973); Vincent P. Lannie, *Public Money and Parochial Education: Bishop Hughes, Governor Seward, and the New York School Controversy* (Cleveland: Press of Case Western Reserve University, 1968); John Webb Pratt, *Religion, Politics, and Diversity: The Church-State Theme in New York History* (Ithaca: Cornell University Press, 1967); and Diane Ravitch, *The Great School Wars: A History of the New York City Public Schools* (Baltimore: Johns Hopkins University Press, 2000). For a fresh interpretation that rejects the warfare paradigm, see Benjamin Justice, *The War That Wasn't: Religious Conflict and Compromise in the Common Schools of New York State, 1865–1900* (Albany: State University of New York Press, 2005). The best source on the Philadelphia Bible wars is Michael Feldberg, *The Philadelphia Riots of 1844: A Study of Ethnic Conflict* (Westport, CT: Greenwood Press, 1975). See too Tracy Fessenden, "The Nineteenth-Century Bible Wars and the Separation of Church and State," *Church History* 74.4 (December 2005): 784–811.

169. Ray Allen Billington, *The Protestant Crusade, 1800–1860: A Study of the Origins of American Nativism* (New York: Macmillan, 1938), 143.

170. William H. Seward, *The Works of William H. Seward,* ed. George E. Baker (New York: Redfield, 1853), 2:215; American Bible Society petition, quoted in *New York Observer,* May 18, 1844; *American Protestant Vindicator,* August 5, 1840—all cited in Billington, *Protestant Crusade,* 145, 157, 148.

171. "Remonstrance of the Public School Society, by their Executive Committee, to the Honorable, the Common Counsel of the City of New-York" (March 2, 1840), in *Report of the Committee on Arts and Sciences and Schools of the Board of Assistants, on the Subject of Appropriating a Portion of the School Money to Religious Societies, for the Support of Schools,* 385, quoted in Hamburger, *Separation of Church and State,* 222. This was not the end of it. In 1842 New York's legislature sided with Bishop Hughes and Governor Seward when it passed the Maclay Bill, which restricted state support to schools that offered nonsectarian education.

172. Michael Katz, *The Irony of Early School Reform: Educational Innovation in Mid-Nineteenth-Century Massachusetts* (Cambridge: Harvard University Press, 1968), 145;

Hamburger, *Separation of Church and State,* 219. One evangelical denomination that, at least for a time, went the way of the Catholics was the Presbyterian Church, USA (Old School), which built hundreds of its own parochial schools. Old School Presbyterians were loath to submit to the bugaboo of nonsectarianism since they too had distinctive teachings (in this case, Reformed theology), which they wanted their children to learn. Lutherans also built a vast network of religious schools, many of them for non-English speakers.

173. Cincinnati *Commercial,* March 31, 1870, cited in Robert Michaelsen, *Piety in the Public School* (New York: Macmillan, 1970), 101; William Torrey Harris, *Report of the Commissioner of Education for the Year 1897–98* (Washington, DC: Government Printing Office, 1899), 2:1564, quoted in R. Laurence Moore, "Bible Reading and Nonsectarian Schooling: The Failure of Religious Instruction in Nineteenth-Century Public Education," *Journal of American History* 86.4 (March 2000): paragraph 22, http://www .historycooperative.org/journals/jah/86.4/moore.html.

174. Thomas Nast, "Fort Sumter," *Harper's Weekly,* March 19, 1870. See Benjamin Justice, "Thomas Nast and the Public Schools of the 1870s," *History of Education Quarterly* 42.5 (Summer 2005), http://www.historycooperative.org/journals/heq/45.2/justice.html.

175. "General Assembly," *Biblical Repertory and Princeton Review* 18 (1846): 439, quoted in Moore, "Bible Reading and Nonsectarian Schooling": paragraph 7, http://www.history-cooperative.org/journals/jah/86.4/moore.html; Michaelsen, *Piety in the Public School,* 101.

176. The Blaine Amendment, 4 Cong. Rec. 5580.

177. John Ireland, "State Schools and Parish Schools" (1890), quoted in Neil G. McCluskey, *Catholic Education in America: A Documentary History* (New York: Bureau of Publications, Teachers College, Columbia University, 1964), 132; Samuel W. Brown, *The Secularization of American Education* (New York: Teachers College, Columbia University, 1912), 1. On religion in the McGuffey readers: Raymond G. Hughes, "An Analysis of the Fourth, Fifth, and Sixth McGuffey Readers" (PhD diss., University of Pittsburgh, 1943).

178. Moore, "Bible Reading and Nonsectarian Schooling," paragraph 27, http://www.historycooperative.org/journals/jah/86.4/moore.html. There is some disagreement about how widespread these schoolhouse pieties were. Surveys conducted by the US Commissioner of Education in 1896 and 1903 found that Bible reading was common in about 75 percent of urban school districts; see "Bible Reading and Religious Exercises in the Public Schools," *Report of the Commissioner of Education* (Washington, DC: US Office of Education, 1903), 2:2445, cited in Michaelsen, *Piety in the Public School,* 168. However, Moore reports in "Bible Reading and Nonsectarian Schooling" that during the last half of the nineteenth century Bible reading was not mandated in any southern state and was actually against the law in Washington and Idaho (paragraph 14).

179. Henry Ward Beecher, "The Common School as an Element of National Unity," *Christian Union,* December 4, 1869, quoted in Michaelsen, *Piety in the Public School,* 116; Westerhoff, *McGuffey and His Readers,* 105; Elson, *Guardians of Tradition,* 43. Many studies have explored the religious and moral content of nineteenth-century school-books. Unfortunately, each depends on subjective judgments about what counts as "religious" and "moral." But what is plain in the aggregate is that religious content declines markedly over the course of the century, replaced in many cases by lessons on morality. In *Two Centuries of Change in the Content of School Readers* (Nashville: George Peabody College for Teachers, 1930), R. R. Robinson tracks a decline in religious content, from 85 percent before 1775, to 22 percent between 1775 and 1825, to 7.5 percent between 1825 and 1875, and 1.5 percent between 1875 and 1915; see table VI, cited in Nietz, *Old Textbooks,* 52. At the beginning of that period, religious content outnumbered moral content by a factor of ten to one; by the end of the period, moral content surpassed religious content by a factor of five to one. See also Harold C. Warren, "Changing Conceptions in the Religious Elements in Early American School Readers" (PhD diss., University of Pittsburgh, 1951); and Tingelstad, "Religious Element in American School Readers." The latter documents a decline in religious content in Webster's spellers from 47 percent in 1804–1829 to just 10 percent in 1829 and beyond. Elson sees one notable exception to this secularization trend: "Catholic schoolbooks retain throughout the century the same kind of sectarian religious zeal exhibited by Protestant books in the first part of the century" (55).

180. John T. McGreevy, *Catholicism and American Freedom: A History* (New York: Norton, 2003), 114.

181. Booker T. Washington, quoted in Cremin, *American Education: The National Experience,* 518. On public school enrollments, see the same source, 179.

182. Metzger, *Academic Freedom in the Age of the University,* 29, 43. On the "revolution" in higher education, the classic is Veysey, *Emergence of the American University.* The account that follows relies heavily on a new generation of scholars responding to Veysey's arguments: Marsden, *Soul of the American University;* Roberts and Turner, *Secular University;* D. G. Hart, *The University Gets Religion: Religious Studies in American Higher Education* (Baltimore: Johns Hopkins University Press, 1999); James T. Burtchaell, *The Dying of the Light: The Disengagement of Colleges and Universities from Their Christian Churches* (Grand Rapids, MI: Eerdmans, 1998); and especially Julie A. Reuben, *The Making of the Modern University: Intellectual Transformation and the Marginalization of Morality* (Chicago: University of Chicago Press, 1996). Much of this new scholarship traces the seeds of higher education's secularization to religious people. Marsden blames liberal Protestants, characterizing the modern university's ethos as "Liberal Protestantism without Protestantism" (48). Burtchaell calls "pietism" to task (842).

183. Eliot, "Experience with a College Elective System" (1895), quoted in Marsden, *Soul of the American University,* 188; Eliot, *Educational Reform: Essays and Addresses* (New York: Century Co., 1898), 43, quoted in Marsden, *Soul of the American University,* 192.

184. Upton Sinclair, *Goose-Step: A Study of American Education* (Pasadena: Upton Sinclair, 1923), cited in Marsden, *Soul of the American University,* 195; Anna K. Kendrick, "Harvard's Secularization: How a College Lost Its Faith," *Harvard Crimson,* March 8, 2006, http://www.thecrimson.harvard.edu/article.aspx?ref=511919; Reuben, *Making of the Modern University,* 83; Andrew Dickson White, "Scientific and Industrial Education in the United States," *Popular Science Monthly* 5 (1874): 187–88, quoted in Reuben, *Making of the Modern University,* 83.

185. Roberts and Turner, *Secular University,* 78. This development imposed on humanities courses a burden they cannot sustain, an unfair burden that distorts and cheapens the study of art and literature by putting both at the beck and call of the nation's moral agenda.

186. Absalom Peters, *College Religious Institutions: A Discourse* (New York: John F. Trow, 1851), 13, quoted in Cremin, *American Education: The National Experience,* 401; William Ernest Hocking, "The Religious Function of State Universities," *University of California Chronicle* 10 (1908): 464, quoted in Reuben, *Making of the Modern University,* 124; Clyde W. Votaw, "Religion in Public School Education," *Religious Education Association: Proceedings of the Fifth Annual Convention* (Chicago: Executive Office of the Association, 1908), 166–67, quoted in Reuben, *Making of the Modern University,* 125.

187. George Marsden, *The Outrageous Idea of Christian Scholarship* (New York: Oxford University Press, 1997), 23; Marsden, *Soul of the American University,* 333. Marsden's observation regarding religion's disappearance from college curricula is confirmed by Robert Michaelsen, who observed in "The Study of Religion: A Quiet Revolution in American Universities," *Journal of the American Academy of Religion* 37.4 (April 1996) that by the 1930s the study of religion "had fallen on evil times" in both public and private universities (182).

188. On church growth: Finke and Stark, *Churching of America.*

189. Richard Hofstadter, *Anti-Intellectualism in American Life* (New York: Vintage Books, 1963), 59, 145, 154.

190. Boylan, *Sunday School,* 138; Hofstadter, *Anti-Intellectualism,* 55, 59.

191. Hatch, *Democratization of American Christianity,* 4, 35, 125; Peter Cartwright, *The Autobiography of Peter Cartwright,* ed. Charles L. Wallis (New York: Abingdon Press, 1956), quoted in Hofstadter, *Anti-Intellectualism,* 102–3.

192. Christopher Lasch, "The Anti-Intellectualism of the Intellectuals," in his *The New Radicalism in America, 1889–1963: The Intellectual as Social Type* (New York: Knopf, 1965), 286–349; Ralph Waldo Emerson, "Circles," in his *Essays: First Series* (Boston: J. Munroe and Company, 1841), http://www.rwe.org/works/Essays-1st_Series_10 _Circles.htm; Walt Whitman, "Notes (Such as They Are) Founded on Elias Hicks," in

his *Prose Works* (Philadelphia: David McKay, 1892), http://www.bartleby.com/229/5021
.html. Emerson and Whitman are both cited in Schmidt, *Restless Souls,* 224, 230.

193. B. B. Edwards, *Writings of Professor B. B. Edwards* (Boston: J. P. Jewitt, 1853),
2:497–98, quoted in Hofstadter, *Anti-Intellectualism,* 87.

194. O. C. Edwards Jr., *A History of Preaching* (Nashville: Abingdon Press, 2004),
476; Dewitte T. Holland, *The Preaching Tradition: A Brief History* (Nashville: Abingdon
Press, 1980), 52; Perry Miller, *The Transcendentalists: An Anthology* (Cambridge: Harvard University Press, 1950), 8; Charles L. Campbell, "A Not-So-Distant Mirror: Nineteenth Century Popular Fiction and Pulpit Storytelling," *Theology Today* 51.4 (January
1995): 578, 577.

195. Harriet Beecher Stowe, *My Wife and I* (New York: J. B. Ford and Company,
1872), 1–2, quoted in Campbell, "A Not-So-Distant Mirror," 574; Hatch, *Democratization of American Christianity,* 57. By 1855 novels accounted for half of the books printed
in the United States. See Brown, *Word in the World,* 50–51.

196. Ann Douglas, *The Feminization of American Culture* (New York: Knopf, 1967),
146; David S. Reynolds, "From Doctrine to Narrative: The Rise of Pulpit Storytelling
in America," *American Quarterly* 32.5 (Winter 1980): 495.

197. Henry Steel Commager, *The American Mind* (New Haven, CT: Yale University
Press, 1950), 165; Hofstadter, *Anti-Intellectualism,* 112, 108, 114.

198. Edwards, *History of Preaching,* 813. On megachurches, see Donald E. Miller,
Reinventing American Protestantism: Christianity in the New Millennium (Berkeley and Los
Angeles: University of California Press, 1997).

199. On Jesus as polymorph: Prothero, *American Jesus.*

200. Phillips Brooks, *Lectures on Preaching: The Yale Lectures on Preaching, 1877*
(Grand Rapids, MI: Baker, 1969), 5; R. R. Reno, "The Great Delayer," *First Things* 145
(August/September 2004), http://www.firstthings.com/ftissues/ft0408/reviews/harp.htm.

201. Some have argued that moralism trounced piety among Puritans during the
colonial period. This is the position of Joseph Haroutunian, *Piety Versus Moralism: The
Passing of the New England Theology* (New York: Henry Holt, 1932); and Perry Miller,
The New England Mind: From Colony to Province. However, in *The New England Soul:
Preaching and Religious Culture in Colonial New England* (New York: Oxford University
Press, 1986), Harry S. Stout argues persuasively that this view is based on a faulty
reading of a special class of occasional sermons rather than the entire corpus of New
England preaching. Doctrinal Puritanism was alive and well, Stout demonstrates, into
and through the Revolution.

202. Thomas Paine, *The Rights of Man* (1791–92), http://www.ushistory.org/paine/
rights/singlehtml.htm.

203. Patrick Henry, "'And I Don't Care What It Is': The Tradition-History of a Civil
Religion Proof-Text," *Journal of the American Academy of Religion* 49.1 (March 1981): 38.

On civil religion, the classic text is Robert N. Bellah, "Civil Religion in America," *Dae-dalus* 96.1 (Winter 1967): 1–21.

204. William Lee Miller, *Piety on the Potomac: Notes on Politics and Morals in the Fifties* (Boston: Houghton Mifflin, 1964); Patrick Henry, "'And I Don't Care What It Is,'" 38; Herberg, *Protestant-Catholic-Jew,* 282, 46, 101, 14. For a more recent rendition of Eisenhower's "faith in faith," consider President George W. Bush's chief of staff Andrew Card, who said that the president had an easier time dealing with foreign leaders who were people of faith. "The President doesn't care what faith it is," Card said, "as long as it's faith"; see Jeffrey Goldberg, "The Believer: George W. Bush's Loyal Speechwriter," *New Yorker,* February 13, 2006, 64.

205. Herberg, *Protestant-Catholic-Jew,* 274; John Courtney Murray, *We Hold These Truths* (New York: Sheed and Ward, 1960), 138; Arthur A. Cohen, *The Myth of the Judeo-Christian Tradition* (New York: Harper and Row, 1970); Mark Silk, "Notes on the Judeo-Christian Tradition in America," *American Quarterly* 36.1 (Spring 1984): 82.

206. Noah Feldman, *Divided by God: America's Church-State Problem—and What We Should Do About It* (New York: Farrar, Straus and Giroux, 2005), 228, 231.

207. Richard N. Ostling, "Americans Facing Toward Mecca," *Time,* May 23, 1988, 50; John L. Esposito, *Islam the Straight Path* (New York: Oxford University Press, 1992), quoted in "The Judeo-Christian-Islamic Heritage," http://www.islamfortoday.com/esposito01.htm; William Safire, "Goo-Goo Eyes," *New York Times,* May 7, 1995, SM32. (Safire is quoting New York Senator Daniel Patrick Moynihan.) The term *people of the book* originates with Muslims; it is a translation from the Arabic phrase *Ahl al-Kitab.*

208. "President George W. Bush's Inaugural Address," White House, January 20, 2001, http://www.whitehouse.gov/news/inaugural-address.html; Tad Szulc, "Abraham: Journey of Faith," *National Geographic* 200. 6 (December 2001): 90–129. The *National Geographic* cover read, "Abraham: Father of Three Faiths."

209. Richard John Neuhaus, "While We're At It," *First Things* 135 (August/September 2003), http://www.firstthings.com/ftissues/ft0308/public.html. On the study, which fixed the U.S. Muslim population at 1.9 million: "In Brief," *Washington Post,* October 27, 2001, B9.

210. *United States v. Seeger,* 380 U.S. 163 (1965); Eck, *New Religious America,* 335, 23. The Pluralism Project's URL is: http://www.pluralism.org.

211. Dickinson W. Adams, ed., *Jefferson's Extracts from the Gospels* (Princeton, NJ: Princeton University Press, 1983), 413, 403.

212. Stephen Batchelor, *Buddhism Without Beliefs* (New York: Riverhead, 1998). See also Stephen Batchelor and Robert Thurman, "Reincarnation: A Debate," *Tricycle* 6.4 (Summer 1997): 24–27, 109–16. Even the Dalai Lama has succumbed to this temptation. See his *The Art of Happiness: A Handbook for Living* (New York: Riverhead, 1998). For a critique of contemporary American Buddhism, see Stephen Prothero, "Boomer Buddhism," http://archive.salon.com/books/feature/2001/02/26/buddhism/print.html.

213. "Toward a Declaration of a Global Ethic," http://www.religioustolerance.org/parliame.htm; William James, "The Will to Believe" (1896), http://falcon.jmu.edu/~omearawm/ph101willtobelieve.html.

214. John W. Nevin, *The Anxious Bench: The Mystical Presence* (New York: Garland Publishing, 1987), 37; Orestes Brownson, "Protestant Revivals and Catholic Retreats," *Brownson's Quarterly Review* 3.3 (July 1858), quoted in James D. Bratt, ed., *Antirevivalism in Antebellum America: A Collection of Religious Voices* (New Brunswick, NJ: Rutgers University Press, 2006), 258, 260.

215. Baltimore Catechism, http://www.truecatholic.org/baltp1.htm#Part1; Garry Wills, *Bare Ruined Choirs: Doubt, Prophecy, and Radical Religion* (Garden City, NY: Doubleday, 1972), 15–16, quoted in Allitt, *Religion in America Since 1945,* 82.

216. H. L. Mencken, "To Expose a Fool," *American Mercury* (October 1925), 158–60, http://purple.niagara.edu/chambers/mencken.html; David F. Wells, *No Place for Truth, or, Whatever Happened to Evangelical Theology?* (Grand Rapids, MI: Eerdmans, 1993), 136, 95, 292.

217. Robert Wuthnow, *The Restructuring of American Religion: Society and Faith Since World War II* (Princeton, NJ: Princeton University Press, 1988).

218. Similar divisions have been proposed by others. In *The Spiritual Self in Everyday Life: The Transformation of Personal Religious Experience in Nineteenth-Century New England* (Boston: Northeastern University Press, 1989), Richard Rabinowitz divides his subjects into: "doctrinalists," whose religious experience emphasizes understanding and whose key word was *soul;* "moralists," whose religious experience emphasized the will and whose key word was *character;* and "devotionalists," whose religious experience emphasized the emotions and whose key word was *personality* (xxviii–xxx). Richard J. Mouw finds four options when it comes to twentieth-century American Protestant understandings of the Bible. In "The Bible in Twentieth-Century Protestantism: A Preliminary Taxonomy," in *The Bible in America: Essays in Cultural History,* ed. Nathan O. Hatch and Mark A. Noll (New York: Oxford University Press, 1982), he calls these approaches "doctrinalism" (142), "pietism" (144), "moralism" (145), and "culturalism" (147). Finally, D. G. Hart, in *The Lost Soul of American Protestantism* (Lanham, MD: Rowman and Littlefield, 2002), finds just two salient types of modern American Protestants: "confessionalists" and "pietists" (xxvii–xxix). Following Ninian Smart, I might expand my list to include liturgical Christians (who emphasize the ritual dimension), institutional Christians (who emphasize the social dimension), and narrative Christians (who emphasize the mythic dimension).

219. See Peter J. Boyer, "A Church Asunder," *New Yorker,* April 17, 2006, 54–65.

220. Alliance of Confessing Evangelicals, "The Cambridge Declaration," accessible through http://www.alliancenet.org/.

221. *The Lutheran Book of Worship* (Minneapolis: Augsburg Publishing House, 1978), 121.

222. Jeff Sharlet, "Killing Religion Journalism," *Revealer,* October 11, 2004, http:// www.therevealer.org/archives/timeless_000970.php. When religion does get attention, Sharlet adds, it is typically covered not as serious news but "as either innocuous spirituality or dangerous fanaticism, perfume or mustard gas."

223. Author interview with Khyati Joshi, May 2006. I derived public, private, and homeschooling enrollments from two sources: U.S. Department of Education, National Center for Education Statistics, "Parent and Family Involvement in Education Survey of the 2003 National Household Education Surveys Program," Table 1, http://nces .ed.gov/pubs2005/2005043.pdf(5); and U.S. Department of Education, National Center for Education Statistics, "Homeschooling in the United States: 2003," http://nces .ed.gov/pubs2006/homeschool. On religious studies courses: Ernest Boyer, "Teaching Religion in the Public Schools and Elsewhere," *Journal of the American Academy of Religion* 60.3 (Autumn 1992): 517–18.

224. Recent treatments of these issues include: Kent Greenawalt, *Does God Belong in Public Schools?* (Princeton, NJ: Princeton University Press, 2005); DelFattore, *Fourth R;* and James W. Fraser, *Between Church and State: Religion and Public Education in a Multicultural America* (New York: St. Martin's Press, 1999). See also Robert Michaelsen, *Piety in the Public School;* and Donald E. Boles, *The Bible, Religion, and the Public Schools* (Ames: Iowa State University Press, 1965).

225. *McCollum v. Board of Education,* 333 U.S. 203 (1948), 235–36.

226. *Abington v. Schempp,* 225, 300.

227. *Stone v. Graham,* 449 U.S. 39 (1980), 42; *Edwards v. Aguillard,* 482 U.S. 578 (1987), 607.

228. *Abington v. Schempp*; Martin Marty, "Around Religion, About Religion, of Religion, and Religion: The Issues of Public School Teaching Today," *Religion and Public Education* 15.4 (Fall 1988): 393.

229. Carter, *Culture of Disbelief.*

230. W. A. Nord, "Religion-Free Texts, 711–15. Roman Catholic schools currently account for 27.9 percent of all private schools, according to S. P. Broughman and N. L. Swaim, *Characteristics of Private Schools in the United States: Results from the 2003–2004 Private School Universe Survey* (Washington, DC: National Center for Education Statistics, 2006), http://nces.ed.gov/pubs2006/2006319.pdf (9). Conservative Christian schools account for 26.2 percent but are growing much more quickly. I obtained the latter figure by adding from table 3 half of the Baptist schools plus all of the following affiliations: Assembly of God, Calvinist, Christian (unspecified), Church of Christ, Church of God, Church of God in Christ, Lutheran Church—Missouri Synod, Wisconsin Evangelical Lutheran Synod (9). On growth in Islamic schools: Shelia M. Poole, "Back to School: Islam in the Class," *Atlanta Journal-Constitution,* August 24, 2005, 4F.

231. Nord and Haynes, *Taking Religion Seriously,* 9, 16.

232. "Religion in the Public Schools: A Joint Statement of Current Law" (1995), http://www.ed.gov/Speeches/04-1995/prayer.html#4; "Archived Information," http://www.ed.gov/inits/religionandschools/secletter.html; *The Bible and Public Schools: A First Amendment Guide* (New York: Bible Literacy Project and Nashville: First Amendment Center, 1999), 7. The first of these documents reads, in part: "The history of religion, comparative religion, the Bible (or other scripture)-as-literature (either as a separate course or within some other existing course), are all permissible public school subjects. It is both permissible and desirable to teach objectively about the role of religion in the history of the United States and other countries." Positions similar to the second document are taken up in "A Parent's Guide to Religion in the Public Schools" and "A Teacher's Guide to Religion in the Public Schools," both available through the Freedom Forum at http://www.firstamendmentcenter.org/about.aspx?item=FAC_publications. The complete list of institutions endorsing the third document is: American Association of School Administrators, American Federation of Teachers, American Jewish Committee, American Jewish Congress, Anti-Defamation League, Association for Supervision and Curriculum Development, Baptist Joint Committee on Public Affairs, Christian Educators Association International, Christian Legal Society, Council on Islamic Education, National Association of Evangelicals, National Association of Secondary School Principals, National Association of Churches of Christ in the U.S.A., National Council for the Social Studies, National Education Association, National School Boards Association, People for the American Way Foundation, Union of American Hebrew Congregations.

233. "Teaching about religions has been included to some degree in every one of the national and state standards documents in social studies as well as many language arts (literature) and arts (visual arts, music and dance) standards," according to Susan L. Douglass, *Teaching about Religion in National and State Social Studies Standards: Executive Summary* (Fountain Valley, CA, and Nashville, TN: Council on Islamic Education and First Amendment Center, 2000), 21. However, Douglass also found that religion is still "treated superficially overall" and that in U.S. history standards, attention to religion "tapers off after the colonial period" and "finds little mention in connection with study of the 20th century" (22). On school district policies, see three examples in Charles C. Haynes and Oliver Thomas, *Finding Common Ground: A Guide to Religious Liberty in Public Schools* (Nashville, TN: First Amendment Center, 2001), 178–220. For one educational group's endorsement of teaching about religion, see the National Council for the Social Studies, "Study About Religions in the Social Studies Curriculum" (1998), http://www.socialstudies.org/positions/religion.

234. "Biblical Ignorance," *Chicago Tribune,* May 12, 2005, 22.

235. One widely disseminated formula, reprinted in Haynes and Thomas, *Finding Common Ground* (75–76), distinguishes between constitutional and unconstitutional teaching about religion like this:

- The school's approach to religion is *academic,* not *devotional.*
- The school strives for student *awareness* of religions, but does not press for student *acceptance* of any religion.
- The school sponsors study *about* religion, not the *practice* of religion.
- The school may *expose* students to a diversity of religious views, but may not *impose* any particular view.
- The school *educates* about all religions; it does not *promote* or *denigrate* religion.
- The school *informs* students about various beliefs; it does not seek to *conform* students to any particular belief.

236. Anne Juhasz and Leslie Wilson, "Should Students Be Well Read or Should They Read Well?" *NASSP Bulletin* 70.488 (March 1986): 78–83; Marie Wachlin and Byron R. Johnson, *The Bible Literacy Report: What Do American Teens Need to Know and What Do They Know?* (New York: Bible Literacy Project, 2005), 15, 6. On Shakespeare and the Bible, see three works by Naseeb Shaheen: *Biblical References in Shakespeare's Tragedies* (Newark: University of Delaware Press, 1987); *Biblical References in Shakespeare's History Plays* (Newark: University of Delaware Press, 1989); and *Biblical References in Shakespeare's Comedies* (Newark: University of Delaware Press, 1993). For a follow-up to the 2005 *Bible Literacy Report,* see Marie Wachlin and Byron R. Johnson, *Bible Literacy Report II: What University Professors Say Incoming Students Need to Know* (Front Royal, VA: Bible Literacy Project, 2006).

237. "President George W. Bush's Inaugural Address," White House, http://www
.whitehouse.gov/news/inaugural-address.html; Luke 10:30–37; Wachlin and Johnson, *Bible Literacy Report,* 14, 16. President Jimmy Carter began and ended his inaugural address by quoting from and referring to Micah 6:8: "He hath showed thee, O man, what is good; and what doth the Lord require of thee, but to do justly, and to love mercy, and to walk humbly with thy God"; see http://www.yale.edu/lawweb/avalon/
presiden/inaug/carter.htm. President Bill Clinton's first inaugural quoted from Galatians 6:9: "And let us not be weary in well-doing, for in due season, we shall reap, if we faint not"; see http://www.yale.edu/lawweb/avalon/presiden/inaug/clinton1.htm.

238. The U.S. District Court ruling in *Doe v. Porter* can be viewed at: http://news
.findlaw.com/hdocs/docs/religion/doeprtr020802mem.pdf. See also the 6th United States Circuit Court of Appeals ruling: *Doe v. Porter,* 370 F.3d 558 (6th Cir. 2004). The NCBCPS Web site is: http://www.bibleinschools.net/sdm.asp. On the Florida lawsuit, see David Levenson, "University Religion Departments and Teaching about the Bible in Public High Schools: A Report from Florida," *Religious Studies News,* March 2002, 3, 7, 10. For a critique of the NCBCPS approach by an SMU biblical studies professor, see Mark A. Chancey, "The Bible and Public Schools: Report on the National Council on Bible Curriculum in Public Schools (NCBCPS)," http://www.tfn.org/files/fck/Bible
Curriculum.pdf, and his "The Revised Curriculum of the National Council on Bible

Curriculum in Public Schools," http://www.tfn.org/religiousfreedom/biblecurriculum/media/revisedcurric/index.php. See also the NCBCPS press release responding to Chancey, "National Council on Bible Curriculum Responds to Attack by Anti-Religious Extremists," August 4, 2005, http://www.bibleinschools.net/media%20day/8-4-5/Response%20to%20TFN.pdf. Courses of this sort led in the 1980s and 1990s to a series of lawsuits in which the courts tried to draw the line between constitutional teaching about religion and the unconstitutional preaching of it. See, for example, *Hall v. Board of Commissioners of Conecuh County,* 656 F.2d 999 (5th Cir. 1981); *Crockett v. Sorenson,* 568 F. Supp. 1422 (W. D. Va. 1983); *Herdahl v. Pontotoc County School District,* 933 F. Supp. 582 (N. D. Miss. 1996); *Chandler v. James,* 985 F. Supp. 1062 (M.D. Ala. 1997); *Gibson v. Lee County School Board,* 1 F. Supp. 2d 1426 (M.D. Fla. 1998). In the last of these cases the courts upheld one Bible course but overturned another, demonstrating that in these circumstances too the devil is in the details.

239. *Edwards v. Aguillard.*

240. "Clinton's Memo: Religious Expression in Public Schools," http://www.ffrf.org/fttoday/1995/august95/memo.html; *McCollum v. Board of Education.*

241. Charles Colson, "Reversing Memory Loss," *Christianity Today,* August 6, 2001, 88.

242. *McCollum v. Board of Education.*

243. Emile Lester and Patrick S. Roberts, *Learning about World Religions in Public Schools: The Impact on Student Attitudes and Community Acceptance in Modesto, Calif.* (Nashville, TN: First Amendment Center, 2006), http://www.firstamendmentcenter.org/PDF/FirstForum_ModestoWorldReligions.pdf.

244. In a 1986 Gallup poll 79 percent said they would not object to "teaching about the major religions of the world" in public schools and 75 percent said they would not object to "using the Bible in literature, history and social studies classes." See George Gallup Jr. and Robert Bezilla, *The Role of the Bible in American Society* (Princeton, NJ: Princeton Religion Research Center, 1990), 22. More recently, nearly three-quarters of Americans said that they supported "using the Bible in literature, history, and social studies classes" in public schools; see Mark Gillespie, "Most Americans Support Prayer in Public Schools," Gallup Poll, July 9, 1999, http://poll.gallup.com.

245. W. A. Nord, *Religion and American Education,* 212.

246. For data on the study of religion for undergraduates: American Academy of Religion, "Survey of Undergraduate Religion and Theology Programs: Data Analysis," http://www.aarweb.org/department/acadreldocs/surveydata-20040309.pdf.

247. Marsden, *Soul of the American University,* 5, 430; Nord and Haynes, *Taking Religion Seriously,* 80; W. A. Nord, *Religion and American Education,* 316. For a book-length elaboration of this argument, see George M. Marsden, *The Outrageous Idea of Christian Scholarship* (New York: Oxford University Press, 1997).

248. Marsden, *Soul of the University,* 440.

249. Jay D. Wexler, "Preparing for the Clothed Public Square: Teaching About Religion, Civic Education, and the Constitution," *William and Mary Law Review* 43.3 (February 2002): 1219; "Mission," The Pluralism Project, http://www.pluralism. org/about/mission. php. See also James W. Fraser's pitch for "a love of diversity" and "multiculturalism" in *Between Church and State,* 5–6. For an intelligent discussion of the moral aims of religious studies, see the transcript of "Religion and Moral Education," one of the sessions in a May 2003 conference held at the Freedom Forum in Arlington, Virginia, on "Teaching About Religion in Public Schools: Where Do We Go from Here?": http://pewforum.org/events/0520/discussion5.pdf.

250. Karen Armstrong, *The Great Transformation: The Beginning of Our Religious Traditions* (New York: Knopf, 2006), xiii, 392.

251. Armstrong, *Great Transformation,* xi, 393.

252. Michael Novak, *The Rise of the Unmeltable Ethnics: Politics and Culture in the Seventies* (New York: Macmillan, 1972).

253. Hofstadter, *Anti-Intellectualism,* 103. Hofstadter is quoting evangelist Peter Cartwright, who is himself paraphrasing the condescensions of "learned and gentlemanly ministers." The Ingersoll quotation is: "Everybody talks about the Bible and nobody reads it; that is the reason it is so generally believed"; see Col. Robert Green Ingersoll, "Lectures of Col. R. G. Ingersoll, Vol. I," http://mirrors.xmission.com/gutenberg/etext05/ingr110.txt.

254. Feldman, *Divided by God,* 7, 8, 237. As Feldman notes, his proposal goes "against the trends of the last several decades, which are for stricter regulation of public religious symbolism and more permissive authorization of government funding and support for religion" (237).

255. The three versions of the Ten Commandments all appeared in Angie Brunkow, "Which Commandments?" *Omaha World-Herald,* January 22, 2005, 1E. The original sources are *The Tanakh: The Holy Scriptures* (Philadelphia: Jewish Publication Society, 1985); "A Traditional Catechetical Formula," in *Catechism of the Catholic Church* (Washington, DC: US Catholic Conference, 1991); and *The Constitution of the Presbyterian Church (U.S.A.): Part I: Book of Confessions* (Louisville: Office of the General Assembly, 1999).

256. Michael Foust, "Christians, Muslims Worship Same God, Bush Tells Reporters," Baptist Press, November 20, 2003, http://www.sbcbaptistpress.org/bpnews .asp?ID=17133.

257. "Bin Laden's Fatwa," *News Hour with Jim Lehrer,* http://www.pbs.org/newshour/terrorism/international/fatwa_1996.html; "Al Qaeda Threats on New Tape," *CBS News,* November 24, 2004, http://www.cbsnews.com/stories/2004/09/09/terror/main 642411.shtml.

258. Emerson, *Letters of Ralph Waldo Emerson,* 3:290.

259. "Jihad Against Jews and Crusaders," *Christian Century* 119.5 (February 27, 2002): 28–29.

260. On polling data on evolution: Frank Newport, "Almost Half of Americans Believe Humans Did Not Evolve," Gallup Poll, June 5, 2006, http:/poll.gallup.com.

261. "News in Brief," *Washington Post,* February 24, 1996, B7.

262. "Religion and the Founding of the American Republic," Library of Congress, http://www.loc.gov/exhibits/religion/rel04.html.

263. North Carolina senator Jesse Helms, quoted in Albright, *Mighty and the Almighty,* 82; "Remarks by William Bennett," http://www.forerunner.com/forerunner/ X0407_Remarks_by_William_B.html; Pat Robertson, "1992 Republican Convention," http://www.patrobertson.com/Speeches/1992GOPConvention.asp.

264. "2001 Interview with Mullah Omar," UPI, http://about.upi.com/AboutUs/ index.php?ContentID=20051018123324-7609&SectionName=AboutUs/.

265. George M. Marsden, *Understanding Fundamentalism and Evangelicalism* (Grand Rapids, MI: Eerdmans, 1991), 1.

266. "The Second Gore-Bush Presidential Debate," October 11, 2000, http://www .debates.org/pages/trans2000b.html; President John F. Kennedy, "Radio and Television Report to the American People on Civil Rights," June 11, 1963, http://www.jfklibrary. org/j061163.htm. In the 2000 debate Gore responded, "I also believe in the Golden Rule."

267. Nina Bernstein, "Mrs. Clinton Says G.O.P.'s Immigration Plan Is at Odds with the Bible," *New York Times,* March 23, 2006, B5.

268. Prothero, *American Jesus,* 8.

269. Walter H. Capps, *The New Religious Right: Piety, Patriotism, and Politics* (Columbia: University of South Carolina Press, 1990), 99.

270. J. C. Hallman, *The Devil Is a Gentleman: Exploring America's Religious Fringe* (New York: Random House, 2006), xv.

Index